ARGONAUTS
TO
ASTRONAUTS

OTHER BOOKS BY MAURICIO OBREGÓN

Ulysses Airborne

The Caribbean as Columbus Saw It
(with Samuel Eliot Morison)

Mauricio Obregón

ARGONAUTS TO ASTRONAUTS

Cop. a

HARPER & ROW, PUBLISHERS

NEW YORK

Cambridge
Hagerstown
Philadelphia
San Francisco

London
Mexico City
São Paulo
Sydney

1817

Parts of this book are based on lectures given by the author at the University of the Andes in Bogotá, Harvard University, and the University Center in Dubrovnik, Yugoslavia. Parts have been adapted for *El Tiempo* of Bogotá, the Colombian Navy, *Diogenes* (UNESCO-CIPSH), *Smithsonian Magazine,* and *Harvard Magazine*.

This work was published in somewhat different form in Spain and in Colombia under the title *De los Argonautas a los Astronautas,* © Mauricio Obregón, 1977. Libreria Editorial Argos, S.A. 1977, Circulo de Lectores 1978.

FIRST EDITION

Designed by C. Linda Dingler

Library of Congress Cataloging in Publication Data

Obregón, Mauricio.
  Argonauts to astronauts.
  Bibliography: p.
  Includes index.
  1. Discoveries (in geography) 2. Explorers—Biography I. Title.
G80.027   910′.9   78-2155
ISBN 0-06-013193-4

80 81 82 83 84 10 9 8 7 6 5 4 3 2 1

To Madronita,
who stood by me

CONTENTS

Illustration Credits:

M.O.	*Mauricio Obregón*
C.O.	*Cristina Martinez-Irujo de Obregón*
S.O.M.	*Sancho Obregón Martinez-Irujo*
J.O.	*Javier Obregón Martinez-Irujo*
M.F.	*Maria Figuerola of Ed. Argos-Vergara*
J.F.N.	*James F. Nields*
S.E.M.	*Samuel Eliot Morison*
D.C.	*David Crofoot*
M.V.	*Marta Villavecchia*

PROLOGUE

To discover is to rend the veil, to push back the frontier of Infinity. It is not just to bump into the unknown, to explore it, and perhaps to forget it; to discover is to give form to what has been uncovered and to pass it on to posterity. And for this, the unforgettable language of poetry is best.

As the memory of the West awakens, the peoples of Egypt and of the Near East explore their rivers and their coasts. But our universe begins to take form only when, in the thirteenth century B.C., the Argonauts and Odysseus unveil the seas which are to be our heritage; and Homer, the greatest of poets, describes the world as a turquoise island within which a ring of earth protects the known Sea from the roar of the Infinite Ocean. Ocean is the cradle and the tomb of the gods, who form with men and women a single hierarchy, imperfect and therefore real.

Greeks, Phoenicians, Romans, Muslims, and Norsemen gradually string a necklace of the sea's bays and its gulfs, but all-encircling Ocean does not recede until Columbus and Magellan present the sixteenth century with a world complete and without an Infinite, a world sprinkled with different human races. This is a world that the Renaissance can possess, and its Quixotes can mold it to their own destinies under the gaze of a God who, in spite of Christ's sacrifice, is distant because He is perfect.

Iberians, Britons, Frenchmen, and Dutch exhaust this world; and the air, which is also a sea, is soon explored by the Montgolfiers in the eighteenth century, by the Wrights at the threshold of the twentieth, then by Lindbergh and by Gagarin. Finally, NASA (an organization, not a hero) carries men from our world to its satellite and shows us again our little green island surrounded by the blackness of space, an island now full of peoples so unaccustomed to solitude that they cannot hear the poetry of the new Infinite or read its legends. But our youth is already searching; what new generation of gods will come thundering out of deep space?

My intention here is to try to live again this saga of discovery, passing from the windy clarity of the Aegean, through the mad harmony of La Mancha, to the silent kettledrum of space, and to see how each reflected the changing posture of our souls, where we gradually create our universe out of the whole cloth of Infinity.

In order to listen for the poetry of the past, we will not sail reproductions of ancient ships or rely on obsolete equipment and provisions; it is not these that have really changed, but the cumulus of our knowledge, which cannot be annulled. Rather will we use all means, classic or new, to follow the voyages of discovery, to throw light upon those parts of them which chroniclers left dark, to push back the border that separates legend from history, and to look beyond the frontiers of science where new myths will soon be born, then legends, and finally history.

In order to cover this territory in one lifetime, we will trace the great winds on photographs taken from satellites, ride jet planes across the empty expanses of ocean where these winds have always been constant, fly high in light planes to get a cartographer's view, then skim the sea to observe harbors through the eyes of a lookout at mast height. This will enable us to discard useless alternatives quickly, to sail and row only when we have chosen the most likely identifications, reexamining with respect but without obligation those which were accepted by generations less mobile than ours. Winds, stars, and the findings of archaeologists, divers, linguists, and climatologists will help us to propose a solution to Homer's ancient riddle; to reconstruct the good ship *Argo;* to trace Jason's and Odysseus' courses; to identify Columbus' discoveries in the Caribbean; and to locate Magellan's mysterious landfalls in the Pacific Isles. And science fiction may even help us to part the curtains of outer space.

We are concerned with those who created legends capable of becoming history. So, wherever we go, we will try to converse not only with heroes but with those who, less heroic, still managed to make themselves heard across the centuries. And heroes or not, we will talk of their worlds, their gods, their women, their music, and their ships. For who can create legend without these?

We will always try to document and illustrate our findings and— though the mixture may dismay some historians—to relate them to our own adventures. For past and present belong to a single perspective; still today one can walk through pine forests that were green when Jason and Odysseus sailed. Wherever we find it necessary, we will not disdain informed speculation frankly identified as such, for not only navigators but also historians and scientists need intuition as much as they need facts. In the Archives of the Indies and the Columbian Library of Seville, in the Archives of Simancas, in the Bibliothèque Nationale of Paris, in the Library of the Vatican, and wherever news of the discoverers is to be found, we will study the chronicles and the charts of each journey. But having done our research, we will leave our desk to speak from a creaking deck, from a roaring plane, or from the teeming silence of the bottom of the seas which God made for our pleasure.

So, let us depart, but first let me remember my mentors. Without Samuel Eliot Morison I might never have weighed anchor, for it was he who taught me always to look before writing, as together we followed the voyages of Columbus, the Norsemen, Cabot, Cartier, and Magellan; and without Rafael Obregón and his schooner *Tarena* I would have been short of sail. As I write, Sam and Raf are dead; they went like Odysseus, having really lived. Without Maurice Baird-Smith's *Mesouda*, Hernán Echavarría's *Gaira*, the Chilean Navy's *Orompello*, Admiral Pugh's barge at Guam, Jim Nield's *Baron*, and Andrés Soriano's *Kingair*, I would certainly have made much less way. And without the friendship and encouragement of Nicolás Gómez Dávila, Marguerite Yourcenar, Enrique Uribe White, and John Parry, I might well have hesitated to press my travels (roughly equivalent to four equatorial earth orbits) between the covers of this book—where in any case they would have been illegible without the patience of my secretary, Elsa Bonilla de Coy.

Indispensable to me were Rosario Parra, Director of the Archives of the Indies in Seville; the late Spyridon Marinatos, Director of Antiquities of Greece; Necati Dolunai, Director of Archaeology of Turkey; the Rev. Alberto Lee López, Director of the National Archives of Colombia; Alec Bright, Design Director of the Gold Museum of Bogotá; Professor Louis-André Vigneras and Katherine Romoli, historians: Kenneth L. Franklin and Clemente Garavito, directors of the planetariums of New York and Bogotá; José Maria Martínez Hidalgo and the late Admiral Julio Guillén, directors of the naval museums of Barcelona and Madrid; Captains Laurio H. di Stefani and Max Justo Gedes, historians of the Argentine and Brazilian navies, and Frank McLear, naval architect; my photographers, David Crofoot, Cristina Martinez-Irujo, and Sancho Obregón; and my illustrator, Javier Obregón. Also Antonio de la Cova; Marta and Javier Villavecchia; Colleen Solomon; Judith Rude; Jorge Cornet of AVIANCA; and the personnel of IHC-PANAM. Last but not least, my thanks to my editor Frances Lindley, whose scalpel was painful but unfailing.

Had I not encountered friends all over the world who, recognizing in my quest some reminder of their own dreams, were quick to help, my enjoyment would never have been the same. I trust this shows between my lines.

Punta Gloria
Santa Marta, Colombia
September 1979

The Known World Grows (*M.O. and M.F.* Schematic)

The world of the Argonauts
and Odysseus, thirteenth century B.C.

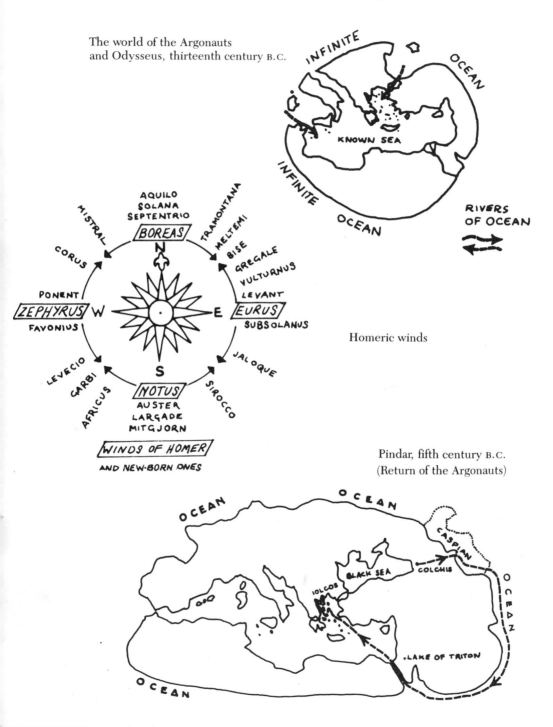

INFINITE OCEAN

KNOWN SEA

INFINITE OCEAN

RIVERS
OF OCEAN

AQUILO
SOLANA
SEPTENTRIO
BOREAS
N

MISTRAL

CORUS

TRAMONTANA
MELTEMI
BISE
GREGALE
VULTURNUS
LEVANT

PONENT
ZEPHYRUS   W
FAVONIUS

E   EURUS
SUBSOLANUS

Homeric winds

LEVECIO
GARBI
AFRICUS

S

JALOQUE

SIROCCO

NOTUS
AUSTER
LARGADE
MITGJORN

WINDS OF HOMER
AND NEW-BORN ONES

Pindar, fifth century B.C.
(Return of the Argonauts)

OCEAN

CASPIAN

COLCHIS

BLACK SEA

IOLCOS

OCEAN

LAKE OF TRITON

OCEAN

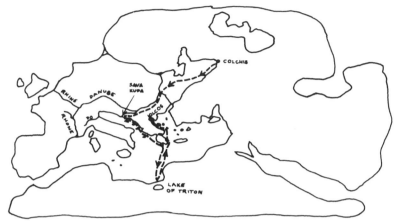

Apollonius, third century B.C. (Return of the Argonauts)

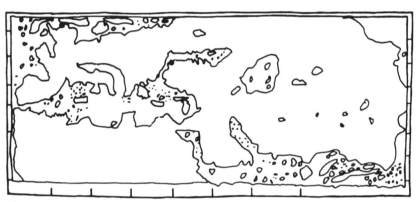

Idrisi, 1145–1192

Henricus Martellus, 1489: Behaim's additions (....) 1492 globe

Waldseemüller, 1507 (Christening America)

Ribero, 1529

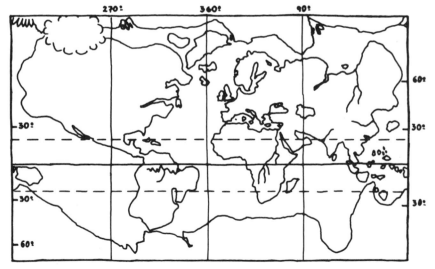

Mercator, 1569

Part One

HOMERIC ISLAND AND INFINITE OCEAN

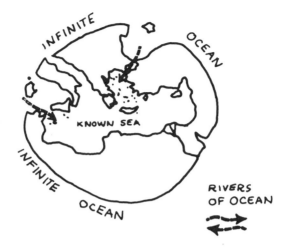

The world of the Argonauts and Odysseus, thirteenth century B.C.

Sun as the only god; but by the next century, when Jason and Odysseus sailed, the seaborn gods were back. We shall begin by trying to establish their relationships.

Jason's and Odysseus' gods were in their third generation. They were no longer abstractions like Chaos or distant realities like Uranus (Heaven) and Gaia (Earth), the youngest of whose children, Cronus and Rhea, in turn begot the gods of Olympus, headed by Zeus. Cronus had long since emasculated Uranus, whose severed genitals had struck from the surf of Cyprus the spark that became Aphrodite, goddess of passion. Similarly, Athena, goddess of intelligence, was born out of a Lybian lagoon while her father, Zeus, devoured her mother, the goddess of wisdom, so that Athena would be his creation alone. Zeus ruled from Olympus over his brethren, among whom he divided creation, establishing a feudal order in which men were simply inferior beings within a universal hierarchy.

From this feudal order, unbroken from Zeus to the lowliest of slaves, an uncomplicated sense of proportion emerged, possible only in the constant presence of God and of Death (presences that the twentieth century desperately tries to avoid). Although each god had his favorite vices and, to satisfy them, used his divine powers as far as he dared, he knew that to avoid a return to Chaos he must respect existing covenants with other gods, with demigods, and with men. These last covenants, from which justice was born, were later renewed by Abraham, by Moses, by Jesus, and by Muhammad; and each of them, one must admit, started something difficult to explain without God.

1
MYTHS, METEORS, AND MARINERS

Gods and Goddesses

Out of the Chaos of the Infinite Ocean, islands of order emerged. As men
went down rivers to the sea, their intelligence sketched the myths that
would enable them to explain what they explored, and their memory the
legends that would make it possible for them to pass on the story. So
when the Argonauts sailed east and Odysseus west to the limits of an
earthbound sea, a sea already teeming with gods, their adventures were
handed down from generation to generation, and Homer's[1] poetry
molded them at last into History, which is a symphony of gods, elements,
and men, its theme song legend, its harmony myth.

Homer's world was a green ring of earth surrounding the known Sea
formed by the Western Mediterranean and the Aegean. Around it roared
the Infinite Ocean, which fed the Sea through two rivers of Ocean, one
from the East, where Helius, the Sun, rose from the Elysian Fields, and
the other from the West, where the Sun descended into Hades.

Mythology and Science have always known whence life first came. To
those who listen, the Gregorian chant of the waves speaks as clearly of
gods as does the multitudinous rocking of the atoms. Out of the Infinite
Ocean the gods arose: in Babylon and in Egypt, Nun and Apsú floated
above the all-encircling waters; in Hesiod's *Theogony*, Gaia, the Earth
(more daughter than mother), was supported by her sons, Sea and Ocean;
in Homer's *Iliad*, Ocean engendered Chaos and all the gods: and in
Genesis, the Spirit of God moved first over the waters. Even today the
Kogi Indians, Colombia's great mythologists, begin their Genesis: "When
all was dark, our mother was the Sea." In the fourteenth century B.C.
Amenhotep IV (Akhnaton) and his lovely Nefertiti tried to establish the

To his brother Poseidon, Zeus gave dominion over the Sea and over earthquakes; we will soon see that the combination of sea and quake is logical and that neither Poseidon nor his son Aeolus, master of the winds, ever forgave a mistake. To his brother Hades, Zeus gave the kingdom of the dead. Taciturn Hades sometimes seems to have been the most powerful of the gods, for few were the souls who escaped him. Even when he stole Zeus' daughter Persephone and left the world temporarily without Spring, Zeus dared not punish him.

Hera was both the sister and the wife of Zeus, but the father of the gods relieved the monotony of his own infinite wisdom with a fruitful succession of amorous adventures. (Jealous Hera tried to keep up with him by producing Hephaestus, the lame blacksmith, on her own.) Besides Hera, two goddesses stood closest to Zeus, perhaps because they were both motherless, and also because in myth, as in everyday life, order and disorder must stand together: Athena, who brought light to men's eyes, and Aphrodite, whose passion blinded them.

Zeus filled the world with his children. We have seen that on Wisdom Zeus begot Athena (just as in the Judeo-Christian tradition Wisdom, who played while God compassed the Sea with its bounds, was the first to be possessed by Him). On Hera Zeus begot Ares, the god of war, who in turn made love to Hephaestus' wife Aphrodite, producing the Amazons, who would watch the Argonauts sail by. On Mnemosyne, goddess of memory, Zeus begot the Muses, and on Demeter, Persephone (Spring). On Leto he begot Apollo (Perfection), who founded Delphi in the shadow of Parnassus where the prudent Oracle alternated with ecstatic Dionysus, again harmonizing order and disorder. Zeus loved as many women as goddesses: on Leda he begot Clytemnestra, Helen of Troy, and Argonauts Castor and Pollux (the boxer); on Alcmene he begot Heracles, the Argonauts' tedious superhero; and on Maia, Hermes, the messenger of the gods and forefather of Odysseus.

From these and from many other heaven-and-earth unions came a great court of demigods, nymphs, and sirens, among whom three great families stand out: those of the first heroes. Our very simplified family tree of the gods shows that those who adorn the earth with their adventures, like Odysseus, are descended from Atlas, the earth-bearer; those whose fiery passions destroy everything they touch, like Medea, are descended from Helius, the Sun; and those whose caution sometimes leads them to treachery, like Jason, are descended from Poseidon, the treacherous Sea. There are of course exceptions: cautious Penelope is an Atlantid, and loving Nausicaa belongs to the family of Poseidon. Gods enjoy exceptions.

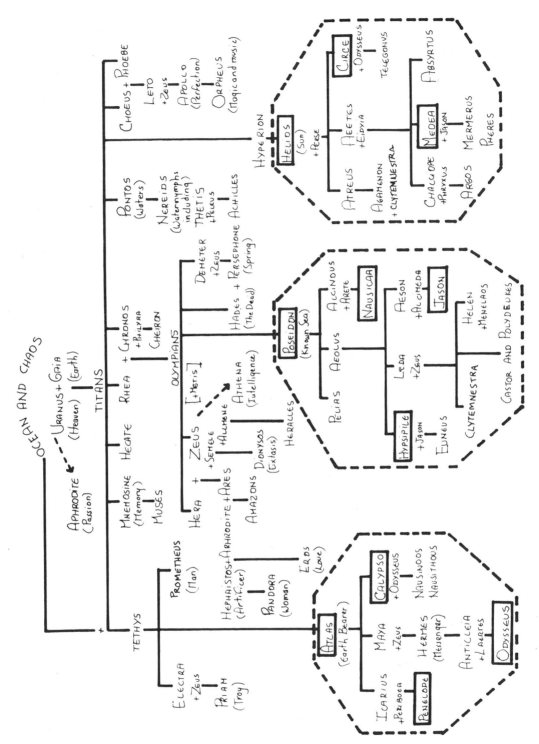

Simplified family tree of the Gods (*M.O. and J.O.*)

Homer's heroes lived in a complete and transcendent world peopled by gods and goddesses whose virtues and vices they shared. Gods often became men, and men and women became constellations, while the earth, the sea, and the winds communed with their tutelary deities. So Jason and Odysseus must deal with gods as real as wind and wave. Jason's patroness was Hera, goddess of survival, and survival was Jason's vocation, not victory or love, for love does not thrive on prudence. Odysseus' mentor, on the other hand, was Athena, and the wily and victorious Ithacan never lacked the love of women or of nymphs, for love gains strength from intelligence.

Having flown formation with an eagle down the god-invested canyon of Delphi, I myself need no further evidence; but for those who have not heard the robes of the ageing gods rustling like leaves in the wind, I must confess how once, in a moonless Mediterranean, I saw one of their sirens.

Standing in the narrow bow of a heavy *llagút,* I grasped the long, heavy trident while my oarsman rowed slowly and silently and the third member of our crew distributed brandy against the cold. The shallows passed, unreal, through the circle of light thrown by our high lantern, and we seemed to be suspended between watery earth and space-black sky. Occasionally, using a feather, we sprinkled the water with oil, stilling the slightest ripple and turning the sea into a crystal from which not even the rocks could draw a sigh. My arm began to ache as I watched for my quarry, and I was no longer sure if it had been hours or whole nights since I had last speared a sleeping fish.

Suddenly, and without a sound, she drifted naked into the magic circle, her golden locks afloat. I could not help tensing to spear her, but in that very second she raised her eyes and smiled, and the boatman, an ever-practical Mediterranean, cried, "Watch it, woman, you are going to get hurt!" Lightly, the siren disappeared into the night, and as we rowed back to the beach, none of us dared break the silence. The days passed, and in the village I sometimes recognized the smile, but never the eyes.

Homeric women shaped not only the heroes' lives but the way they would end them, for the features of death are chiseled by life. They were joined to their husbands by the gods (Helen of Troy's cuckolded husband, Menelaus, was careful to point this out). Married women were the center of the family, which was at least as important as the state, and they retained their own property (Penelope speaks of "*my* servant Dolios who watches *my* orchards"). But wifely infidelity was far from irreparable, and Menelaus soon forgave Helen; concubines and their children were treated with respect; and all women were admired as much for their intelligence as for their beauty (Antinous, leader of Penelope's suitors, spoke of her as an "incomparable schemer with a wonderful brain"). To punish Prometheus, the first man, for stealing their fire, the gods ordered Hephaestus to fashion Pandora, the first mortal woman, out of clay. Clever Prometheus refused her, but, endowed as she was with all the graces and all the arts, she easily got his brother, Epimetheus, to marry her. Then she opened the forbidden box that Zeus had given her as dowry, and all the plagues of mankind emerged, leaving only Hope.

Elements

Despite Pandora, the gods' favorite weapons were not women but the elements, and before setting sail we must learn to know and to respect them, and we must determine how much they have changed.

In the second century B.C., Hipparchus of Rhodes established that the different parts of the globe inclined more or less toward the sun according to the seasons, and he divided the globe into five climates or inclinations. In the middle were the *tropics* (the Greek word means the keel of the globe); north and south of the tropics were the two temperate zones, where men lived, and beyond them were the two polar zones. Still today the latitudes (or tropics) of Cancer and Capricorn limit the zone on which the sun's rays fall vertically, and the temperate zones end in the Arctic and Antarctic circles, beyond which the sun never altogether rises in winter or altogether sets in summer. But now we know that the limits of the climates that characterize these zones vary constantly with the skirtlike undulations of the circumpolar vortices, which always spin out of the west, as stubborn and as capricious as goddesses.

In the tropics, the sun produces huge "balloons" of hot air that rise and make room for cold polar air; and since the earth's surface revolves fastest at the equator, the resulting winds do not blow out of the north and south but out of the northeast and southeast. Most of our discoverers followed these great constant winds around the world with Helius, the Sun. But if things were that simple, Aeolus, god of the winds, would have been out of work, so valleys locally channel the winds (pouring powerful Mistrals, for example, down the Rhone and onto the Mediterranean) and continental mountain ranges prevent the great winds from passing from sea to sea, obliging them to circle clockwise over northern waters and counterclockwise in the south. We shall see how clever mariners came and went by following these winds around the oceans.

Near the equator, where the northeast and the southeast trade winds collide, the intertropical convergence zone changes its latitude with the seasons (roughly, between 15°N and 15°S), alternately flooding different parts of the tropics with rain and with dry, steady winds, and producing the punctually changing monsoons which will enable us to explain Elcano's sixteenth-century route to the Spice Islands, and the Caribbean *Brisa*. Finally, the ground heating of the air, its deflection by hills, and the continual struggle between light fronts of hot air and heavy fronts of cold (which can advance at a thousand kilometers per day) build storms around which the winds circle compulsively, producing semimythological effects such as this: in the northern temperate zone, if the wind is on one's right, one is probably flying or sailing into better weather, and if it is on one's left, into worse.

As it rises, warm air cools and its vapors condense, giving birth to clouds: cotton wool cumuli up to some fifteen thousand feet, sheets of stratus up to twenty, and feathery cirrus up to thirty. If the updraft is strong enough, Zeus' anvil begins to thunder, and the infernal cumulonimbus boils with the god's lightning up to some sixty thousand feet. I got into one once in an old and overloaded DC-3, and with wheels and flaps down and elevators full forward, I still shot up at more than three thousand feet per minute, until the god grew tired of me and threw me out like a toy.

But Hera always calls her family back to order, and the morning sea breeze returns to the waves in the evenings as if to sleep with the Nereids, the daughters of Ocean. Each nation grows familiar with its prevailing winds, so much so that the ancient Greeks identified directions with winds whose personality, smell, and taste they easily recognized. Out of the north sprang Boreas, like a dry white wine; out of the east steady Eurus blew, smelling of earth and tasting of bread; out of the south Notus raged with fiery passion; and out of the west stormed Zephyrus, the variable, with its promise of rain. Still today out of the north unmistakable Mistrals, Meltemis, Santa Anas, Harmattans, and Tramontanas worry Frenchmen, Greeks, Californians, Nigerians, and Catalans (who tend to commit suicide when it blows out of the north); while out of the south equally characteristic Siroccos, Khamsins, Nodos, and Foens craze Italians, Levantines, Yugoslavs, and Swiss (who prefer to commit their rare crimes of passion when it blows out of the south). And the trades blow steadily out of the east, while storms brew in the west.

So the great winds and their standard-bearers, the clouds, have not changed, and they will treat us as they treated Jason or Magellan, even though today we watch them from satellites and make computer forecasts that are more reliable—if less convincing—than those the Greeks got

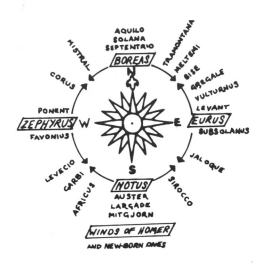

Homeric winds (with some modern names)

from the entrails of birds or those today's fishermen infer from the ominous blush of a dawn or the promissory glory of a sunset.

The currents of Ocean and of Poseidon's enclosed Sea are produced by the rotation of the earth, by the great winds, and by fast-flowing, deep-sea rivers. As with air masses, cold waters displace warm; in addition, salt waters displace fresh waters. The Greeks' Rivers of Ocean still exist: the Straits of Gibraltar and the Hellespont carry the surface currents with which the Atlantic and the Black Sea repay the sunny Mediterranean for the water it loses by evaporation and by slipping its saltier brine under theirs.[2] The sea is also attracted by Sun and by Moon, and when the two are in line with the wind, water piles up as in the Canadian Bay of Fundy, where tide levels vary by as much as fifteen meters.

Most waves are born of the wind, and storms can easily build them over thirty meters high and send them across the Atlantic. But Poseidon is master not only of the sea but of earthquakes, and quakes and eruptions can build sixty-meter waves that travel around the world at a thousand kilometers per hour. When Krakatoa blew its top a century ago near Sumatra, its force, equivalent to some hundred hydrogen bombs, was felt in the English Channel thirty-two hours later; and around the fourteenth century B.C. the Aegean island of Thira, or Santorin, exploded with the power of a thousand hydrogen bombs, hurling out waves that apparently destroyed cities all around the Eastern Mediterranean. Some have even speculated that it was Thira's tidal wave which bore Odysseus out of the known world, but those of us who have suffered the yearly Meltemi find the explanation (and the adjustment of dates) unnecessary. In any case, Ocean continues his violent courting of his mother-daughter Earth, and as he carries her away, continents separate (nearly two centimeters every year), leaving deep valleys like the mid-Atlantic trench in the sea-bottom, while great plates of earth crust jostle each other, raising long spines of volcanoes like those which border the American Pacific.

During the last four billion years the constant vagaries of winds, waters, and continents have, like Zeus, spread life all over the earth and its oceans (it is significant that blood serum has the same salinity as primeval sea water). But we have seen that Hera will not stand for much disorder, and the passion which Aphrodite bequeaths to all living creatures soon results in an orderly evolution (which Apollonius sketches as he tells the story of the Argonauts). Eventually every family of beings adapts to certain conditions; each sea and each sky knows its denizens, and navigators learn to recognize them. Pelicans, for example, never fly much more than twenty-five nautical miles from shore (Columbus wrote in his diary that "an alcatraz . . . will not stray twenty leagues from land"), and sharks and dolphins stay close to shore in temperate waters, but in the tropics they roam the high seas (their habits will help us to locate Magellan's Shark Island). Birds stake their claims on air currents and even defend them: once, while soaring over the Chilean Andes, I heard a loud "bang" whenever I turned my glider in front of a particular cliff, and I wondered if its tail was going to fall off. I discovered to my relief that the noise was made by the feathered owner of the air current I was using, who was trying to drive his talons into the metal intruder.

These richly various forms of life require a balance in the biosphere, the eggshell of habitable space which separates the bottom of Homer's wine-dark sea from the mythical heights of Olympus. About half of the seventeen trillion kilowatts of sunshine which Helius sends to earth every day is reflected back into space, and it is the other half that maintains our temperature and evaporates the seas so that they can water the land. Bacteria fertilize the earth with nitrogen "fixed" from the atmosphere so that plants can photosynthesize oxygen, and men and animals consume it to produce energy.

But ubiquitous man can upset these cycles. We already number four billion—half of us Asian, and half of those, Chinese—and it seems that by the end of the century we may be six billion, though like all statistical projections, this one will need frequent revision (the curve already seems to be leveling off). If our fires continue to carbonize more and more oxygen and to destroy the forests that produce it, the atmosphere's veil of carbon dioxide, which has increased more than ten percent in the last century, could turn the world into a hothouse which the sun's rays would penetrate but from which reflected infrared rays could not escape. It seems that up to the middle of the twentieth century this effect raised our mean temperature a couple of degrees, but since then the temperature has dropped enough to reduce northern summers by some three weeks, perhaps because the smoke and dust we keep pouring into our atmosphere reflect increasing amounts of Helius' energy before it reaches us. If this tendency continues, our "population problem" could solve itself tragically, for an average drop of 3°C. could so reduce the intensive agriculture on which we depend that a quarter of humanity might die of hunger (when we come to the Vikings, we shall see that something of the sort actually happened to the first Greenland colony). Helius, Poseidon, and Atlas, the heads of our three Olympian families, impose their balance without pity, and it is still difficult for us to distinguish their short-term whims from their long-term decrees. Nevertheless, if we do not learn to respect them, we may end up like the two neighbors we shall soon visit: Venus, an inferno, or Mars, a frozen desert.

Fortunately, we seem to be learning, and we are perhaps in time to save most of the beasts that watched the Argonauts sail by. So, for the period which will occupy us, the sea, the earth, and their inhabitants are as constant as the great winds, and, correcting for the obvious short-range changes wrought by tides, quakes, eruptions, erosion, and the migration of plants and animals, we shall face the same coasts the discoverers faced. And the gods, far from dead, will continue to speak to us in the grave language of wind and wave, even if we seldom stop to listen.

It may seem strange, but what has changed most in the centuries that concern us is the firmament. Though the stars have hardly moved within their own constellations, each year all of them together gain about a day on the sun. Thus, even though our calendar is designed to correct this, the sun's position among the stars on any given date today is different from what it was for the Assyrians and for the Egyptians—a fact that greatly confuses our astrologers. What is more (Hipparchus observed this in the second century B.C.), the earth, as it spins on its way around the sun, wobbles sleepily like a top, its poles completing every twenty-six thousand years a circle in space whose diameter is about a third of that of the globe. Consequently, when we refer to Homer's stars, we will have to figure that the projection of the north pole lay then between Kochab on top of the bowl of the Little Dipper and Giansar in Draco's tail, and that all the other stars circled around that point just as surely as they circle today around Polaris, our own North Star. In the days of Jason and Odysseus, the pole lay even farther back in the heavens, near Thuban in Draco.

Homer mentions more than once the zenith of the stars, so it is logical to suppose that Jason and Odysseus knew very well which stars faithfully overheaded their home ports—at least within five degrees, which is as close as one can judge the vertical without instruments. Only one generation separated the two seafarers, and only one degree separated their home ports, so I calculate that for both of them the principal home stars were Arcturus in Bootes, Vega in Lira, Capella in Auriga, Deneb in Cygnus, Mirfak in Perseus, and Cassiopeia's entire "M," each of them in its season clearly recognizable with the naked eye. So, though the Homeric navigators could never tell how far east or west they had gone, they could quite easily judge whether they were north or south of their home latitude, that is, the one traveled by their home stars. Then they could sail north or south to get under that latitude and sail home east or west toward the home stars' rising or setting. This method, known as latitude sailing, was used by the Polynesians not long after the Argonauts. To sail north or south was no problem, for Boreas in the north and Notus in the south were easy winds to recognize during the day, and at night Orion (Heracles) always stalked the Big Dipper or Bear in the north from his zenith in the south. The Bear was Callisto, the nymph who dared to make love to Zeus and was transformed by jealous Hera into a beast which never bathed in the sea; we shall see how this astronomically accurate legend will help us locate Homer himself.

Ships

Let us return to life on our own planet, which has gradually produced organisms adaptable to different climates and, therefore, increasingly inclined to travel and to discover. To begin with, let us attempt a reconstruction of *Argo*, the ship in which our first discoverers will sail, trying, without etymological pretensions, to connect the names of its component parts with modern words that will help us to remember them.

Homer calls merchant ships round (in other words, beamy) and says that they were driven by twenty oarsmen and a great sail. Warships like *Argo* were *macra*, or great (that is, long and narrow), and could be whipped up to high speeds by fifty oarsmen, whose number later gave rise to the name *pentekonter*. Their massive oak keel was called *tropis* (as in tropics), and it protruded forward of the hull in a *steira* (like a steer's

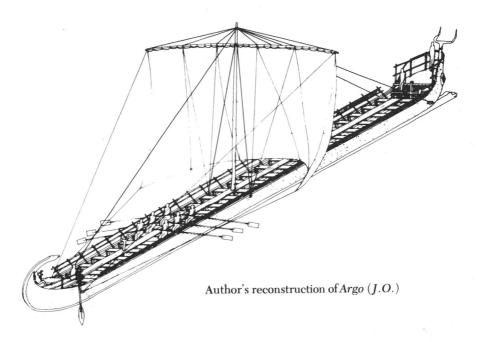

Author's reconstruction of *Argo* (*J.O.*)

horn). Homer says, "about the steira the surging wave sang aloud," and I think the steira's purpose was not to ram other ships—all fighting was still done on shore—but rather to cleave the water, just as a similarly shaped prow does on some modern ships. The hull rose a meter and a half above the keel; it was carvel-built of pine planks carefully formed with an adze and supported by frames called *stamina* (strong). The planks were sewn together end to end with *sparta* (esparto grass or papyrus cord), a method still used for small boats in the South Pacific, in Scandinavia, and in Araby. Homer almost always describes his ships as "black," so it seems clear that their hulls were tarred; Odysseus' ships are sometimes referred to as purple cheeked, but I think this was because of their purple bow ornaments, which depicted wheels or eyes.

Unless we assign two men to each oar (a tempting solution but contrary to contemporary evidence), to accommodate fifty oarsmen the hull must have measured some twenty-eight meters on the waterline, plus another two for the flying stern. It cannot have been much wider than three meters at its beamiest point, because Homer refers to two beams some two meters long which transfixed the black hull fore and aft of the oarsmen where it narrowed slightly. These beams were called *threnoi* (they groaned like a threnody) and their exposed ends served as stirrups for coming aboard. When the wind was steady, I think they were also used to make fast the sheets or *pous* (as in push) that held the tacks of the sail. But when the wind was treacherous, the pous surely passed around the threnus to gain friction, and were then held in the helmsman's grip. (When we come to the Renaissance, we shall see that Homer's threnoi can help us answer an old question about caravels). Twenty-five benches served also as crossbeams or thwarts, probably joined along their middle by a wooden gangway; on each gunwale, leather thongs secured the oars to their *kleis* (keys or tholepins). Draft must have been about a meter, so the gunwales were not much more than half a meter above water, and long wicker *pararrumata* (rail or parapet) kept the crests of waves from breaking into the ship.

Fore and aft of the threnoi were two small *ikria* (creaking decks). On the foredeck stood the first officer, singing out the beat to his oarsmen, and sometimes a lookout or, when approaching a hostile beach, a couple of lancers. On the afterdeck reclined the *archos* (the captain or archsailor), perhaps accompanied by a fair passenger like Medea, wrapped in skins. On the edge of the afterdeck sat the *kybernetes* (the helmsman, who governs), steering the ship with a steerboard called *pedalion* (a foot in the sea). The decks also protected the ship's stores, which consisted mainly of live sheep and goats, sacks of grain, and, more important, skins full of wine concentrated under the sun (just like today's *Trockenbeerenauslese*). The wine was watered according to each occasion and tasted strongly of the nose-wrinkling pine resin then used to tighten wood vats (retsina wine is still artificially flavored in Greece).

The fir mast, called *histos* (for hoisting the sail), was some twelve meters high. Stepped through its perforated *mesodome* (the "partners" in the middle thwart) and into its *histopede* (mast step) on the keel, it was steadied by leather stays called *tonoi* (each of which, as every sailor knows, sings out its own "tone" in the wind). The white square sail was called *histia;* it was made of several pieces of woolen or linen cloth (cotton was apparently still rare) and was held in place by a net called *histion*, as Viking sails would be two thousand years later. It hung on a ten-meter horizontal yard called *epikrion* (above the *kria* or decks), which was raised or lowered with leather halliards called *kaloi* (kalliards?). These were made by cutting a spiral out of a hide and then twisting and stretching it to dry in the sun, as cattlemen still do in Colombia. The sail was brailed up to the yard with lines of papyrus or of grass and made fast to the gunwales.

Cordage in general was known as *hopla* (it makes one hop), but each line had its own name in order to confound the landlubber who watched openmouthed as a proud pentekonter beached its stern, its perforated anchorstone or *eune* (eunuch) over the bow, its mast lowered aft onto the *histodoke* (mastdock), and the oarsmen backwatering. When the sternpost, curved like a scorpion's sting, was high enough on the beach, the men jumped ashore and, shouting and shoving as each successive wave lightened the ship, slowly beached its entire length. On the beach they steadied the ship with a row of stones, perhaps their own ballast stones, called *hermata* (like Hermes' pillar).

Sketchy and few are the contemporary illustrations of such ships that have come down to us, but it is interesting that the earliest was found in Iolcus, Jason's home, and is still to be seen in the Museum of Volos. Divers have now found the remains of a Mycenaean ship below Cape Gelidonya in Southern Turkey, and these confirm many Homeric details, especially the wicker rail, which Arab *lamu* dhows still use. Nevertheless, our best information comes from a careful sailor's reading of the Homeric texts, beginning with the description of the boat which Calypso helped Odysseus build. But caution is necessary: On the beach near Troy, Hector raised his arm and rested his hand on the sternpost or *aphlaston* (it comes last), and it has therefore been supposed that the sternpost can have been no more than two meters high. But when one constructs the ship one realizes that the sternpost must surely have stood some three meters high when the ship was beached; so I suggest that, unless Hector was on horseback, he can only have gripped the base of the sternpost.

On the other hand, the height of the mast is clear: When Odysseus' warship was wrecked off Sicily, the mast fell aft and crushed the helmsman's skull, so it must have been twelve meters high—two meters below deck level and ten meters above. (At first this seemed to me too high for stability, and I wondered if it might not have been the yardarm that brained the helmsman; but on completing my drawings I found that

Seventeenth century B.C. ship, restored by Theochares (urn discovered in Iolcos [Volos] in 1956) *(M.O. and M.F.)*

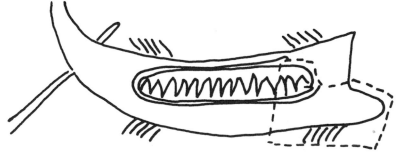

Doric ship *(M.O. and M.F.)*

Bronze Age ship, Asine urn, twelfth century B.C. *(M.O. and M.F.)*

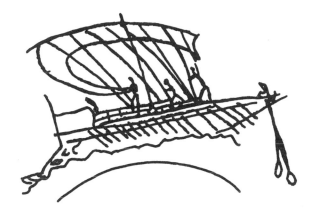

Sixth century B.C. ship *(M.O. and M.F.)*

Iolcos ship (top center) (Volos Museum) *(M.V.)*

the twelve-meter mast suggested by Homer was actually necessary for the ship.) As for the sail, Homer says that with a favorable wind, the mast was first stepped and the yard and sail were then hoisted. When the wind died, the sail was brailed up to the yard, which was then lowered, and the mast unstepped and stowed horizontally. So our guess as to rig seems pretty safe. The number of oarsmen seems equally clear: Homer says that each of Achilles' warships carried fifty oarsmen to Troy, and when he tells us how Odysseus transported cattle in a cargo ship, he refers to twenty oarsmen, and that number is confirmed in clay records found at Pylos.

If some still find my reconstruction of *Argo* unlikely, they should compare it with our photograph of today's training barge, which is equivalent to half of *Argo* without sail, and with the drawing, made by one of Captain Cook's men, of a fleet of seventeenth-century Polynesian praus, the nearest propelled by more than forty paddlers, and those on the horizon under sail.

Ships such as *Argo* could not sail close to the wind. When it blew adverse but light, they lowered the yard and mast and rowed, and when it freshened, they either beached or in steep coves hove overboard the perforated anchor stone (I spotted one on the sea bottom near Ithaca and, diving closer, found it was still being used by a fisherman). It took the Argonauts twelve hours to row thirty miles to Samothrace from Lemnos and again from there to the Hellespont, so they made two and a half knots

Modern training shell (*Harvard Magazine*)

Polynesian prow, eighteenth century B.C. (Drawn by an officer serving under Captain Cook)

rowing. Odysseus' son Telemachus sailed one hundred miles from Pylos to Ithaca in twelve hours before a god-sent wind, and Nestor made the same time over the same distance from Lesbos to Geraistos (today's Carystus) in southern Euboea. So they made eight knots, a pretty god-sent speed but not out of line with the modern formula for maximum hull speed, 1.6 times the square root of the waterline in feet. Five knots is a more likely average speed under sail, and that is what *Argo* made from Cape Acherusias (Ereğli) to Cape Carambis (Cape Kerempe) and again from Sinop to the Amazons' river, Thermodon, one hundred twenty miles in twenty-four hours.

Like all good sailors, Homeric navigators tended to be cautious and usually preferred to sail within sight of land and in the summer daytime. At night, during storms, or in winter, their ships generally rested on the beach. Let us leave them there and prepare to sail with the Argonauts.

NOTES

1. Some say that Homer never existed and that the *Iliad* and the *Odyssey*, after being handed down orally by generations of bards like Alcinous' blind singer, were finally written down by some scribe. But the magic of Homer's name is such that the Homeridae of Chios dedicated themselves for centuries to the tradition that it was their island that saw the poet's birth, and great cities still vie for the honor. The way the epics are constructed satisfies me that they must finally have been written down by one great poet. I hope our navigations will show that this poet must either have been a sailor or have lived where men knew the sea. Who but a sailor could have written this: "There are times when the great sea is darkened by a soundless swell. It knows that a gale is on its way; but that is all it knows, and the waves cannot begin their march . . . till the wind sets in steadily from one side or the other."

2. In the Straits of Gibraltar the surface current flows into the Mediterranean counter to the current at the bottom of the sea. During World War II, German and Italian submarines used both currents to transit the straits with engines turned off so that the British could not detect their throbbing.

2
THE
ARGONAUTS
AND
ODYSSEUS

Chroniclers, Harbors, and Heroes

As soon as I heard that the yacht *Mesouda* was sailing for the Ionian Sea, I flew to Athens and drove directly to the port city of Piraeus on the off chance of getting one last look at Odysseus' kingdom, and the usual search through port police offices and bustling moorings enabled me to join her crew *(Mesouda* is Arabic for happy woman). We sailed at night to the Diaporioi Islands and, under a full moon, dove over a sandy bottom strewn with fragments of ancient urns. It is of course forbidden to take any home—yet on our way back we found a huge dredge sucking up sand, urns and all. So much for archaeological conservation!

Waiting our turn, we sailed deep and narrow through the Corinth Canal; the next day, off the Trizonian Islands in the Gulf of Corinth, our cruise was almost ended by a sudden zephyr, a dragging anchor, and a nonstarting engine. We spent the night in the fortified harbor of Navpaktos, where, in 1571, Don John of Austria and his armada made ready to protect the Mediterranean from the Turks at Lepanto, then we sailed out into the Ionian Sea through the Gulf of Patras, into which Zephyrus was piling up a good chop. One by one the islands which made up Odysseus' kingdom rose from the horizon: wooded Zakinthos to port, high Cephalonia to starboard, and under it Odysseus' rugged Ithaca itself. At night we sailed north into the stage-lit harbor of the island of Paxos and moored stern-to under the phoenix sign of the Greek colonels' government, but when we thought we could settle down to exchanging ouzo and songs in the local taverna, women in black began to bewail the mobilization of their men for Cyprus. At midnight the colonels' sign was removed by a couple of policemen; a new Trojan war had returned Greece to parliamentary democracy.

Next for Corfú, where, according to tradition, both Jason and Odysseus stopped on their separate voyages home and where the Venetians, the English, and the French seem to have agreed to leave some of their best colonial architecture. As we entered the beautiful harbor, I reflected on the differences between the *Argonautica* and the *Odyssey;* for Jason may well have reentered Greece here, but not, I think, Odysseus.

Both heroes sailed in the thirteenth century B.C., when Nebuchad-nezzar I ruled Babylon, when in Egypt Karnak and Luxor were only two centuries old and Abu Simbel had not yet been started, and when Moses and his Israelites, heirs perhaps of the monotheism of Akhnaton, aban-doned Rameses II. The epics forged from the adventures of Jason and Odysseus were transmitted through four centuries of unbroken oral tradition, a feat made possible by the uncluttered minds of the bards and by a golden thread of standard descriptive phrases such as "the wine-dark sea" and "the rosy-fingered dawn." But in the eighth century B.C., when the time came to write the stories down, the fates of the two epics and therefore the precision of their details diverged.

To me the dramatic unity of the *Odyssey*, complete with flashbacks, shows the voice of a single great poet.[1] On the other hand, we first glimpse the *Argonautica* in minor references by Homer and Hesiod around the beginning of the eighth century B.C. The earliest known complete, though brief, account of the Argonauts' adventure appears in Pindar's fourth *Pythian Ode* in the fifth century B.C., and this is amplified by Herodotus and embroidered by Aeschylus, Sophocles, and Euripides in the sixth and fifth centuries. A final version is achieved only in the third century B.C. by Apollonius of Rhodes, the librarian of Alexandria, who had to complete his epic in Rhodes because of the controversy it created. Not only does his *Argonautica* give most of the details we need to retrace Jason's route, but its *scolia,* or footnotes, refer several times to other complete accounts unknown to us. (Could it be that when the great library of Alexandria burned, we lost an *Argonautica* by Homer?) Consequently, while we can rely almost entirely on the Homeric version of the *Odyssey*, which has come down to us complete from the days when it had to be memorized in full for the Olympic games, we will have to take into account five centuries of references for the *Argonautica*.

Fortunately, we are most concerned with the Argonauts' outward voyage to Colchis, where they discovered that the Black Sea was not a gulf of the Infinite Ocean but a finite sea bounded by the high Caucasus, and the chronicles are in agreement on this leg of the voyage. The Argonauts' return, on the other hand, is described by each chronicler in accordance with his contemporaries' view of the world (nevertheless, I hope to show that geographic sense can be made of it). We will use Apollonius' account as our basic guide, filling it out wherever necessary with details from other chroniclers. Our technical "backup system" will be the sailing directions that Scylax prepared for Darius the Great around the fifth century B.C. (to which Apollonius, as librarian of Alexandria, may well have had access) and also, of course, our own estimates of what a ship like *Argo* could in fact have done.

Jason sailed from Pagasae, the port of Iolcus, at the head of the great Pagasaean Gulf, a round inland sea some fifteen nautical miles in diameter, situated above the northern tip of the island of Euboea (Evia), which protects southeastern Greece from the Aegean. Today's capital is Volos, third in importance among Greek ports, a lively city crowned by Mount Pelion, exuberant in summer and snowcapped in winter. West of the city lie the ruins of Roman Demetrias, under which local tradition says that Pagasae, the port, is buried—but this makes no nautical sense to me. Iolcus itself, on the other hand, is traditionally supposed to be inside the city of Volos. After much enquiring in that city, I found my way to a workingmen's quarter a few blocks inland from the mouth of the river and covering the top of a low hill whose flanks are ringed by ancient walls. When I enquired, an old man pointed to a piece of column embedded in the sidewalk and said, "Yes sir, Iolcus is everywhere." Here, I suggest, is not only Iolcus but also its port, awaiting a team of archaeologists well-heeled enough to buy and excavate the entire quarter.

Pindar tells us that King Pelias of Iolcus, a descendant of treacherous Poseidon, usurped the throne of his half brother Aeson, Jason's father, and that an oracle warned him that his challenger would arrive wearing only one sandal. Young Jason, who was brought up on Mount Pelion by Cheiron the Centaur, went down to Iolcus to claim his throne and made the mistake of declaring in public his willingness to give up the rest of his rightful inheritance in exchange for the crown. Luckily, on the way down he carried an old crone across the river, who turned out to be Hera in disguise; unluckily, one of his sandals remained stuck in the mud. Wily old Pelias, thus forewarned, offered to give up not only the throne but the entire inheritance if Jason would prove himself by sailing "to the end of the world" to recover the golden fleece.

The fleece came from the winged golden ram on whose back Pelias' ancestor Phrixus and his sister Helle had escaped their stepmother's wrath. Helle fell from the ram's back and disappeared between Europe and Asia, thus christening the Hellespont, but Phrixus' soul haunted Pelias with the threat of a seven-year famine for Iolcus if the golden fleece was not brought home. Jason could not refuse the public challenge, so, consoled by Acastus, Pelias' son, who impulsively decided to join the expedition, he began to put together his crew.

Jason was a handsome northern aristocrat with long blond hair who carried two spears, one for throwing and one for thrusting, and covered his woolen underwear (typical of his country, Magnesia) with a leopardskin. Pindar tells us that he was *amekanos*, not very resourceful, unlike Odysseus, to whom Homer often refers as *politropon*, the wily one. But Jason did have one redeeming virtue, and that a very aristocratic one: He knew how to pick men who possessed the skills he lacked. This is

Jason watching Heracles. Fifth century B.C. Greek urn (*State Antique and Gem Collection, Munich*)

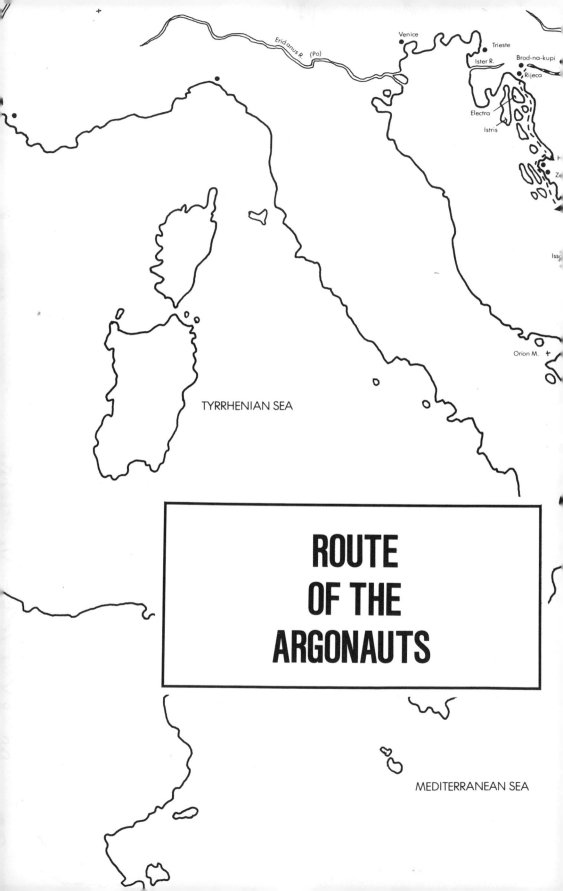

Eridanus R. (Po)

Venice

Trieste

Ister R.

Brod-na-kupi

Rijeca

Electra

Istris

Z

Iss

Orion M.

TYRRHENIAN SEA

ROUTE
OF THE
ARGONAUTS

MEDITERRANEAN SEA

BLACK SEA

Caucasus Mts. 3,000 m

Colchis
Cochisaea

Phasys R.

Plain de Ares

Paleostomi Lagoon

COLCHIDES

bis

ast of Egalus

Sinop

C. Bafra

Deltas of the
Assyrians

Philyra's Cave

Hopa

BYZERES

Sacred Mt.

C. Zeus

Ares Is.

C. Zephir

Rize

BECHEIRI

Boyabat

Hacys R.

C. Chiva

Unye

Keresos

Tripoli

Trebizond

MACRONES

Kastamonu

Pharnakia

HLAGONES

Termyscira

Thermodon R.

Aksu R.

TIBURENI

NDINI

ASSYRIANS

Iris R.

CALIBES

perhaps why, while the *Odyssey* bears the name of its central hero, the very name *Argonautica* indicates that it is the story of a shipload of heroes. The Western discovery of the globe thus begins with a team—a sort of ancient NASA.

First Jason recruited Argus, the engineer, to build the ship that was to bear his name. For balance he chose the musical wizard who could best handle what an engineer does not understand, Orpheus, son of Apollo and the Muse Calliope. Next came Tiphys, the great helmsman, supported by Zetes and Calais, the winged sons of Boreas, the north wind. Then Mopsus and Idmon, two seers, balanced by the boxer Pollux, and Castor, his twin. Lynceus, the lynx-eyed, came with his mad brother Idas, who saw reality beyond appearances and fearlessly sang out the truth. Fleet Aetalides, son of Hermes, was backed by Ancaeus, the young giant who knew the stars. Peleus, Achilles' father, came with Telamon, father of "big" Ajax; Oileus, father of "little" Ajax; and Menoetius, father of Achilles' beloved Patroclus. All four sons would be heroes of the Greek expedition against Troy, no doubt inspired by the deeds of their Argonaut sires. Finally, amidships would row Heracles, the heavy club-carrying superhero, cloaked in his lion skin and waited upon by his beauteous page, Hylas.

For a while Jason's lack of enthusiasm postponed departure, and the Argonauts grew so impatient that they wondered whether Heracles should not take over Jason's command. But Heracles refused. When even *Argo*'s talking keel (Athena's gift) protested the delay, crazy Idas insulted Jason, Idmon and Tiphys defended him, and only Orpheus' lyre averted a mutiny. Tearfully, Jason gave the order to sail.

The Argonautica

The weeping of the women of Iolcus receded as Orpheus' lyre set the rhythm of the oars and *Argo* glided through the morning mists, across the sleeping gulf, and out into the sea, passing between Mount Klimo, almost a thousand meters high, and the steep peninsula of Trikeri, or Tisea.

Across the centuries an echo of Orpheus' song has come down to us. A cuneiform musical score engraved on a clay tablet dating from about the time of the Argonauts was found not long ago in Ugarit, Syria. Interpretated on a reconstructed lyre, it sounds as if it could well have paced a long-distance oarsman.[2]

Jason's tutor, Cheiron the Centaur, heard the song and galloped down to the beach, followed by his wife Chariclo carrying the infant Achilles so that he might watch his father Peleus sail by, and begin to

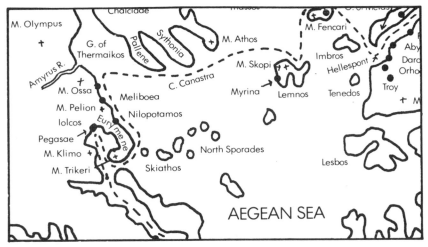

Route of the Argonauts—Iolcos to the Hellespont

dream of Troy. Wise Cheiron, who would voluntarily give up his immortality to become the constellation Sagittarius, was the great tutor of heroes, perhaps, as Machiavelli points out, because a great leader needs animal instincts as much as he needs human virtues. The Centaur could have come down to any of the beaches that cling to Mount Pelion's skirts, but tradition says he galloped into the surf at Milopotamos under high Tsangarada, and anyone who has swum off this white beach surrounded by rocky caverns will tend to agree.

As *Argo* rounded dark Cape Sepias, Notus, the south wind, blew at last. The tired Argonauts stepped the mast and hoisted the sail, and the "tone" of the stays took over Orpheus' song. Fish played in the roiling wake as *Argo* left the island of Skiathos to starboard and ran with the current up the magnificent coast of Magnesia and under Mount Pelion, whose seaward slopes are always perfumed and dressed for summer with herbs, flowers, fruit, walnut, pine, and olive. But when "Dolop's tomb" was in sight (any one of the high rocks that rise out of this theatrical seacoast), the wind left *Argo*'s sail and the Argonauts decided to beach her at Amphetae, "the last port of call," happy to spend two days offering sacrifices—in other words, feasting. I suggest they did so on the beach at Choreftion, which means "the place for ceremonies or choirs," under steep and shady Zagora.

Notus returned; the Argonauts sailed past Meliboea, today's Melivia, and Eurymene, today's Rizo, then under two-thousand-meter Mount Ossa, up the scarred flanks of which the Titans of old tried to pile Mount Pelion in order to challenge Olympus. They passed the mouth of Amirus, today's Pinios, the river that still plows a broad furrow through dusty Thessaly to create the verdant valley of Tempe and fills it with the song of the nightingale. In the evening they were abeam snowcapped Olympus, three thousand meters high, and dared not waste the favorable wind, for they knew that out of the cumulonimbus which so often crowns the great mountain such sudden storms swoop down that no sailor can doubt that Zeus is punishing his misdeeds (I saw two dinghies sunk by such a storm). They crossed the Gulf of Thermaikos at night and ran past the Pallene peninsula, where, Apollonius says, Cape Canastra rises out of the sea. Certainly, as one first sights it in the moonlight, Canastra looks like an island. The second Chalcidic peninsula, Sythonia, was also left behind, and dawn gilded *Argo*'s sail under two-thousand-meter Mount Athos, prow of the third peninsula.[3] Thus in twelve hours *Argo* sailed some sixty nautical miles, which fits our estimate of five knots.

The wind died down again, and the Argonauts rowed toward five-hundred-meter Mount Skopia, beckoning them over the horizon to the island of Lemnos. Here Queen Hypsipyle had led the island women to massacre all the men (except the queen's father) for not paying attention to their wives as well as to their slave women. (Oddly, it was also the birthplace of Aphrodite's mischievous son, Eros.) The ferocious Lemnian women prepared to fight off the Argonauts, but, sweet-talked by Aetalides, they soon submitted to the sailors—all but Heracles, who sulked on the beach with a few henchmen and finally harangued his philandering comrades. "Let us leave Jason here," he cried, "since his idea of glory is to repopulate Lemnos. We must sail on." So Jason was forced to leave. In time, Queen Hypsipyle would bear his son Euneus, who would be the reigning king of Lemnos when Agamemnon's expedition to Troy sailed by (cautious as his father, Euneus' only contribution to the Trojan war would be the good wine of his island).

Lemnos is a butterfly-shaped island whose body is green and whose wings are studded with rocky heights. There, eagles soar in search of tortoises, and today's amateur archaeologists have to help push their taxis up deeply rutted roads while women in black dresses and white veils ride by on donkeys and smile indulgently. To the northeast lie the sprawling ruins of Ifestia, or Hephaistia (Greeks spell as they wish), a great city with two harbors, but it flourished long after the Argonauts left. To the southwest the ruins of steep Poliochni overlook a long beach on which Heracles could well have strutted while his shipmates made love, but Poliochni itself was in ruins long before the Argonauts arrived. Cozy Myrina, on the other hand, which still bears the name of Hypsipyle's mother, is the first port one sees when one sails over from Mount Athos, whose shadow, says Apollonius, falls upon the Lemnian capital. Con-

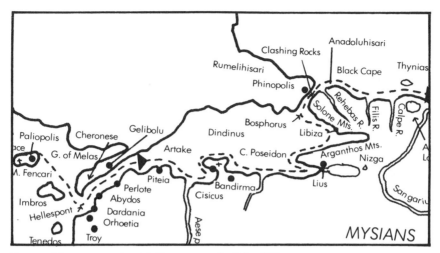

Route of the Argonauts—Hellespont to the Isle of Thynias

sequently, I propose to leave the Lemnian women and their foolish husbands under this pretty port.

On the northeast corner of Lemnos there is an ancient sanctuary of the Cabires, the sect that founded the mysteries of Eleusis and Samothrace. Samothrace is an island of goats, sulphurous waters, and magnetic stones, whose two-thousand-meter Mount Fengari (Moon Mountain) is visible from the Lemnian sanctuary. I think this is where the Argonauts left Lemnos, after Orpheus had been initiated by the Cabires into the mysteries which still seem to haunt Samothrace. From Lemnos they rowed twenty nautical miles in eight hours (not even Heracles could row more than eight hours in one day), for an average of two and a half knots, which is again close to our estimate. Once on Samothrace, they probably beached *Argo* in the bay of Paliopolis, which today is silted up.

Another full day's rowing (for about the same distance) brought *Argo* to the Chersonese, "with the Thracian coast to the left but leaving the island of Imbros to the right," says Apollonius, accurately describing the safest route. He also says that at dawn they were ready to enter the bleak Hellespont as soon as the wind changed to the south, a correct description of the only condition that will allow a ship like *Argo* to sail into the River of Ocean. The prevailing current of about four knots is always adverse here (we have seen why) except when the wind has blown plenty of water out into the Aegean and then veers to the south. Making the best of this rare piece of luck, by evening *Argo* had traversed the strait "along its Roetian coast, past Ida, Dardania, Abydos, Percote, and Piteia"—in other words, hugging the Asian shore just as a modern yachtsman would—and "rowing and sailing at the same time," says Apollonius, as though he were a sailor.

The following morning the Argonauts entered the broad Propontis, or Sea of Marmara, sailed past the mouth of the Aesepus River (today's Gönen), and beached *Argo* in the evening on the isthmus of Artake (today's Erdek), a pleasant little port where gentle south winds silver the leaves of the olive trees that watch over vineyards strewn with the ruins of the ancient capital. "On the Phrygian coast," says Apollonius, "there is a high peninsula whose isthmus barely surmounts the waves," and he goes on to say that its Mount Dindimium is shaped like a bear and that from its summit one can see Thrace, the Mysian Mountains, and even the Bosporus. The isthmus is in fact so low that Alexander the Great had to build it up into a causeway, and, though I was never able to spot the bear, I have flown low past Dindimium, today's Kapidağ, and seen the magnificent view Apollonius describes.

Here the Argonauts paid their respects to King Cizicus and got a good night's rest, after which they brought *Argo* around the peninsula to Chitus, which, Apollonius says, is also called Pandermos, "the cozy port" (its name means "wrapped in skins," as in epidermis, which has survived to this day in its Turkish version, Bandirma). The Argonauts made allies of King Cizicus and his Doliones by slaughtering the monstrous savages who periodically came down from Bear Mountain, but when *Argo* sailed on and was forced back at night by a shift in the wind, the Doliones thought they were being invaded. In the ensuing Skirmish Cizicus lost his life, and his young queen, Cleite, hanged herself on hearing the news. Jason, who prudently preferred not to leave enemies where he might have to call again on his way home, cleared up the error at dawn and buried the king with full Greek honors. After a further stay of twelve days Mopsus saw a hawk light on *Argo*'s sternpost and the Argonauts took their leave with a great sacrificial feast on the mountain. Tiphys exchanged his anchor stone for a heavier one, leaving many generations to venerate here the anchor the Argonauts left behind.

They rowed away to the east, confident that Zephyrus would soon blow out of the west, but, despite the omen of the hawk, Zephyrus was not eager to take over, and beyond the Rhyndacus River (today's Sisaria) the oarsmen began to tire. Only Heracles rowed harder and harder; he broke his oar, fell overboard, and clambered aboard again, furious at having no work to do (obviously not a real Greek). But apparently a good wind soon sprang up, for at dusk *Argo* entered the harbor of Cius, today's Gemlik, where the high mountains Apollonius mentions dominate Iznik, ancient Nicaea, where Pliny would serve centuries later as Trajan's governor and later still the Nicene Creed would be produced and the first Crusade end in a shambles. While the Mysians feasted the Argonauts,

Heracles looked for a spruce out of which to fashion a new oar, and Hylas, his pretty squire, wandered off to a stream and was spirited away by its nymph. Heracles refused to leave without him, and after a long wait and much debate, when the morning star brought a favorable wind, Jason and Tiphys decided to sail anyway. One has the feeling that Jason, who was not usually so decisive, quite liked the idea of going on without the superhero (who would later take his revenge by killing the two sons of the wind which now wafted *Argo* away).

Argo rounded Cape Poseidon, today's Boz Burnú, and the Argonauts beached her "under the morning star." Here King Amycus and his Bebryces met them with a challenge. No crew could sail from that beach until one of its members had beaten the burly king at fisticuffs. Jason, as usual, had the man. Taciturn Pollux put up his fists, punched the king over the ear, and split his skull. For good measure the Argonauts massacred the Bebryces and strewed their bodies "like logs" around the beach on which they themselves then slept wrapped in their skins and cloaks—all but Pollux, who wandered off into the night, brooding over what he had done, and never returned. The distance is right, and so is the beach, for all this to have happened near today's Gebze.[4]

The following day *Argo* entered the narrow Bosporus and, thanks to Tiphys, rode out one of the sudden waves which still surprise these waters. Then, says Apollonius, where the strait makes a great curve to the right and just before the Black Sea comes into view, Notus again turned into Boreas, the dominant north wind (Bora still to the Turks, but Meltemi to modern Greeks). The ship sought shelter at the port of Phineus the blind prophet (it is still marked Phinopolis on some old maps), where the strait makes two broad curves, turns right at Buyuk-deré, and then runs straight into the Black Sea, as described by Appolonius. This port is probably today's Tarabaya, one of the best yacht basins in the Bosporus.

Jason requested Phineus' instructions for reaching Colchis, but the prophet whom the gods had condemned to a blind, hungry, and fetid existence as punishment for seeing the future too clearly offered his services only on one condition: The Argonauts must first rid him of the stinking Harpies who, at every meal, swooped down to claw the food out of his mouth. Again Jason had the men for the job. A great feast was prepared, and as soon as the batlike beat of the Harpies' wings was heard, Zetes and Calais, the sons of Boreas, took to the air. The first recorded aerial dogfight ended with the Harpies forced down and grounded on a distant isle, their lives spared only "because they were the hounds of Zeus." Grateful Phineus, bathed and fed, then warned Jason of the

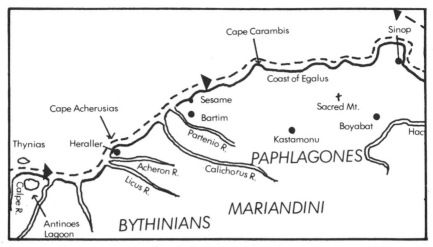

Route of the Argonauts—Isle of Thynias to Sinop

Clashing Rocks that closed like jaws on anyone who tried to pass through the narrowest point in the strait, and instructed him to send forth a dove just ahead of *Argo* so that the rocks would clash and part again, and then to row like mad on top of the wave that would form before the rocks clanged shut once more. If Jason must pray, said Phineus, he should do so at once, for there would be no time when *Argo* was riding the surf. Beyond this advice, despite Jason's pleading, there was little the seer would say about the rest of the voyage, except that the return route would be different. Phineus had learned that, while men punish prophets who do not satisfy their expectations, gods punish those who poach on their perfect knowledge of the future.

The dove lost its tailfeathers and *Argo* its sternpost, but the Argonauts made it through the rocks, which remained anchored to the bottom. Surrounded today by the "Devil's Currents," these reefs must still be watched carefully as the sailor passes Rumelikavagi, one of the narrowest stretches of the strait, which is guarded by two castles, Rumelihisari, "the castle on the Roman side," and Anadoluhisari, "the castle on the Anatolian side." Defensive traditions die hard, and these narrows, where one finally sights the Black Sea, are still a military reservation.

Finally *Argo* rounded Apollonius' Black Cape, today's Kara Burnú (still marked by what looks like a pile of dark tombstones), and entered the Black Sea. This schizophrenic sea cannot decide whether it belongs to the Mediterranean or to the Caspian. I have seen it as sun-drenched and blue as the Mediterranean, with only a thin line of cloud on the horizon, and in no time at all I have watched the north wind gallop out of the limitless steppes and transform the thin cloud into the black shroud that surely gave the sea its name. At sight of it, Jason hesitated, but Tiphys egged him on, and with Boreas on their beam and the strange peaks of Colone (today's Alam and Chatal Dağ) to the south, they ran past the rivers Rehebas (today's Riva) and Filis, which now flows into the sea at Agva. But even brave Tiphys was tempted to strike sail and drop anchor as the island of Thynias came into view, for it was topped by a huge apparition. Fortunately, Orpheus could explain it: it was his father, Apollo. My explanation is more pedestrian: Thynias, which I think is the island of Kefken, is backed by the strangely colored dunes of the bay of the same name, from which Boreas still sends columns of yellow dust high into the air under the shadow of Babi Dag, the Mountain of the Old Man.

The next day the rivers Calpe and Sangarius (today's Sakarya) were left behind, and as *Argo* reached the mouth of the river Lycus (today's Karasakar), the wind died and the Argonauts rowed to the beach under "high Cape Acherusias, where the river Acheron flows out of Hades' Cave in which silence never reigns, near flat stone reefs barely washed over by the waves." Here King Lycus, the wolf, whose dominions stretched from the river that bore his name to the Amazons' Thermodon, gratefully received the Argonauts who had rid him of his enemy Amycus. He even offered them his son as guide. But Hades, too, claimed his due: Idmon the seer was killed by a wild boar, and Tiphys the incomparable helmsman died of a fever.

In my view, all this happened in today's port of Ereğli, the Turkish version of the name Heraclea. Around Ereğli wild animals still abound, and Kurbagali Deré ("the gully of the frogs") is still pocked with huge caverns, some containing the remains of Byzantine shrines sunk in black pools whose frigid breath rustles the leaves that frame the caverns' entrances. Even Apollonius' flat stone reefs are still visible beyond Baba Burnú (The Old Man's Cape), and when I enquired if any Mycenean tombs had been found here, an old man smiled and said, "When the Greeks were still here (before Kemal), they showed me two *tumuli* on top of Baba Burnú. Unfortunately, I cannot show them to you, for the cape is a military reservation."[5]

Jason's lamentations soon produced the volunteer helmsman he needed: young Ancaeus, son of the sea god, whose knowledge of the stars would prove indispensable on the Argonauts' return voyage. Zephyrus was blowing again, and *Argo* sailed past "the fertile lands of the Maryandini," Apollonius' accurate description of the only part of this coast that does not fall sheer into the sea. The Argonauts visited the tomb of Sthenelus, Heracles' old comrade, whose ghost dazzled them. This shore

Kurbagali Deré (Hades' Cave) *(S.O.)*

Amasra (The Tomb of Sthenelus) *(S.O.)*

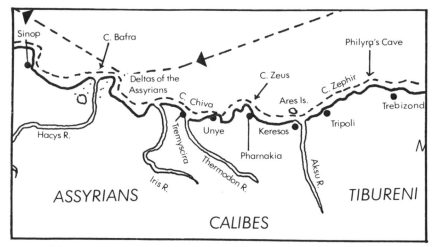

Route of the Argonauts—Sinop to Trebizond

is dotted with high vertical rocks and my choice for Sthenelus' tomb is the one that marks the entrance to the walled port of Amasra, framed by the high mountains Apollonius also mentions, and caressed by the coldest surf in which I have ever swum. Among the rivers Apollonius places here, Sesamus stands out, for this is Amasra's ancient name.

Argo sailed on to Cape Carambis "in a night and a day," almost a hundred nautical miles in twenty-four hours—a speed of just over four knots. This cape, says Apollonius, splits the wind. Today's Cape Kerempe, a name similar enough to Carambis, is famous for changes of wind, and no sailor can tell if Boreas, when he strikes at Kerempe from the Crimean peninsula, will turn east or west.

They left Carambis at dawn, and by the time the sun had set and risen again they were safe behind Cape Sinop, having made a little less than their usual four or five knots. This cape, a high peninsula rather like the rock of Gibraltar, was named for the astute virgin who gave herself to gods and to men on one condition, that they respect her virginity. The Argonauts rested here for twelve days and were joined by volunteers claiming to be survivors of Heracles' earlier expedition.[6] Before sailing on from Sinop, they made the pilgrimage to Apollonius' "Sacred Mountain."

From Amasra I climbed almost vertically over a thousand meters to the pass where Boreas formed a perfect dynamic updraft on which eagles soared effortlessly above a tall stand of pine through which the sun dappled the mossy ground. Then I descended into a wide valley

Rock Temple at Salarkoy (The Sacred Mount) (*S.O.*)

Door to the Altar of Sacrifices
(The Sacred Mount) (*S.O.*)

with a steep hill at its center, below which lay a medieval village of stone, wood, and slate, guarded by a modest minaret. As I approached the hill, I focused my binoculars on its summit and spotted what looked like the entrance to a cave temple. A gaitered shepherd led me into the village, where we were surrounded by clean-faced women with large round loaves under one arm and handsome children (many of them blond) hanging on to the other. Hard pressed to keep up with my guide, I climbed the hill, passed under a high colonnade surmouted by a lion and a broken eagle, both carved out of the live rock, and entered a small, dark chamber full of the buzzing of bees.

As my eyes grew accustomed to the dark, I recognized the sacrificial stone altar, its channel still reddish from the animals' blood. But the shepherd would not let me rest; he beckoned me frantically out of the temple, then led me into a small cave behind the crest of the hill, up a vertiginous stone stairway, and out onto a pulpit overlooking the village. Under a sky streaked with clouds scudding before Nodos, it was easy to imagine the dramatic mysteries that must have been performed here before Byzantium transformed the ancient temple into a Christian shrine. It is here, I feel sure—off the road from Amasra to Kastamonu and some thirteen kilometers before Boyabat—that the Argonauts sacrificed at Apollonius' holy mount.

With Zephyrus brisk in their sail, the Argonauts passed the Halys River, today's Kizil Irmak, the red river that flows into the sea at Cape Bafra, and then the Iris River, today's Yesil Irmak, the green river that flows into the sea at Cape Chiva. Apollonius calls these "the fertile deltas of the Assyrians," and the deltas of the two rivers are still the best lands for rice on this whole coast. Here Scylax locates "Assyria" and places a second river "Lycus," which brings us close to the border between King Lycus and the land of the Amazons.

"The land of the Amazons," says Apollonius, "is watered by the hundred mouths of the river Thermodon." The fact is that from here on it is impossible to sail far without passing the mouth of a river and since they all flow from behind the same coastal range, the supposition that they all come from one great current is understandable. One of these mouths belongs to today's Terme, which the first illustrated *Ptolemaic Atlas* (maps by Crivelli, Bologna, 1477) clearly marks "Thermodontis F. (river)." Apollonius says also that the Amazons sacrificed on a black rock, and not far from here there is a second Kara Burnú, as black as the one we rounded after entering the Black Sea. Just beyond this cape *Argo* was brought to port in the mouth of the Terme, where crescent-shaped fishing boats still moor today.

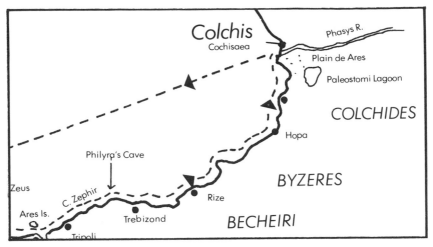

Route of the Argonauts—Trebizond to Colchis

The Argonauts had learned enough from the Lemnian women not to get involved with Amazons, and without dallying, they passed the land of the Chalybes, "who spend their days digging and forging iron surrounded by soot, flames, and black smoke" (probably the West's first encounter with iron). There is still plenty of coal along this coast, and there must also have been plenty of fire, judging from the range of extinct volcanoes that now frames it. *Argo* rounded Zeus' Cape, probably today's Yasun Burnú, or Jason's Cape, whose greenish flanks topped with humid verdure still shroud it in mystery. Then the ship ran along "the coast of the Tibureni" until the wind died down, and as the island of Ares, god of war, came into view, a squadron of war birds launched an attack on the ship. The crew covered *Argo* with their shields and raised an infernal din by banging their swords on them, and this, with the swishing of their helmet plumes, was enough to scare away the war god's birds. No islands are marked on our maps of this coast, but just beyond today's Giresun (ancient Keresos, where the Roman General Lucullus would discover cherries) and facing the mouth of Aksú Dersi stands a high rock out of whose wooded summit a pile of ruins shines white. Local tradition identifies these remains with Mars, the Roman successor of Ares, and as I watched one falcon after another dropped out of the sky, leaving me with my mouth open. That evening at the inn, I talked to a man who carried a hooded falcon on his wrist, and he said proudly that this was where the best falcons come from. Ares' birds are not extinct.

Phineus, the blind prophet, had told Jason to put in at this inhospitable island for a pleasant surprise, and as usual the seer was right. The sons of Phrixus, Jason's ancestor who flew to Colchis on the golden ram, had been wrecked here while escaping from King Aietes, and, after a little persuasion, the eldest, Argeus, agreed to join *Argo* and guide her to the land of the golden fleece. With the wind in her sail, *Argo* passed a coast where, Apollonius says, savages made love in the open and took great care of the father while the mother was giving birth. It is a handsome coast, covered today with hazelnut trees, here growing under a minaret, there under a Greek, a Roman, or a Byzantine ruin; and it is still studded with the small log huts that Apollonius describes and calls *mossines*, which today's Mosinoes still use.

In a day and a night, says Apollonius, the Argonauts came to the cave where Cronus made love to the nymph Philyra and, caught in the act by his wife Rhea, fled in the form of a stallion, leaving Philyra to give birth to Jason's tutor Cheiron, half god, half stallion. Twenty-four hours at some six knots means one hundred fifty nautical miles, which puts *Argo* at Trebizond, an ancient outpost of Greece that is still framed in sunlit olive groves. Here, in the centuries ahead, Xenophon would march into the surf shouting "Thalassa!" (the sea) after leading his ten thousand men all the way from Babylon; and, in 1451, Comnenius, last of the Byzantine emperors, fleeing the Crusaders' sack of Constantinople, would complete

Güzelhissar Cave at Trebizond
(Philyra's Cave) (S.O.)

the Byzantine millennium. The most likely cape for Philyra's cave was, as usual, located in a military reservation, but the director of the museum was able to get permission for me to search, and there, to his delight and mine, was the great cave. "With a two-thousand-year-old book in your hand you have found a cave which I did not know," he said. "Why don't you stay here and excavate it with us?"

Trebizond marks the end of the wooden *mossines*, which are replaced east of here by primitive stone dwellings surrounded by tea plantations. Apollonius says that after leaving Philyra's cave the Argonauts ran along a coast peopled by many races, Macrones, Becheiri, Sapeires, and Byzeres, and Scylax also places them all along the same coast. Today this is the rough land of the Lazes, a prehellenic race which speaks a Turco-Georgian dialect and which, according to Turkish wags, is so primitive that the men spend all their time in mock feuds (*kan davas*) while their women do the work and give birth.

At last the majestic Caucasus Mountains rose above the eastern horizon and the Argonauts reached the far corner of the Black Sea.[7] As night fell, Argus, the son of Phrixus, guided them into the mouth of the Phasis River, which I think is today's Rioni, which flows into the sea at the Russian port of Poti. To their left stood Aia, the Colchian capital (the Russians may some day find it under the sea), and to their right stretched the plain of Ares, where a dragon as long as *Argo*, says Pindar, guarded the oak over which the golden fleece was draped, "flashing in the sun like Zeus' *aegis*." Mast and sail stowed, *Argo* glided slightly into the rushes that framed the river's mouth, and, dropping their stone anchor, the exhausted Argonauts fell asleep.

Next day crazy Idas goaded the reluctant Jason into requesting the fleece directly from King Aietes, son of Helius. The king received Jason—and reacted like Pelias. He did not refuse outright, but he stated impossible conditions: Jason would first have to yoke the king's two fire-breathing bulls and plow his field; then sow dragon's teeth and slay the warriors who sprang from them; and finally vanquish the monster guarding the fleece. But Eros' dart had pierced the heart of Aietes' young daughter Medea, her skin the color of the moon, her eyes like green wine, her hair like a sunset. (I find Apollonius' description of Medea's sudden love for Jason the best part of his *Argonautica*; it is the first blush of a romanticism that would not bloom for more than fifteen hundred years.) Medea's love transformed Jason into a true hero, and the magic powers she obtained from her godmother, the great witch Hecate, enabled Jason to pass all Aietes' tests and finally to win possession of the golden fleece.

Their mission accomplished, the Argonauts set fire to one of Aietes' fleets and, taking Medea with them, sailed for home. But the princess had betrayed her father, and, as Apollonius says, "Every wrong brings a greater evil." To avenge young Argus' alliance with the Argonauts, his mother, Medea's elder sister, was slaughtered in a blind fury by Aietes, their father. And this launched the series of horrors that during *Argo*'s return transformed Medea from a loving maiden into a hateful witch and Jason from a reluctant hero into a desperate vagabond.

The Problem of Argo's Return

With *Argo*'s homeward voyage, the frontier that separates legend from history recedes again into the mist. Phineus told Jason that the return route would be different from the outbound, which still makes nautical sense, for to sail west along the whole length of the southern coast of the Black Sea is to buck the prevailing winds and currents. Yet each chronicler of the voyage home has offered a route consistent with his own knowledge of geography and navigation, and we are going to have to pick and choose.

The most extreme route is that proposed in 40 B.C. by one of the latest chroniclers, Diodorus Siculus, perhaps because he thinks he knows more geography than he really does. He sends *Argo* up the Don, which he calls Tanais, then, after a long portage, up the Volga, and finally, with several more portages, from river to river and out into the Gulf of Finland. From there he has *Argo* sail to the North Sea, down the Atlantic coast, and back into the Mediterranean. We will see that the Vikings did in fact transport ships comparable to *Argo* from the Gulf of Finland to the rivers of Russia and out into the Black Sea. However, the rigors of Diodorus' hypothetical voyage around northern Europe, added to the fact that the Argonauts (in particular, the astronomer Ancaeus) would have known that they were sailing hopelessly north of their home stars, make me reject his route without further comment.

Pindar is more realistic. He suggests that the Argonauts emerged from Colchis directly into the Eastern Ocean, then sailed around to the Red Sea, carried *Argo* for twelve days across a desolate land, and came out into the Mediterranean through Triton's lake "in the land of Nile, where Zeus Ammon reigns." In his view, then, the Argonauts escaped Aietes up the Phasis River, carried *Argo* some one hundred fifty kilometers up the Transcaucasian valley to the Kura River, and finally sailed down the Kura to the Caspian, which Pindar considered a gulf of Ocean along whose shores one could reach the Red Sea. This tradition still lives in Tiflis, the

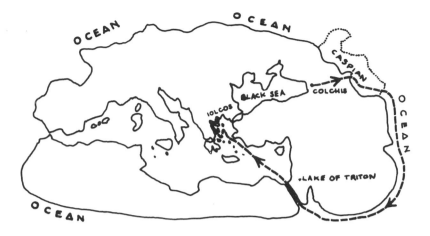

Pindar, fifth century B.C. (Return of the Argonauts)

capital of the Soviet Republic of Georgia, whence the Transcaucasian highway and canal do lead to the Caspian.[8] If one could somehow transport *Argo* from the Caspian to the Persian Gulf, the rest of Pindar's proposal would make sense, and Triton's lake could be the salt lake that is now part of the Suez Canal.[9] But anyone who knows the mountains that surround Teheran and Tabriz knows that it would be impossible to carry a ship from the Caspian to the rivers that flow into the gulf.

Apollonius comes closest to a practical route, but he includes two side trips of which we must immediately dispose. Once he gets the Argonauts into the Adriatic, he makes them enter "Eridanus," today's Po River (which Scylax considers to be another mouth of the Rhone). Then he brings them out through the real mouth of the Rhone (near Marseilles) and back along the Hyères Islands and Elba into the Tyrrhenian Sea. From there he has them follow the route of Odysseus, complete with Circe, the Sirens, the volcano (Stromboli), the floating islands (the Eole), Scylla and Charybdis (Messina), and home via Scheria, the land of fair Nausicaa. After which, having senselessly sent the Argonauts north again into the Adriatic and back south, Apollonius has them blown by Boreas from Cape Malea to Africa, exactly like Odysseus, there to get lost in Triton's lake and later to visit Crete. These wanderings make no nautical sense if Jason was trying to get home with the golden fleece as directly as possible, as he surely must have been. So I suspect that both side trips were added by Apollonius in order to display his knowledge of Homer. If we exclude them, his return route becomes altogether practical.

According to Apollonius, *Argo* began her homeward voyage by

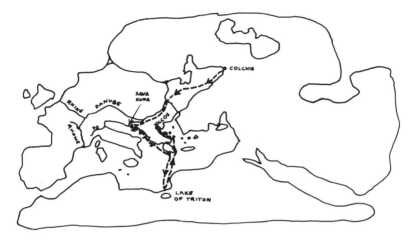

Apollonius, third century B.C. (Return of the Argonauts)

sailing west from Colchis only as far as the Halys River on Cape Bafra, some one hundred seventy-five nautical miles. This would have taken less than twenty-four hours at the eight knots *Argo* could make with the god-sent wind that Medea surely conjured up for the first day of their flight. At the mouth of the river, says Apollonius, they paused to make sacrifices in honor of Hecate, to whom, as we have seen, Medea owed her magic powers. This done, they went back to sensible seamanship and, instead of continuing west along the coast, headed northwest across the Black Sea to the mouth of the Ister, which we know as the Danube. They put in at the "triangular isle, Peuce," which the great river still forms between its two mouths at Sfantu Gheorghe and Sulina, on the border of today's Rumania and the USSR.

Here, at a cove dedicated to Artemis, the goddess of the hunt, the Argonauts ran into a squadron of pursuing Colchians led by Apsyrtus, Medea's younger brother. Jason vowed to surrender Medea, and even to send Aietes the purple mantle of Queen Hypsipyle as a peace offering, in return for being allowed to sail home with the fleece; and Apsyrtus, persuaded, came to him. Unflinching, Jason killed the youth and drank his blood in Medea's presence, whereupon the Argonauts massacred the leaderless Colchians. Then, hearing that yet another Colchian squadron barred the Bosporus, they sailed up the Danube to a smoke-filled abyss—surely the famous Iron Gate of Turnú-Severin, where the river rushes down a deep gorge at a speed of some fifteen knots—which they must have passed by dragging *Argo* upstream from the banks.[10]

Tradition sends *Argo* all the way up the river, even to its source at

Donaueschingen in Germany, but *Argo* could not possibly have sailed up that far. She might have gone as far as Sigmaringen, thence to be carried and pushed over gently rolling country to Lake Constance and around the Rhine cataracts, and then to sail up the Aare River. Finally, she could have crossed lakes Biel, Neuchâtel, and Leman to the Rhone, after a total of some sixty kilometers of portages. But even this route is unnecessarily complicated. At today's Belgrade, not only is the Danube five degrees north of Iolcus—Jason and his navigator Ancaeus, watching their home stars, would begin to worry about going too far north—but the Danube there takes a very definite turn northward. The Sava River, on the other hand, runs into the Danube straight out of the west, and at Sisak *Argo* could have continued to sail west on the Kupa River as far as Brod-na-kupi ("the Kupa's ford"). There only thirty kilometers of hills dotted with lakes would have separated her from the Adriatic.

It is here, I think, that the Argonauts organized their only portage, a short but not an easy one, for some of these lakes lie over three hundred meters high in the mountains. Yet the feat is not impossible if one remembers that in those days two things were plentiful which today are scarce: help from the press-ganged Celts whom Apollonius mentions and who in fact were already there, and time, weeks or months of it, punctuated with sacrificial feasts. To this day, the city of Pula on the tip of the Istrian peninsula (which existed in Apollonius' time) prides itself on having been visited by the Argonauts.

If I am right, *Argo* was pushed over the hills on wooden rollers and joyfully returned to the brine below Istria. But another problem arises: According to Apollonius, the Argonauts immediately sailed to the island of Electra, which, everyone knows, is Samothrace in the northern Aegean, five hundred nautical miles away. Mercifully, Scylax rescues us again by placing a second island of Electra, which today bears the unpronounceable name of Krk, right where we need it. Then, says Apollonius, the Argonauts followed a river down to Hilas, and indeed from Krk to the south a chain of islands creates the riverlike Podgorski or Velebitski Channel, which ends near Nin, north of Zadar. Mycenean remains have been found at Nin, and Hilas could well have been Nin's ancient name, since this coast was peopled by the Hili, or Illyrians. (If someone were to excavate the beautiful round tumulus which is today surmounted by a small shrine just outside Nin, he might well find the bronze tripod that Apollonius says the Argonauts buried here.) Finally, south of Zadar the Dalmatian coast begins to clothe its stones with olive and with cypress, and *Argo*, scenting home, sailed easily to the Liburnian islands, Issa, Corcyra Nigra, and Melita (today's Vis, Korcula, and Mljet), and then into Nymphae, today's walled Dubrovnik, where there are still plenty of nymphs. It used to be called Ragusa, which I like to think was originally Argusa.

From here on—eliminating the two Homeric side trips—Apollonius brings *Argo* home through familiar waters, around the Peloponnese and Cape Sounion, and up into the Gulf of Euboea past Aulis, where later Agamemnon's fleet would gather to attack Troy. Word of the golden fleece and of red-haired Medea had surely gone before them, and the Argonauts' entry into their beloved Gulf of Pagasae must have been a sight to see.

The end of Jason's story centers on Medea, who sank into the evil that springs so easily from unrequited love, especially in one who has called down the magic of Hecate, always surrounded by the hissing of flames and the howling of dogs. Having betrayed her own father and allowed her brother to be murdered before her eyes, Medea, when she finally reached Greece, fed the murdered Pelias to his daughters at a feast. Then Jason, who seems to have loved no one, decided to leave her and marry Glauce, the only daughter of Creon, king of Corinth. He explained to Medea that having brought her from the end of the world to the center of civilization, he had the right to seek his own royal destiny. Her love now burning with a frozen flame, Medea reassured Jason that not only would she look after their children but would send a wedding present to his new bride: the cloak Medea herself had made from the golden fleece. On the wedding day, Glauce threw the resplendent cloak about her young shoulders, and the fleece, leprous with so much treason, stuck to her flesh and destroyed it. Medea, before leaving with old Aegeus, cut her children's throats, and Jason, the cautious prince, knowing at last that neither regal pomp nor human warmth was to be his lot, ended his days wandering far into the north in search of the tomb of Cronus, father of the Centaur. He was not the last whose false love transformed a maiden into a witch, just as gods unheeded are transformed into stones and the music of a careful life, not really lived, turns into noise.

The first step in our discovery of the globe has been accomplished. Thanks to his crew and to Medea, *amekanos* Jason has covered the almost one thousand nautical miles that separate Iolcus from Colchis—three hundred to enter the "gulf" of the Black Sea and six hundred to find that it is closed at Poti. And he has returned, not only with the fleece but with the news that the Black Sea is not a gulf of the Infinite Ocean but another sea to the scale of man, like the Aegean or the Eastern Mediterranean. The Ocean no longer roars behind the Bosporus; in the east it now awaits

Alexander and Islam behind the high Caucasus, while westward it awaits Odysseus beyond the Straits of Tunis.

The Odyssey

In the generation that follows the Argonauts, it is Odysseus' turn to push back the Infinite, this time westward from Tunis, where the island of Ogygia has thus far marked the end of the world, to the Pillars of Hercules, where the Ocean will await Columbus.

For Odysseus, a squat, red-bearded, and wily Mediterranean, the voyage of the Argonauts was like the conquest of the air for us— legendary, yet so recent that a conversation with one's elders can revive it. Apollodorus actually includes Laertes, Odysseus' father, among the Argonauts, and Valerius Flaccus makes wise king Nestor the only hero to sail both to Colchis and to Troy (not impossible, perhaps, for a bon vivant who always insisted on olives with his wine. Each generation tries to add its heroes to the epic stories). Achilles, who as a child saw *Argo* sail past the beach below Mount Pelion, grew up to become the touchy hero of the *Iliad,* and we have seen that he was not the only Argonaut's son to fight at Troy. Troy itself concerns us only because Homer's description led Schliemann to discover it southeast of the mouth of the Hellespont, and it was from Troy that Odysseus began his voyage home.

Odysseus and the Sirens.
Early fifth century Attic urn
*(Reproduced by courtesy of
the Trustees of the British Museum)*

After sacking and burning the city, Agamemnon and his brother, Menelaus, argued in front of their drunken troops about the return to Greece. Agamemnon decided to stay on the Trojan beach long enough to offer the proper sacrifices, but Menelaus, Nestor, Diomedes, and Odysseus ran their black ships into the surf and immediately made the short crossing to nearby Tenedos island (today's Bozcaada). From Tenedos, all except Odysseus sailed for Lesbos and thence directly to Geraistos at the southern end of the island of Euboea, one hundred twenty nautical miles of open sea in twenty-four hours (a speed of five knots). Obviously they were in a hurry to get home before Boreas (which at the close of the *Illiad* blew on Patroclus' tomb) brought in the autumn storms.

Odysseus, unlike Jason, was *peirates*, one who likes to push his luck; the opportunity of sacking one more Asian city and at the same time pleasing his commander-in-chief was irresistible. His decision was probably influenced also by the wily side of his character. A canny sailor, never frightened by men or gods but respectful of the sea, he naturally preferred to thread the southern Sporades and the Cyclades toward home rather than risk a storm in open water.

After putting in again at the Trojan beach to pay its respects to Agamemnon, I think the Ithacan squadron of twelve ships coasted southward along the coast of Asia Minor, not north to Thrace as tradition has it, which would have meant bucking the wind. Odysseus sacked Ismarus, the port of the Cicones (which I locate near today's Izmir because Homer tells us that the Cicones' inland allies counterattacked with war chariots, a typically Asian tactic), and thence, mourning his dead, sailed with the freshening wind to Ikaria. There he sat out the inevitable storm, probably on the southeastern beach, which still offers good shelter. When Boreas abated, the Ithacan squadron sailed from island to island across the Aegean to Cape Sounion, where Odysseus' helmsman was buried with ceremony (another tomb waiting to be found).

This duty done, the fleet tried to round Cape Malea, the highest of the Peloponnese "fingers," which even modern sailboats approach with caution. But Boreas was up again, and though the Ithacans hastily struck their sails and rowed like mad toward land, they were blown past the island of Cythera to Africa, where the Lotus-eaters almost convinced them to remain.

The land of the lotus has traditionally been identified with the island of Djerba, but here again I differ. Our Greek meteorological map of the Meltemi and our satellite photo both support my hypothesis that Odysseus hit the African coast south of Benghazi, at the bottom of the Gulf of Sirte, which is closer to where Scylax places the Lotus-eaters. It is also the

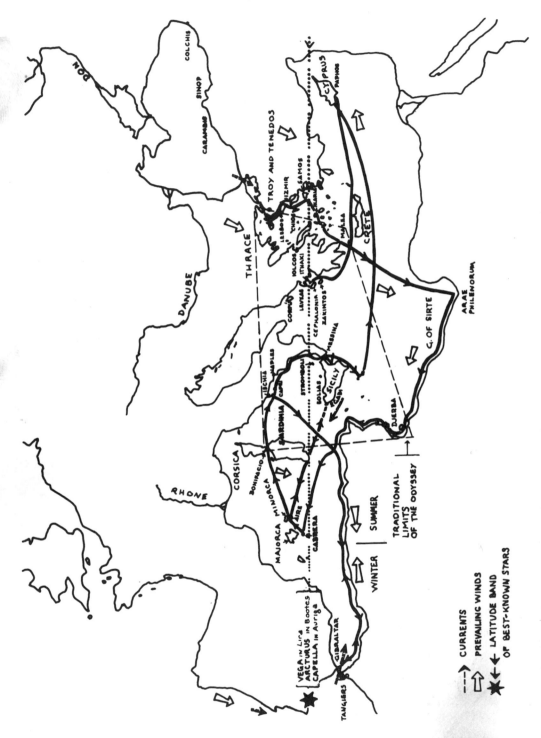

Route of Odysseus (*M.O. and M.F.*)

Cape Malea (*C.O.*)

site of the Triton's lake, where, according to Apollonius, Jason almost ended his homecoming—and it is interesting to note that Apollonius assumes that Jason would have fetched up there after being blown away from Malea. From Benghazi to Tripoli, with its ruins of the Roman city of Leptis Magna and its Italian olive groves, the coast today looks so empty that when I decided to fly low to look for the Lotus-eaters' port, miles of ocher desert under one wing and turquoise sea under the other almost made me despair. But suddenly a small rocky headland appeared out of the flat coast, and, as I circled, we photographed the ruins which topped it and the submerged harbor visible below. Scylax calls this place Fontes Ammonii, and Crivelli's *Ptolemaic Atlas* labels it Arae Philenorum. I consider it a much better location than Djerba for the Lotus-eaters.

Homer says that Odysseus tied his drugged scouts under their benches and rowed away from the land of the lotus. I suspect that he thought he was in Egypt, whither the Meltemi did in fact blow Menelaus as he was taking Helen of Troy back to Sparta. Therefore, instead of rashly rowing out into the open sea, Odysseus rowed along the coast as long as it ran to the northwest in order to set sail for Greece from its northernmost point (exactly what Appolonius describes Jason as having done). My hypothesis takes Odysseus from Sirte to Carthage, where the coast finally turns southwest and where Odysseus must have awaited Notus in order to sail north to Greece—sailing, in fact, into the Gulf of Tunis. All this differs from tradition, which holds that he sailed from the island of Djerba into the Tyrrhenian Sea—where the rest of the *Odyssey*, as described by Homer, will certainly not fit.

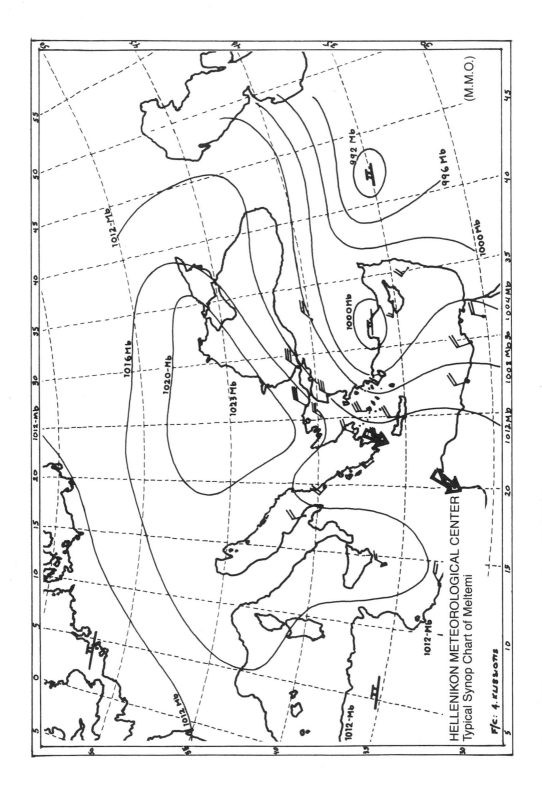

The Meltemi (Greek meteorological chart) (*M.F.*)

The Meltemi (satellite photo) (*NASA*)

Gulf of Sirte (The sunken port of the Lotus-eaters) (*C.O.*)

In the Tunisian Gulf the Sirocco often turns suddenly into a Tramontana, so the northeaster probably caught Odysseus in deep water. Though he struck his sails and tried to row north toward the mountains of Sicily (which are not unlike those of the Peloponnese), he was slowly forced westward toward the Balearics. Off the southeastern coast of Majorca the island of Cabrera, with its small port, is just like the island where Homer next describes the Ithacans' feasting on the goats that give Cabrera its name. From here Odysseus could see the smoke of the fires of the Cyclopes, a race of cave dwellers who preferred not to work for their food. They would not be out of place in the caverns that pock the eastern coast of Majorca, whose mountains frame one of the most generously fertile plains of the whole of leisure-loving Spain.

Neighboring Minorca's caves are like those of eastern Majorca, and the very first cave I entered was full of sheep. In one such cave Odysseus and his scouts were trapped by the giant Polyphemus, the Cyclops who devoured half a dozen Ithacans before their wily leader gave him undiluted wine, blinded him with a burning stake, and tricked him into rolling back the stone door so that his sheep could go to pasture. Clinging to the sheep's bellies, the surviving Ithacans escaped. Minorca is a land of stones (here Hannibal raised his best slingshot warriors), and the wounded giant tried to sink Odysseus' ship with a salvo of huge boulders. But his roar was drowned out by Odysseus' famous laugh, which still seems to ring around the great stone *talayots*, or towers, the tabletopped *taulas*, and the long *navetas* shaped like upturned boats, which are strewn without explanation all over Minorca. I think the first were watchtowers, the second columns to hold up the roofs of artificial caves, and the third ex-votos put up by the Cyclopes to ward off ships such as those which brought Odysseus (Homer tells us that the Cyclopes had no boats).

The squadron sailed to the island of Aeolus, king of the winds. In front of Mahón, the Minorcan capital, there is today an island called the Isle of the Wind, whose high rock coast, gilded by the setting sun, reminds one of Homer's "coast of bronze." Here Aeolus gave Odysseus the zephyr he needed to sail home, as well as a leather pouch that he warned him not to open. For nine days the fleet sailed east, and Odysseus never rested until in the morning mists he thought he saw his home islands.[11] Exhausted, he fell asleep, and immediately Eurylochus, the ship's troublemaker, opened Aeolus' leather bag. Out leaped Eurus, the east wind, and the hapless fleet was blown back to Aeolus, who refused to have anything further to do with its godforsaken crew.

Odysseus now knew approximately which way he had to row for home, but after covering two hundred fifty nautical miles in six days (an

Balearic Cave (Cave of the Cyclops) (*C.O.*)

The Isle of the Wind (Aeolus' floating isle) (*C.O.*)

Bonifacio (The Laestrygones' port) (*C.O.*)

average speed of just under two knots), he came up against the barrier
formed by Corsica and Sardinia. Recognizing that this was not home, he
looked for a way through and found the Strait of Bonifacio, where the port
of the same name, with its high and narrow entrance, answers exactly to
Homer's description of Telepylus, the port of the Laestrygones. (Tradition has always placed it here but has never explained why Odysseus,
supposedly in the Tyrrhenian Sea, should have passed westward through
the strait when he obviously should have been heading east; we have
solved the problem by bringing him to the Balearics first.) The fleet
sought shelter inside the deep port, but Odysseus preferred to moor his
own ship to a rock outside the harbor's mouth. As usual the wily one was
right, for the Laestrygones turned out to be vicious giants who bombed
the trapped fleet with huge rocks hurled down from their city high above
the port. Only Odysseus' ship escaped, eastward through the strait.

Before following Odysseus further, let me propose a solution to
another Homeric riddle. The bard tells us that in Telepylus, "sunrise and
sunset follow each other so closely that if a man did not need sleep, he
could earn double wages as a herdsman and as a shepherd too"—a
statement that has given rise to all sorts of conjectures. Some have sent
Odysseus far enough north for him to discover the midnight sun, and I
myself flew all the way to the Canary Islands to see if he might have sailed
far enough south to be impressed by the shortened twilight of the tropics.
But neither solution makes nautical sense because both wind and stars
would surely have discouraged him. Instead, my answer to the riddle is
very down-to-earth: On Corsica, as on Minorca, sheep often shelter from
the sun in caves, and the shepherd who leads them out to pasture in the
cool evening could well meet the cowherd bringing his cattle home for the
night to be milked in the early morning.

Odysseus' lonely ship next reached the island of Aeaea, where the sorceress Circe, the younger sister of Medea's father, became the first of a series of women who both helped and hindered him. Monte Circeo on the Italian coast and east of Bonifacio has always been identified with Aeaea, but Homer leaves no doubt that Circe lived on an island. By watching the passage of his home stars, Odysseus probably knew that from Bonifacio he must sail somewhat south of east to reach home. For both reasons, I prefer to place the sorceress on the island of Ischia to the southeast. Ischia was known of old as Aenaria, a name not unlike Aeaea, or as Pithekoussai, the isle of the apes, an image that fits Homer's description of an island full of wild animals. That the name has moved to the coast does not worry me; historical names are nomads.

Spotting a column of smoke, Odysseus sent Eurylochus with a patrol to investigate, and the troublemaker, having learned at Telepylus from his captain, stayed outside while his men entered Circe's castle and were transformed by the sorceress into wild pigs. Back at the beach, Eurylochus suggested leaving right away, but Odysseus, who had been forced to abandon his fleet at Telepylus, refused to forsake his men— perhaps because the presence of a woman, sorceress or not, interested him—and marched to Circe's castle. On the way, Hermes, his forebear, intercepted him and gave him the magic herb he needed in order to recover his scouts and to make Circe his for a year. During their long dalliance, young Elpenor got drunk, fell off Circe's roof, and broke his neck, and several Mycenean tombs have in fact been found on Ischia. One of them, perhaps Elpenor's, was topped by a wine jug and contained a cup inscribed with a reference to Nestor.

Circe did everything possible to retain her lover, but finally released him on one condition: She would tell him how to get home if he first sailed to the River of Ocean "where the sun goes to its death" and there consulted with the dead. The northeast wind would take him there, she said, and the River of Ocean's current would start him back. In fact, the summer winds tend to blow out of the east along the North African coast, and the surface current in the Straits of Gibraltar runs back into the Mediterranean. Moreover, Homer's description of the stony beach on which Odysseus landed, the tall forests through which he passed, the volcanic landscape that is the antechamber of the western entrance to Hades, and the caverns that still bear mythological names, all indicate that Odysseus reached the western end of his journey near today's Tangiers. Thus he found that the Western Mediterranean, like the Black Sea, was not a gulf of Infinite Ocean but a finite sea into which the Eastern River of Ocean flowed.

The *Odyssey*'s Book of the Dead is an emporium of legends, only a few of which we can note here. As soon as Odysseus poured sacrificial blood into the great ditch, his mother, Anticleia, arose to give him his first news of home, reviving his desire to return and wreak vengeance on the impudent suitors who occupied his palace and pursued his wife. Next, the seer Teiresias warned Odysseus of trials ahead and prophesied that death would come to him from the sea in its least bitter form, once he had completed his last voyage, "to a land where no one knows an oar from a winnowing fan" (the Russian steppes?). Finally, the shades of Agamemnon and Achilles both offered Odysseus advice. The commander-in-chief, murdered by his wife's lover, warned him not to trust anyone, not even his wife, when he reached home. And Achilles, hailed by Odysseus as the greatest of all who died at Troy, declared, "Odysseus, my lord, spare me your praise of death. I would rather be the slave of a pauper, but alive, than prince of all these ghosts." Greeks have always loved life above all else.

The passage of time gradually focuses legends into ever clearer history, and Homer's account of Odysseus' return is much more precise than the accounts of the Argonauts' voyage home. The current of the River of Ocean brought Odysseus back into the Mediterranean, and once there, he had no trouble sailing east again, to Circe's island, thanks to the fact that in winter the wind reverses itself along the African coast. At last Circe told him how to get home, and his men rowed him past the Sirens, their ears plugged with wax (I think past Capri, for to sail south from Ischia, one must pass that magic island, still a good place for sirens). According to tradition, Odysseus was tied to the mast; more likely, it was to the mast step, since the mast would surely have been stowed for maximum speed while rowing.

Odysseus followed the Italian coast down to Cape Vaticano and easily picked the more seamanlike of the two routes described by Circe: not via the floating islands (the Eole) and around Sicily, but past Stromboli's volcano, "where even Zeus' doves dare not fly," and through the Strait of Messina, which separates Scylla from Charybdis. Hugging the Calabrian shore, as recommended by Circe (and by modern sailing directions), he avoided Charybdis, where even today small boats must be careful of whirlpools. But the price of his seaman's caution was high: Six of his men were taken by Scylla, the giant octopus.

Thus thanks to Circe's precise instructions, Odysseus finally rounded the Italian "barrier" that had been keeping him from home. But, Homer says, there were clouds over Scylla (even today clouds over Calabria announce a Sirocco), and, once through the strait, the south wind forced

Capri (The Sirens' isle) *(C.O.)*

Stromboli (where Zeus's doves dare not to fly) *(C.O.)*

Odysseus to land on Trinacria, where Circe had warned him not to touch the sun god's cattle. Sicily is triangular and dominated by the sun, and the best cattleland on the island (now adorned by oil refineries) still lies north of Taormina's beach. There, I believe, Odysseus landed and took his rest, and there Eurylochus convinced the hungry crew that Helius' cattle were for eating. Awakening too late, Odysseus hurriedly set sail, but the sun god's revenge was too swift to escape. Off the southeast tip of Sicily the sky darkened while the winds clashed, and, enveloped in "lightning and the smell of sulphur," the ship was lost with all hands, the helmsman's skull split by the falling mast or sailyard. Only Odysseus survived, clinging to a raft he improvised by lashing the mast to the keel with a leather stay. I too ran into trouble off Siracusa when I broke my rudder on a tunny net in a sudden Sirocco, the same wind that now sent Odysseus back to Messina.

But Boreas soon returned, blowing Odysseus' raft to Ogygia, the island which, before the Ithacans entered the Western Mediterranean, was thought to be the end of the world, and which I take to be Malta. Calypso, the lonely nymph, kept him there for seven years and gave him two sons; but finally Zeus, convinced by Athena, sent Hermes to order Calypso to help her lover build a boat to take him away (it is the careful Homeric description of this boat that has already helped us to reconstruct *Argo*). Calypso also gave Odysseus precise navigational instructions: He must sail dead east by the sun, keeping the Big Dipper on his left at night, "the only constellation," in her words, "which never bathes in Ocean's stream."[12]

Odysseus sailed east for eighteen days to Scheria, the longest leg of the *Odyssey*. According to Homer, Scheria was a land distant not only from Ogygia, Calypso's island, but also from Ithaca. So, for me, Odysseus' next landfall could not be Kerkyra (Corfú), which is only sixty nautical miles north of Ithaca; anyhow, to sail from Malta to Corfú one would not head east across the open sea but northeast along the sole of Italy's boot. Eighteen days and nights sailing east from Malta at an average of two and a half knots (not a bad speed for a small, improvised, single-handed sailboat) would carry Odysseus about a thousand nautical miles east—in my view, to Cyprus. Homer's description of the zephyr which caresses Scheria's orchards fits Cyprus well (we shall see that Homer was probably a Cypriot himself),[13] and even Apollonius supports my identification, for he calls Scheria "Drapane" (sickle), a name that recalls the shape of Cyprus. I am sorry to break with the tradition which identifies Scheria with Corfú, because of all the islands of Greece sweet Corfú would perhaps best have framed lovely Nausicaa, princess of Scheria; but if we are to make nautical sense of the *Odyssey*, Cyprus must be her home.

When Zeus decided to allow Odysseus to go home, his brother Poseidon, who hated the Ithacan for blinding his son Polyphemus, was away from Olympus. But, on his way back from "Ethiopia," Poseidon spotted the lonely sailboat (another indication that Odysseus was sailing all the way across the Mediterranean, not just nipping into Corfú) and raised a terrible storm that sank Odysseus' boat.

Once again a woman came to the rescue. The nymph Io protected Odysseus with her veil, and Athena guided him onto the Phaeacian shore, whose description in Homer fits that of western Cyprus. The river mouth near Paphos, I think, allowed Odysseus to swim past the reefs Homer describes and to come ashore near the "double harbor" of Scheria, where Aphrodite was born. Here Nausicaa, "more graceful than Delos' tall palmtree," rescued the exhausted hero and led him to her father's palace after telling him on the way how to gain the king's favor and make an ally of the queen.

King Alcinous, knowing a hero when he saw one, feasted and entertained his guest with the songs of a blind bard whom tradition has consecrated as Homer's self-portrait. He listened fascinated to Odysseus'

Paphos, Cyprus (The double port at Scheria) (C.O.)

story, and after organizing games in his honor sent him home in a ship manned by fifty princes and loaded with gifts of copper, the metal that gave Cyprus its name. The ship, said Alcinous, needed no helmsman, which suggests to me that the Phaeacians may have introduced the West to the lateen sail, with which it would be possible to sail from Cyprus to Ithaca in a steady Meltemi with a steering oar lashed at the proper angle. Joshua Slocum, first and greatest of lone circumnavigators, crossed the Indian Ocean with a lashed tiller in a steady monsoon.

Be that as it may, on Cyprus greathearted Odysseus left a corner of his heart. Timidly but without doubt, Nausicaa declared her love for him, and Alcinous showed how much he regretted that the Ithacan was not for his daughter. Still Odysseus insisted on going home, though he vowed never to forget the white-armed maiden to whom he owed his life.

So, after twenty-years' absence, Odysseus returned to Ithaca, and another three thousand years will not suffice to end the arguments over which of his islands was the original Ithaca and which of their bays his port.

I have sailed and flown low over all the possibilities, and my conclusion once again is down-to-earth: Ithaca is today's Ithaki. It is as steep as Telemachus, Odysseus' son, said it was when he refused Menelaus' gift of horses because there was no room on Ithaca for them to graze, while the islands of Levkas and Cephalonia both have pastures. Odysseus' statement that Ithaca is the island that slopes most to the west has caused a great deal of confusion, but I think he was merely referring to the steeper of its two long coasts.

On Ithaki the favorite contender for Odysseus' harbor has been Porto Andrea in the south, but I found it so unsafe that the first change of wind forced me to sail out of it. Port Vathy, the capital, has no island behind which the murderous suitors could have hidden for weeks while awaiting the return of Telemachus from his search for news of his long-lost father. But when I sailed into beautiful Polis in the northwest of Ithaki, I found a safe harbor and a rocky islet, today's Deskalio, which could have been Homer's Asteris, set in the channel separating Ithaki from Cephalonia. On Cephalonia, well hidden behind Deskalio, a deep blue inlet bearing the name Paleokaravos (port of the ancient ship) could easily have served for the suitors' ambush.

On the northeastern shore of Ithaki itself, just over the island's high, narrow spine, there is another good harbor, Frikes, where Telemachus could have put in after outflanking his enemies. Kalamos, an easy walk for Odysseus from Polis and for Telemachus from Frikes, fits perfectly

Polis, Ithaca (Odysseus' port) (*M.O.*)

Deskalio (Asteris) (*M.O.*)

Homer's description of the site where father and son were reunited at the hut of Eumaeus, the faithful swineherd. There, under Homer's high white cliffs, I have refreshed myself with the cool water of the fountain he knew as Korax.

At the magic hour when the sea stills its sighs so that the song of the cicada can psalm the evening's dying, I rowed across the bay of Polis to a cavern now collapsed by an earthquake. Here, in 1938, the British archaeologist Miss Benton found fragments of copper tripods reminiscent of those which Alcinous gave Odysseus and which Odysseus hid in a cave as soon as he landed on Ithaca. Then I climbed the herb-scented hill to Stavros and was shown around Miss Benton's little Mycenean Museum by her old assistant, Laertes. I have little doubt that the remains of Odysseus' palace will one day be found under the terraced vineyards one climbs from Polis to Stavros, its stones still stained with the blood of the suitors massacred by father and son in the closing scene of the greatest of adventure stories.

Odysseus' most difficult feat had still to be accomplished: to convince Penelope that he really was Odysseus. Neither maiden, nymph, nor sorceress, Penelope was a full-blown, flesh-and-blood woman who had kept the suitors waiting just in case; only when Odysseus had finally got her back in his arms had he really won. Yet no more than Odysseus can we forget Nausicaa, for she possessed a rare virtue: She loved and let live. Her help was as indispensable to Odysseus as Medea's was to Jason, but it had no strings attached and therefore called down no curses. Odysseus, for his part, took no advantage of her. Never did he deny his intention of returning to Ithaca and to Penelope, not even when, for a while at least, he easily returned the love of Circe and of Calypso. Sharp as a reef honed by the surf, there was plenty of subterfuge in Odysseus, but no treason, and anyone who heard his laugh could guess the kind of man he had to deal with. A son of earth-supporting Atlas, as Jason was of Poseidon, lord of the treacherous sea, he knew that the art of giving love is the same as the art of receiving it, and that life is in the texture of its living and has perhaps no goal. So Teiresias' prophecy rang true: Odysseus' life ended like an autumn sunset, aglow with the love of Penelope, of Telemachus, and of the people of Ithaca, on the luminous ridge that separates the bay of Polis from Frikes, where a few tall cypress still guard his olive groves and his vines.

Our Homeric journey is done. Odysseus has found that the Infinite Ocean does not lie west of Tunis but beyond the Pillars of Hercules. Thanks to the perseverance of the Argonauts and the cunning of

Odysseus, the world has grown in two generations from an island of self-contained land and windswept sea to a continent peopled by many races and large enough to include the whole of the Mediterranean and the Black Sea. The Infinite Ocean still terrifies mortals with its roar, but in the west it is now out in the Atlantic, and in the east it is far off in the Indian Ocean.

"Time passes," says Pindar, "and sails fallen limp await the tremor of a new breeze." Many centuries and many seas stretch before us, so let us pass over times during which the known world's dimensions hardly change, to sail again only with those who will conquer Infinity.

NOTES

1. Homer has Calypso say that the Big Dipper is "the only constellation which never bathes in Ocean's stream." How far down the stars swing as they circulate around the celestial projection of the north pole depends exclusively on the latitude of the observer (we have seen that in the eighth century B.C. the pole lay between the stars Kochab and Giansar). Seen from the equator, *all* the constellations rise in the east and set in the west; seen from the north pole, *none* of the visible constellations ever sets. Consequently, the farther north the observer stands, the greater the number of constellations that join the Dipper in never bathing in Ocean's stream. My diagram shows that if Homer had lived above 37°N latitude, Etamin at the head of the great constellation of Draco would from his point of view also have stayed dry above the horizon. In order then for the Dipper to be the *only* constellation that never set, Homer must have been familiar *only* with latitudes below 37°N; and his language places him near Asia Minor. Therefore I propose that he was native of the southernmost and easternmost outpost of Greece, the island of Cyprus. Cyprus did not take an active role against Troy, and Homer is notoriously impartial to Greeks and Trojans.

Having tested my rudimentary astronomy in the musical silence of the planetarium while my two young sons watched wide-eyed, I flew to Cyprus to try my proposal on Vasso Karageorgis, Director of the Archaeological Museum. Far from laughing, he took me down to a locked room in the museum's basement and showed me a collection of implements and furniture which were in use on Cyprus in Homer's time (seventh century B.C.) and are strikingly similar to what archaeologists have shown to have been in use in the rest of Greece in the thirteenth century B.C., when Jason and Odysseus sailed.

Next, trying to find out how the *Odyssey* might first have been written down, I noted that while in Homer's day the rest of Greece had already adopted the Phoenician alphabet, the Cypriots, conservative in writing as well as in furniture, still used pictographs similar to those used in Jason's and Odysseus' time to engrave on clay tablets extensive lists of ships, oarsmen, and supplies similar to Homer's "catalogue of ships."

Consequently, my hypothesis that Homer was a Cypriot answers four ancient questions: why Homer was so sure that the Dipper was the only constellation that never dipped below the horizon; how, in the eighth century B.C., he could describe so well the implements used five centuries earlier; where he could have obtained his detailed and apparently complete "catalogue of ships"; and why he, a Greek, was so neutral in his treatment of the Trojan war.

Homeric star chart

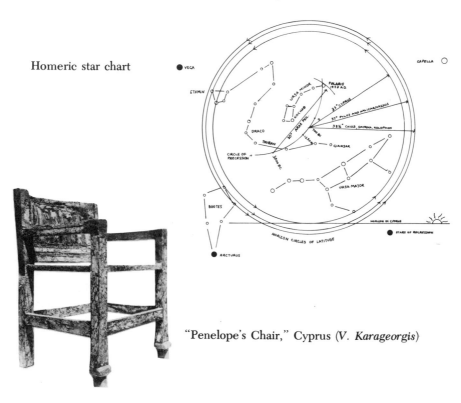

"Penelope's Chair," Cyprus (V. *Karageorgis*)

2. Earlier Babylonian tablets indicate that the lyre was usually tuned to the seven notes of our Western major scale, not to the five of the Eastern pentatonic. Moreover, the ancient score calls for some rudimentary harmony, hitherto considered a medieval innovation. The Babylonian tablets even identify the "unclear" diminished fifth to which we refer when we come to the Renaissance. So Orpheus' song may well be at the origin of our music, just as his mysteries are embedded in our religion.

3. To avoid losing his fleet as Darius did when rounding vicious Cape Nymphaion, Xerxes dug a canal across the neck of the Athos peninsula. Today the canal helps separate Greece from the theocracy of Hagios Ouros, Holy Mount Athos, where some two thousand monks still work peacefully at their Byzantine murals and in their libraries, welcoming pilgrims like me—but not women, who

have been banned here for almost a thousand years. Of the four hundred monasteries which in the fifteenth century housed forty thousand monks, only twenty still stand, but they represent all the Orthodox countries of the world. Their living antiarchitecture, far from being decadent, is the perfect setting for a spiritual retreat, interrupted only by the singing of matins and lauds and counterpointed by the whispering of sea breezes through olive groves.

4. Gebze is ancient Libissa, where Hannibal committed suicide in 182 B.C. I searched for his tomb, but all I found was a circle of cypress solemnly bowing around some fallen monoliths on a high round hill overlooking the beach. This seemed to me a fitting monument, but my Turkish interpreter said, "Poor Hannibal!"

5. Warmed by plentiful *raki,* I amused myself by teasing the local archaeologist about Turkey's invasion of Cyprus. His reply is worth quoting as a cameo portrait of the Ottoman empire: "No, no," he said, "you are mistaken. We Turks, we are not aggressive. You have seen it; we are hospitable Muslims. Of course, *war* we like!"

6. Besides Heracles, Theseus was the only hero supposed to have entered the Black Sea on his own about this time. This legend is difficult to document, though we do know that Theseus belonged to the generation which separated Jason from Odysseus. Theseus' father, Aegeus, married Medea when Jason abandoned her, and Theseus in turn lost his throne to Menestheus, whose fleet sailed for Troy at the same time as Odysseus.

7. High on the Caucasus, Zeus' eagle pecked at the entrails of poor, chained Prometheus. I flew over the Caucasus with a Russian pilot, and when I asked if its wonderful updrafts were used for soaring, he replied that such sports were not allowed near the frontiers of the USSR.

8. In Georgia, vines dating from the time of the Argonauts are still supposed to yield the excellent wine of the region. Ancient maps locate "Iberia" here, and I had to learn to sip the wine while my hosts swilled it down as we tried for hours to relate Georgian with Spanish.

9. According to Herodotus, in the seventh century B.C. Pharaoh Neccho II actually dug a canal from the Red Sea to the Nile so that his ships could sail from the Red Sea to the Mediterranean. It disappeared under the sand until traces of it were found, I am told, by today's Israelis.

10. In the second century A.D., Trajan, under whom the Roman empire reached its greatest extent, breached the Iron Gate by cutting a six-foot path out of the vertical rock and then broadening it with a wooden platform so that his army would be able to march through in good order.

11. We will apply our estimated speeds to the *Odyssey* as we did to the *Argonautica,* but in the *Odyssey* distances and durations are usually multiples of the magic numbers three, seven, and nine and they should therefore perhaps be taken less literally.

12. See note 1.

13. See note 1.

Part Two
THE COMPLETE WORLD OF THE RENAISSANCE

Muhammad and the Archangel (*J.O.*)

3

ISLAM,
THE VIKINGS,
AND THE
RENAISSANCE

Islam: Eurasia

When Alexander the Great invaded the Asian continent and crossed the Oxus[1] and the Indus, his ambition was to reach the Ganges, and so perhaps to sail into the eastern Ocean Sea. But his exhausted troops mutinied, forcing him to march southward across the desert and to sail back to the Persian Gulf in the coastal vessels of Admiral Nearcos. Not even a demigod could reach the oriental boundary of the known landmass; eight centuries had to pass before the Muslims, "God's subjects," finally reached the eastern shores of the Ocean.

The Prophet Muhammad was born in the year 570 A.D. in the city of Mecca in Jazirat al Arab, the "Arabian Island" bounded by two seas and a desert. England's conversion to Christianity was just beginning; the Visigoths were still conquering Spain; Buddhism had just been brought to Japan; and Hagia Sophia, the most impressive church in all Christendom, had but recently been consecrated in Constantinople.

Muhammad received his first divine revelation on Mount Hira, when he was forty years old. His wife Kadija, older and wealthier than he, believed from the first in his One God "who created man and teaches him everything through the scriptures." Thanks to Kadija, the Prophet kept his faith during the two long years he had to wait for the revelations to resume. When they did, his monotheism did not suit the idolatrous merchants of Mecca; in the year 622 A.D., Muhammad and his few disciples had to found their mosque in Yathrib, today Medina al Nabi, "the Oasis of the Prophet," some three hundred kilometers to the north.

From this exodus, or Hegira, the Arab calendar began to count its years while Muhammad continued to write down his revelations in the

Koran. Its five basic precepts, faith, prayer, alms, fasting, and pilgrimage, today guide the lives of more than seven hundred fifty million people from Indonesia to Guinea and from Russia to Madagascar.

God's messenger, the archangel Gabriel, ordered the Prophet to wage war on the unfaithful. His followers began by attacking the annual caravan from Damascus and ended by defeating the Meccans who beseiged Medina. Tribe after tribe of Bedouins joined the victors, and in 628 A.D. Muhammad returned to Mecca at the head of ten thousand men to banish the idols from the Kaaba, the black-shrouded "House of God" which marks the spot where, according to Muslim tradition, Abraham nearly sacrificed his son, and which became the center of Islam.[2]

Before the Koran limited marriages to four, the Prophet consolidated his power by means of a dozen matrimonial alliances. In the year 632 A.D., after proclaiming his last revelation to the faithful on the plain of Arafat, he died in the arms of his favorite wife, Aysha, daughter of Abu Bakr who became the first caliph. The Prophet was buried in Medina.

Rebel tribes were soon subdued by Abu Bakr and their prophets toppled. Then, to the cry of *Alajú Akbar* ("God is Great"), Islam hurled itself against the two great neighboring empires, Byzantium and Persia, and defeated both, taking first Damascus and then Jerusalem from Emperor Heraclius, and, from Persia, the fertile crescent that lies between the Tigris and the Euphrates. In the next century Islam consumed the known world as if driven by the four winds.

Three qualities made the Muslims invincible: the mobility of their warriors, who were almost as easy to supply as their camels and mules; their "holy war," to which the constant presence of God gave a sharpened sense of destiny; and their equally god-fearing clemency toward the vanquished.

Many Jews (whose national identity is still today as dependent on the presence of God as is Islam's) refused to accept Muhammad, but they were allowed to live in peace as long as they paid the annual tax of one

"Fight the Infidels" (Arabic Script) (*J.O.*)

day's wages plus a measure of wheat. Nor did a divided Christianity find it hard to accept a Prophet who shared his title with Christ. "Believe in God, and in what He revealed to Abraham, Ishmael, Isaac, Jacob, Moses, Jesus, and the Prophets: make no distinction between them, and submit only to Him," says the Koran. And the *Hadith*, which with the legal code, *Sharia*, completes Muslim written tradition, says, "When you die, your neighbors will ask what goods you have left; but the Angel will ask what good you have done." The Muslim religion does not complicate matters: no original sin, no monasticism, and (though a Muslim once said to me, "I envy you Christians, only one wife!") no monogamy.

In 642 A.D. the second caliph, Omar, turned west, invaded Egypt, and occupied Alexandria, and in 682, Uqbah Ibn Nafi overran the south coast of the Mediterranean and occupied Tripoli, Carthage, and Tangiers, the last Byzantine bases. When the imperial fleet was annihilated off Licia, the Muslims became masters of the Southern Mediterranean. Having reached West Africa, Ibn Nafi rode his charger into the Atlantic surf off the beach at Agadir and proclaimed, "God is my witness that only the Ocean has put a limit on what I have conquered in His name."

In the meantime, turning east, General Ibn Qasim, seventeen years old, occupied Samarkand and Tashkent, crossed the Oxus and the Indus, and established Islam first in India and then on the frontiers of Cathay. "Always seek knowledge, even in China," says the Koran, and it was from China that the Muslims brought the science of papermaking.

Six centuries later Tamerlane (*Timur*, eastern, and *lan*, lame) still ruled the Muslim East from Samarkand, where today the Soviet authorities preserve his tomb. In Soviet Bukhara, the Muslim *Madrasa*, whose minaret once served as a lighthouse for caravans, is still open to students, and there are active mosques even in Alma-Ata on the frontier of China. At the end of the thirteenth century Marco Polo found Muslims in Sumatra, and in the fifteenth century the Portuguese found them in the Spice Islands.

"Seek Knowledge" (Arabic Script) (*J.O.*)

Turning south in Africa, Islam overran its eastern coast as far as Tanganyika, and its western coast as far as Cape Verde, where in his map of 1500 Juan de la Cosa placed the crescent moon. When Vasco da Gama rounded the Cape of Good Hope, the pilot who led him to India was seventy-year-old Ahmed Ibn Najid. Today in Africa there are twice as many Muslims as Christians, and I have hunted in Nigeria with Muslim Hausas, black as ebony, who still ride like Arabs, turbaned and brandishing scimitars.

Nevertheless, on the shores of the Atlantic and on the islands which look out onto the Pacific, the Muslims of the endless desert and of the endlessly repeated arabesque respected the Infinite Ocean (which they called the Sea of Darkness) and confined themselves to the coastal navigation they had learned from the Greeks. With their lateen sails they could have tacked from island to island into the Pacific, and, even more easily, they could have sailed into the Atlantic from Cape Verde, where the trade winds blow westward. Yet in the east they were content to coast from the Bay of Bengal to the Isles of Spice, and in the west to turn south across the Sahara's sea of sand. There their knowledge of the stars—another Greek heritage—was as useful to them as it was at sea; to this day, most important southern stars have Arab names, not Greek names as in the north.

Ibn Nafi was right; it was the Ocean that set Islam's limits. The Muslims never ventured beyond Eurasia, not even to the Canary Islands and, at the other end of the world, they never sailed beyond the Philippines, where in the sixteenth century Magellan's fleet would meet Moors who spoke Spanish, and where Muslims still fight Christians today.[3]

While Islam became master of half of Africa, it also turned north. In 711, Tariq Ibn Ziyab landed on Gibraltar (*Djeb-al-Tar*, Mount Tariq). His Moors defeated Rodrigo and his Visigoths near Cadiz, cornered the Christians in the mountains of northern Spain, and penetrated into France. There they were finally stopped at Tours in 732 by Charles Martel, Charlemagne's grandfather.

Islamic culture flourished for almost eight centuries in Spain, embroidering the Spanish language with more than four thousand Moorish words, adorning the austere peninsula with jewels like Córdoba and Granada, and producing heroes who, like El Cid in the eleventh century, took the field as often for the Moors as against them. When in 1492 the Catholic sovereigns completed the reconquest of Granada, the defeated Moorish King Boabdil was not the only one who wept. Andalusian song and poetry still cry for the heyday of Islam, as do the fountains of the Alhambra. If Columbus had not met Ferdinand and Isabella in

Granada, the future of Spain would have been hard; she might well have forgotten how to inlay steel with gold, how to sing to the guitar, and how to recite Arab love poems. "Weep not for your robe, daughter of Bakili, or the river will carry away your youth. Come into the shade, and I will weave for you a robe more precious than the one you have lost, a robe made of caresses."

Meanwhile, Islam's capital was as mobile as the Muslims themselves. With the Omayid dynasty (661–750) it passed from Mecca to Damascus, where the exploits of the legendary Bedouin hero Antar, which so inspired medieval Europe, are still recited in public. With the Abassid dynasty it passed to Baghdad (built by al-Mansur in 762 and destroyed by Genghis Khan in 1258), where, at the end of the eighth century, Haroun al-Rashid presided over the Thousand and One Nights. And with the Fatimid dynasty (973–1171) it passed to Cairo, again today the capital of Islam—at least for the present.

Islam means submission to God, and in this sense it is synonymous with our word *enthusiasm* (from the Greek *en theos*, possessed by God). It is precisely enthusiasm, perhaps more than any other emotion, that identifies the Renaissance with Antiquity and distinguishes both from the Middle Ages. It also distinguishes the West, where the quest for God is pursued with enthusiasm, from the East, where God is sought in withdrawal. Consequently, Islam's enthusiasm places it squarely at the source of the Renaissance of the West, as does the fact that, as soon as it found the leisure to absorb the cultures it had conquered, Islam became the bridge by which the West rediscovered its Greek heritage. The combination of Arab enthusiasm with the cultures of Egypt, Greece, Persia, India, and Byzantium produced a constellation of artists and scientists who reaped the wisdom of the ancient world, cultivated it in the Middle Ages, and passed it on to the European Renaissance.

In the seventh century, a few years after the death of the Prophet, the Arabs revived the library of Alexandria. In the eighth, before the time of Charlemagne, Abu Masa Dshafar crowned his chemical research with the discovery of *aqua regia*. In the ninth, while the mosque at Córdoba was being built and Ptolemy's *Geography* was being translated into Arabic, Mohammed Ibn Musa al-Kwarismi wrote the first book on algebra, confounding generations of students after having lulled them into a false security with the decimal numbers Islam had brought from India.

In the tenth century, while the University of Córdoba and the first monastery on Mount Athos were being founded, al-Hazan (Alhazen) codified the laws of physics and al-Sufi, in his *Book of Stars*, mentioned nebulae, those distant galaxies that the seventeenth century had to rediscover. In the eleventh century, while the crypt of Chartres was

Twelfth century map of the world by Idrisi *(Bodleian Library)*

being built, Ibn Sin (Avicena) wrote the canon that dominated Western medicine for centuries. In the eleventh and twelfth centuries, even before the troubadours sang their first love songs in France, Omar Khayyám, a mathematician and astronomer who lived to be almost one hundred, composed the *Rubaiyát;* Ibn Rushd (Averróes) wrote his commentaries on Plato and Aristotle; and Mohammed Idrisi drew the first complete map of Eurasia for Roger II Giscard, the Norseman who then ruled Sicily.

In the thirteenth century, while Genghis Khan led the Mongols west, while the Alcazar was being built in Seville, and while Saint Francis preached in Assisi, Yaqut wrote his *Geographic Encyclopedia* and Ibn al-Baitar his *Pharmacology*. And in the fourteenth century, when the Swiss Confederation was being formed, the Black Death was ravaging Europe, and the Alhambra was being built in Granada, Ibn Batuta's description of his voyages earned him the title of Muslim Marco Polo, and Ibn Khaldun wrote a *History* not unworthy of Herodotus.

"The most sublime homage that can be offered to God is to know His work," wrote Averróes. But although the Muslims measured the circumference of the globe far more accurately than Columbus did, they had no chronometer with which to measure longitude. So the Eurasian continent that Idrisi's map bequeathed to the West appeared so broad that it left no room for America. A single Infinite Ocean still washed the single continent at both extremes.

The Vikings: Beyond

The Vikings, who took their name from their home fjords or *viks*, spread terror in their slim warships from Scandinavia to Sicily and from Ireland to the great rivers of Russia throughout the Middle Ages. At the same time, their peasant brothers, the Norsemen, followed their fortune in beamy *knarrs*. Vessels of both types were recovered from Roskilde Fjord near Skuldelev, Denmark, in 1968, so we know that *knarrs* measured some twenty meters by five, while warships measured up to thirty meters overall but had a beam of not much more than four meters. Both were usually built of oak, their woolen squaresail supported by a rope net and their mast by leather stays; they were steered with a "steer board" on the right-hand side (hence the word starboard). Though their long oars pierced their gunwales, the Viking warships, which carried up to fifty warriors, differed little from *Argo* and, like the Greeks, the Vikings usually coasted in them. But the Norsemen in their *knarrs* became much more daring bluewater sailors. They even used a rudimentary *gnomon* to follow by day the latitude they picked at night from the stars, "running down the latitudes" as Odysseus had done. In their day the Norse were without known rivals as long-range navigators, for the Polynesians would remain hidden in their paradise behind the American barrier for another thousand years. Before the end of the ninth century the Norse had sailed to Iceland, and in 982 Eric the Red, fleeing Icelandic justice, founded his colony in Greenland.

Greenland's name can be explained by the color of its mountains of greenish ice, which are clearly visible during transatlantic flights. But climatologists have deduced, by sampling the polar ice caps, analyzing tree rings, and plotting the variations of ocean temperatures, that from the fifth to the thirteenth centuries, while it was so cold in Southern Europe that the Tiber and the Nile froze over, it was so warm in the North that wine was produced in England (and perhaps in Newfoundland); Greenland, therefore, may well have been truly green. From the thirteenth century to the fifteenth, climate flucuated wildly and the seas were hazardous, and from the fifteenth to the nineteenth the North passed through a minor glacial period—all of which coincides well with the history of Nordic exploration.

The Icelandic sagas, a body of oral history similar to the bardic poems Homer inherited, tell us how the Norsemen sailed west from Greenland in the eleventh century. The sagas were not written down until the thirteenth century (the originals are in the Royal Library at Copenhagen), and they were then almost forgotten until they were published in Latin in

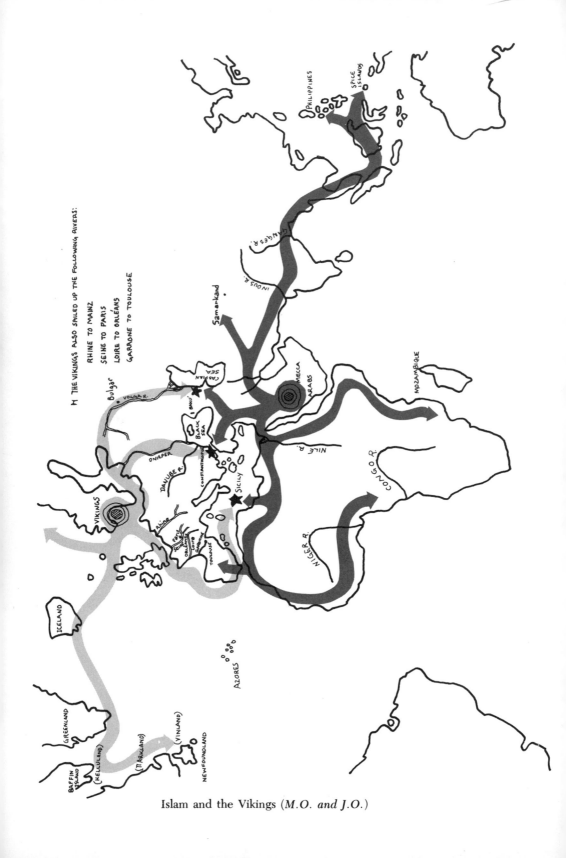

Islam and the Vikings (*M.O. and J.O.*)

the eighteenth century. But, having retraced the Norsemen's route to the West, I am convinced that they did indeed, as the sagas maintain, follow the coast of Baffin Island to Labrador and Newfoundland. It is therefore worth summarizing what the sagas tell us and my reasons for believing them.

Toward the end of the tenth century, Biarni Herulfson set sail from Iceland for Greenland, drifted off his latitude, and came to a flat, wooded coast not at all like the land of the frozen mountains. With the wind he followed the coast to the northeast and returned to Greenland, where he sold his *knarr* to Leif Ericson, son of Eric the Red. Leif was the first Christian in the colony. Up to that time the Norsemen had been pagans, governed by thirty-six *godar* or priests, who in the religious sagas or *Eddas* left us a rough picture of their pantheon (not unlike that of the Greeks). Thor was king of the Aesir, the principal gods, and, like Zeus, hurled lightning and thunder against the giants; Odin, the magician, was like Orpheus; Loki, like Eros; Frey was the god of crops and his sister Freya, like Aphrodite, was goddess of love.

Leif Ericson decided to seek the wood that Greenland lacked in the land Biarni had sighted. In the first summer of the eleventh century (the century of El Cid) he set sail westward with thirty-five men. The sagas describe the coasts he explored: first Helluland, flat and rocky; then Markland, where spruce stood over the Wonderstrands, long white beaches across which a series of streams flowed into the sea; and finally Vinland, where Leif entered a shallow bay beyond an island that guarded the mouth of a strait. There he built shelters where he stayed the rest of the summer and one winter; the sagas say that the sun shone longer there than in Greenland, there was good pasture, and a salmon run flowed from a lake. Grapes or berries were plentiful, and Tyrker, Leif's German godfather, made wine and got drunk, thereby giving Vinland its name. Whether it is possible to make wine so far north has been argued endlessly, but I think our climatologists have given us the answer, and berries may even have fermented by themselves in summer, as *marula* does in Africa. In any case the Norsemen's exploration of America, which was to end tragically, began on a festive note, and in the spring Leif returned to his base with a good cargo of wood and maybe some wine.

Two years later, Thorvald, another of Eric's sons, went back to Vinland to spend two winters in Leif's shelters. This time America met the invasion with Skrellings, dark barbarians who attacked from the sea in canoes and planted an arrow in Thorvald's breast. The surviving Norsemen hurried back to Greenland; three or four years later they mounted a more serious expedition of three *knarrs* and two hundred men and women. In command was Thorfinn Karlsefni, who took along his wife Gudrid, the widowed daughter-in-law of Eric; Freydis, Leif's half sister; and her husband, another Thorvald. Just as Leif had done, they crossed a strait with an island at its entrance, then managed to spend four years in Vinland and in Hop, farther to the south.

In this expedition it was the women who distinguished themselves. Gudrid gave birth to the first European born in America, and, when the Skrellings attacked, Freydis, though she bore the name of the goddess of love (or perhaps because she did), stripped to the waist and, pounding her chest with a short sword as if on a drum, advanced on the redskins (or Eskimos), who retired in disorder. Even so, the expeditionaries could not conquer their fear of the Skrellings and decided to return to Greenland.

Finally, around the year 1014, the brothers Helgi and Finnbogi agreed to return to Vinland with Thorvald and the indomitable Freydis to cut timber. Once there, Freydis had an idea: she convinced her husband that Helgi and Finnbogi had tried to seduce her. She made him so jealous that he and his men massacred the brothers while Freydis took care of the women. Then, sole owners of all the timber they had cut, they returned to Greenland and forgot Vinland.

On the northernmost tip of Newfoundland, in front of the island and strait of Belle Isle, I visited Anse-aux-Meadows in the shallow bay of Epaves, a wide, grassy shore dotted with blackberry bushes and watered by a stream which runs down from a lake. Here Norwegian archaeologist Helge Ingstad showed me the remains of shelters like those found in Greenland, a few implements, and charcoal that has been carbon-dated to the eleventh century—which leaves little doubt that this is Vinland. Then I crossed the strait and continued to the northeast along Labrador's black and forbidding coast, which is visited by icebergs even in summer. Suddenly, as I rounded Cape Porcupine near Hamilton Inlet, I saw fifty kilometers of white beaches, where, from the shade of a beautiful stand of spruce, several streams flow into the sea—surely Markland! Finally, further north and less than five degrees from the Arctic Circle, the rocky coasts of Baffin Island seemed perfect for Helluland.

The Norsemen certainly hit upon America, but the Skrellings did not allow its veil to be lifted and enjoyed another five hundred years of independence, thanks perhaps to our climatologists' "hazardous seas." The Norse exploration of America was forgotten and Vinland (and Hop) vanished, though nineteenth-century archaeologists searched for it from

Labrador to New York.[5] The mother colony on Greenland also disappeared. The skeletons that have been found there are of small, undernourished people, surely victims of the little ice age (1430–1850) that, the climatologists tell us, closed their ports.

Other Vikings opened up Russia by carrying their ships from the Baltic into the Dnieper, the Volga, and the Don—and so down to Constantinople. In southwest Russia and in Sicily they met the Muslims and could have informed them that their countrymen had found land beyond the Atlantic, but apparently they did not. Muslim maps used in medieval Europe, beginning with the one Mohammed Idrisi made for Norseman Roger II, showed one landmass, Eurasia, bounded east and west by the Infinite Ocean.

Neither Islam nor the Norse changed man's view of his universe. Therefore, though both were great explorers, they never became discoverers. But Homer's green island, surrounded by the Infinite Ocean, although it had increased in size, could not satisfy Renaissance man. He had to possess, to measure and to create everything anew, constructing harmonies of logic, of words, of forms, and of color in order to put the stamp of his own personality on life—and thereby conquer death.

Renaissance, Caravels, and Clocks

During the Middle Ages the gods of Olympus took refuge in the North and Christ alone, with his queen mother and his court of angels, archangels, and saints, reassured Western man of God's presence. Columbus' discoveries were made to the sound of the Salve Regina as he garlanded the Caribbean with saints and with virgins, from Montserrat and Nevis (Nieves) to the Eleven Thousand who still reign in the Virgin Islands. When he dedicated his third voyage to the Holy Trinity, three hills awaited his arrival, and Trinidad is the name he gave the beautiful three-cornered island which bears it still.

The old Olympian gods did finally return to Renaissance Italy but bereft of their feudal hierarchy, for Renaissance man no longer needed to impose order upon chaos; the Mediterranean world had made peace with its gods, and only northern barbarians still feared the chaos of the Infinite. The sun-drenched Renaissance wanted simply to possess the Infinite, a pagan attitude without paganism that enabled it to mold creation to its own liking without weakening the Church, which was soon to reach its greatest splendor. Savonarola attempted an evangelical reform and failed tragically; and Friar Bartolomé de las Casas upbraided the Spanish emperor's Council of the Indies because of Spain's treatment of the Indians. "My lords," said he, "look to your souls, for in truth, I fear for your salvation." For once a great and victorious empire suffered from a guilty conscience and in 1542 promulgated the New Laws of the Indies. But most Renaissance heroes, instead of preaching, preferred to fly the pennant of their mysticism while embarked on a personal search for their own place in history.

As the Renaissance advanced, full of confidence, several expeditions penetrated Asia overland. From his debtor's prison Marco Polo in the thirteenth century described the Malay Straits which Columbus would try to find in Panama. At the end of the fifteenth century Pedro de Colvilhao was sent by the King of Portugal to India via the Red Sea, and sailed down the eastern coast of Africa as far as the Zambezi River in today's Mozambique. But the boundless horizons of the sea tend to turn traders into discoverers, and we shall see that the great navigators were more interested in discovery than in trade, even in the Spice Islands, and even though Renaissance Europe was as much addicted to spices as it was to gold.[6] Spices were supposed to preserve food (they do disguise its decay) and to cure many ills, and even to serve as aphrodisiacs. At any rate, that was the illusion fostered in their rich lovers by Renaissance beauties, *viragoes* who sometimes married at the age of eight and soon aspired to the culture of the *vir*. Elegant courtesans *(cortegiane honeste)* were just as respectable as housewives *(massaie)*. Far from sharing the yellow veil of prostitutes "*di candela*," they were hostesses who, like the *hetaerae* of classical Greece, regaled their admirers with their art and their culture, discoursing in Latin and Greek on theology, politics, letters, and music. The music they loved combines the innocence of the Middle Ages with the sophistication of the high Renaissance, which to me seems to portray Columbus, a true son of both worlds.[7]

In the meantime, navigational systems based on Egyptian and Babylonian astronomy sufficed for Jason and Odysseus—and for their Greek, Phoenician, and Roman descendants—to sail the Mediterranean and the Black Sea and even to follow the coasts of the Atlantic north as far as England and south as far as the Canaries. But to face the Ocean's deep the Renaissance had to rediscover latitude and longitude, a system invented in the third century B.C. by Eratosthenes of Cyrene.

The concept of latitude comes directly from Jason's and Odysseus' east-west bands of stars, and longitude simply traces the way a spherical world can be divided north and south like a tangerine. For Columbus the north pole already lay beneath Polaris, which seemed to descend toward the horizon as the observer approached the equator. It was therefore obvious that intermediate altitudes of the pole star corresponded to intermediate latitudes and could be used to calculate them. The altitude of the pole star or of the sun was measured with the astrolabe, which the Muslims inherited from the Greeks, with a quadrant (one-fourth of an astrolabe), or with a cross-staff, all forerunners of the sextants and octants that today's astronauts still use (I have heard them checking their position by the stars).

Longitude was much more difficult to pin down, for in twenty-four hours every star passes through every degree of longitude. Thus, without knowing how much time had elapsed since a star passed through a familiar longitude, a navigator could not use that star to find his own longitude— and no navigator could continually calculate his east-west position by turning an hourglass every half hour, week after week—though estimates could be made by observing an eclipse (or the opposition of a planet with the moon) and comparing its local time with the time predicted in astronomical tables. Each navigator, furthermore, used a different base longitude, some that of the Teide in the Canaries, some that of the Azores, others the line of demarcation of Tordesillas; each had his own notions about the circumference of the globe, although Eratosthenes had calculated it with remarkable precision in the third century B.C.[8] Columbus had the good luck to underestimate the earth's circumference by a third, thereby ignoring the fact that one-third of the globe was covered by the Pacific and consequently locating the eastern coast of Asia almost exactly where America awaited him. Some claim that Columbus knew the earth's circumference very well and purposely understated it, but throughout history ignorance is a much more reliable explanation than ill will.[9]

Today, scientific and technical discoveries are almost immediately put to use, but in those days, even when a discovery was not forgotten, centuries passed before it was put into practice. Mechanical clocks existed when Magellan sailed, but for centuries none was taken on board a ship. The spring clock had been invented around 1470, and in the Society of Antiquaries in London I have seen the clock made in Prague in 1525 for

Renaissance Navigational Instruments (*M.O. and M.F.*)

Quadrant	Cross staff	Astrolabe	Hourglass (sand clock)
			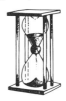

Sigismund I of Poland. It is a bronze cylinder nearly ten inches in diameter and ten inches high, which gives astronomical and astrological data in addition to the hours and the quarters. But to determine longitude, much greater accuracy is required, because the earth at the equator moves more than two hundred nautical miles each quarter of an hour. In fact, the exact position of the longitude which Pope Alexander VI and the 1494 Treaty of Tordesillas fixed as the dividing line between Spain's and Portugal's possessions remained so doubtful that it was impossible to establish to whom the Spice Islands belonged. In 1714 the British Parliament's Longitude Act established a prize of twenty thousand pounds for a shipboard chronometer capable of measuring longitude to an acceptable degree of accuracy, yet not until 1759 did John Harrison's "Number Four" chronometer measure up to that requirement by reaching Jamaica with an error equivalent to just over one nautical mile.[10]

Unable to determine longitude, Columbus and Magellan often ran down the latitudes just like the Homeric sailors and the Polynesians. Otherwise they used "dead reckoning," plotting distance and course to calculate a new fix from an old one, then checking it by crossing their latitude (obtained from the altitude of the sun or of the pole star) with their magnetic compass course. The compass, probably another Arab contribution, was already in general use, and Columbus was the first to establish clearly that on long voyages the compass needle required corrections. Albo, Magellan's navigator, whose latitudes were much more accurate than those of Columbus, corrected his compass needle at night by the stars and at midday with a *gnomon* whose shadow on the compass served to identify North. To measure speed Columbus had no log, so the seconds had to be counted while a floating object passed the ship from bow to stern.[11] I have tried this with a champagne cork, and the formula works: the speed in knots is about half the waterline length in feet, divided by the number of seconds. Close to land Columbus was always careful to use the lead, a knotted line weighted with lead that measures depth and, when tipped with tallow, the quality of the bottom (because sand and shells adhere to the tallow).

All these navigational aids required their rutters (charts), their cosmographies, and their navigational manuals. The first real rutter was that of Scylax of Caryanda in the fifth century B.C.; the first cosmography or description of the known world was Ptolemy's *Geography* in the second century A.D.; and perhaps the first comprehensive navigational manual was that of Pedro de Medina in 1530, which is now in the National Library in Madrid. Clay maps were made in Babylon in 4000 B.C., and Anaximander drew maps of sorts in Miletus in the sixth century B.C., but before the twelfth century A.D. cartography was much more symbolic than scientific.[12]

Truly modern cartography began with the 1154 A.D. map of Mohammed Idrisi and with the Pisan *Portolan Charts* of the late thirteenth century. It bloomed at the Majorcan School, where in 1375 Abraham Cresques embellished his *Catalán Atlas* with a thousand captions and colors. In 1488 a map by the German Henricus Martellus showed for the first time the Cape of Good Hope, which Bartolomeu Diaz had just rounded; and in 1492, just before Columbus set sail, Martin Behaim (the Bohemian) produced the first globe that has come down to us (fifty-one centimeters in diameter and made of plastered papier mâché covered in parchment, it is still preserved at Nuremberg). Martin Waldseemüller christened America in the map he published with his new edition of Ptolemy in 1507, and Schöner made globes before and after Magellan's voyage. Nuño García, Magellan's cartographer, showed the Strait in his *Padrón Real* of 1523 (Turin), one of a series of master charts which successive chief pilots, among them Vespucci, would be charged with keeping up to date. In 1529 Diego Ribero, a Portuguese in the service of Spain, at last showed a well-proportioned world, complete with Pacific, Indies, and all (his map is in the Vatican Library, where it was produced for me as though it were a holy relic, for its colors are fading). Finally, in 1569, in the time of Galileo, Copernicus, and Kepler, the Flemish geographer Mercator initiated the era of exact cartography with the projection that bears his name and is still the most useful for navigation because it allows courses to be laid off as straight lines.

Meanwhile, Jason's and Odysseus' ships had been only slightly improved by Phoenicians, Greeks, and Romans, who caulked them and then transformed them into triremes and galleys. It seems clear that the lateen sail was known in the second or third century, and I think something like one is portrayed in the twenty-second century B.C. mural on the northern wall of the tomb of Asa, at Deir el Gebrawi in Egypt. In the Middle Ages ships became more maneuverable and more comfortable, with tillers, more squaresails, and fore and aft castles, yet they still could not sail close to the wind. There was, in fact, no fundamental change in the art of navigation until the Portuguese, in the fifteenth century, opened the way to discovery with the caravel, which combined a more hydrodynamic hull with a lateen rig and could sail much closer to the wind than anything yet seen in the West. Unfortunately, we have neither the remains nor the plans of a caravel, but from nautical instructions and the small drawings that decorate charts of the time, we deduce that caravels displaced from thirty to seventy tons, drew one or

Henricus Martellus, 1489: Behaim's additions (. . . .) 1492 globe

Waldseemüller, 1507 (America's Christening)

Ribero, 1529

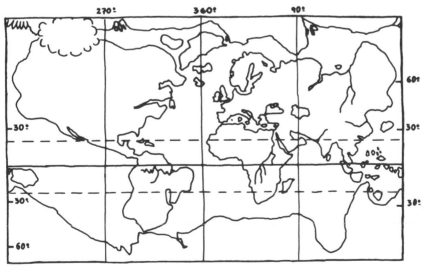

Mercator, 1569

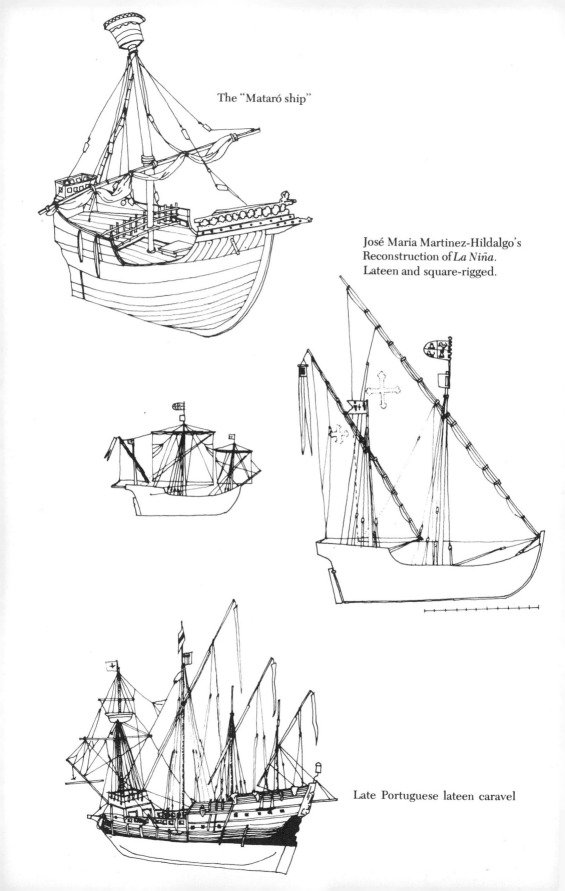

The "Mataró ship"

José Maria Martinez-Hildalgo's
Reconstruction of *La Niña*.
Lateen and square-rigged.

Late Portuguese lateen caravel

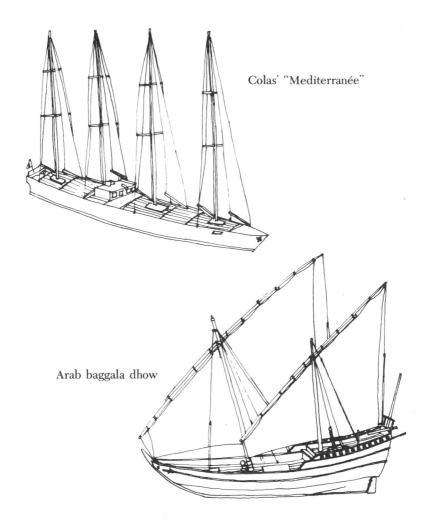

Colas' "Mediterranée"

Arab baggala dhow

two meters, and when necessary could be moved with oars. They measured between twenty and thirty meters on the waterline and had a beam of six to ten meters, so they were proportionately less beamy than other ships. Writings of the period show the caravel to have been a very special vessel; Columbus' log makes almost a hundred references to his *Santa Maria* as a *nao* (a beamy ship) and more than a hundred to the *Pinta* and the *Niña* as caravels. Their name obviously comes from the Greek *karavi* (originally *Karabos*, a scarab) through the Arab *carabo* (a light craft).

The first caravels appeared in Portugal in the fifteenth century and were of low displacement and low freeboard, sharp at bow and stern (though sometimes squared off above the waterline), and with no forecastle so that the yard, as long as the hull, could be brought over with its great lateen sail. At first they were no faster than *Argo*, but as their design improved they achieved up to eleven knots, thanks not only to their high sails but, I believe, to their superior buttock lines that greatly reduced wake turbulence. Soon a foremast and a mizzen on the poop were added. The Portuguese, champion close-haul sailors, built four-masted, lateen-rigged caravels for working close to the wind, a technique similar to that used by Alain Colas to cross the Atlantic alone in 1976. The Spaniards, on the other hand, preferred downwind sailing and kept changing lateen to square sails for higher speed on the wind, until there were completely "square rigged" caravels. Caravels disappeared in the seventeenth century; if there is anything that resembles one today, it is the Arab dhow, especially of the *baggala* or *sambuck* types.

Centuries had to pass before the Marconi rig permitted sailing really close to the wind, and therefore at a good average speed under sail on any course. The West eventually inherited fast catamarans and trimarans from the Polynesians, and today the hydrofoil can lift a small hull out of the water at speeds of almost forty knots under sail. But caravels backed by *naos* were good enough to challenge the Infinite Ocean.

NOTES

1. The river Oxus is today called Amu Darya; it flows northwest from Afghanistan to the Aral Sea.

2. According to the Koran, the Kaaba was built by Abraham with the help of his first son, Ishmael. On the road from Ur of the Chaldees to Canaan, God promised Abraham a son, and while his wife Sarah was still childless, his Egyptian slave Hagar bore him Ishmael. When Sarah gave birth to Isaac, God commanded Abraham to leave Hagar and Ishmael in a desert valley where, as a reward for their submission, He revealed to Hagar the well of Zamzam, near which the Kaaba was built. Its one remaining black stone (twelve inches in diameter) is now part of the fifty-foot-cube shrine that stands empty in commemoration of its cleansing by the Prophet, at the center of the Holy Mosque of Mecca, visited last year by some two million pilgrims (al-Haji).

The Bible, on the other hand, says that God commanded Abraham to sacrifice his son Isaac and that only when he had proved his submission did God allow him to substitute a ram. According to Jewish tradition, this occurred in Jerusalem.

Consequently, Mecca is the center of Islam, and Jerusalem of Israel; and while Arabs trace their descent to Ishmael, Jews trace theirs to Isaac. Today's enemies are blood brothers who share the story of the most dreadful example of total submission to God.

3. Inevitably, the expansion of Islam to the ends of the Eurasian continent gave rise to a long series of wars of succession and also to all sorts of heresies, such as that of the Hashashin or assassins, who, drugged with hashish, spread terror in the name of Islam during the eleventh and twelfth centuries. Their peaceful descendants, the Ishmaelites, still pay the Aga Khan a tribute equivalent to his weight in diamonds, which in 1946 was one hundred twenty kilos.

4. The ship in our illustration is at Viking Ship Hall in Oslo, Norway. It is twenty-two meters long, carried thirty oarsmen, and graced the sepulcher of a Viking lady of the ninth century at Oseberg—perhaps our ferocious friend Freydis.

5. Yale University even bought an old map which purported to show Vinland. Samuel Eliot Morison immediately declared the "Vinland map" false because of the colors of its ink, and I because in front of Asia it shows an unmistakable but inverted image of the Newfoundland of today; whoever added the island forgot that outlines do not "turn tail" when one flattens the sphere. Yale now admits the map is a forgery. In any case, we have seen that winds and currents in the tropics run toward America, and Columbus remarked that near Trinidad he had seen turbaned "Indians" much darker than the rest. I suggest that, well before the Norsemen, some African canoe probably drifted from Guinea to the Caribbean (its occupants could have survived by catching fish and squeezing drinking water out of them). If in fact anyone arrived before the Norsemen, he left even fewer tracks in the sands of history than they, so he certainly was no discoverer.

6. So valuable were cloves, nutmeg, pepper, incense, myrrh, saffron, and ginger that the relatively small quantity of spices Magellan's *Victoria* brought back from Spain enabled the expedition's financier, Cristobal de Haro, to pay all expenses including the imperial tax (his accounts in the archives are neatly perforated to prove it). Even today an ounce of concentrated incense is worth a third of an ounce of gold, and an ounce of essence of myrrh costs twenty-five times as much—perhaps because today it is more important to perfume oneself than to praise God.

The price of things is a story in itself. According to British economist Phelps Brown (in *Forbes*, March 1, 1975), prices in real terms remained almost steady from the end of the thirteenth century until early in the sixteenth. Then, starting perhaps with the flood of American gold and silver (a hundred times more silver than gold), prices multiplied six times by the middle of the seventeenth century. From then to the second World War real prices remained relatively constant except for occasional fluctuations. Today, due perhaps to the flood of so-called Eurodollars and Petrodollars (and Drugdollars), prices have again multiplied by six.

On the other hand, interest rates, which were limited by the Code of Hammurabi (1800 B.C.) to a maximum of thirty-three-and-one-third percent, have decreased steadily (even though in Babylon a debtor could mortgage his wife, his concubine, or even himself for up to three years). Since the decline of the Roman empire, rates have generally fluctuated between six percent and thirteen percent (plus davaluation). Today, oil producers receive each year ten times what Spain got from America in the entire sixteenth century, so, relatively speaking, there must be at least as much money around now as there was in the Renaissance. Perhaps we should expect a super-Renaissance, but I see no sign of it yet.

7. In Raphael's Parnassus, Sappho is the famous courtesan Imperia, who has rested in peace since 1511 in the church of San Gregorio al Cielo under the

legend, "Imperia, Roman courtesan worthy of her name because of the beauty she brought into the world."

As for music, in 1324 Pope John XXII decreed that major chords should be used with great care in church lest their earthiness distract the faithful. Renaissance musicians gave the name of *Diabolus in Musica* to the diminished fifth (two notes separated by three full tones) which, as we have seen, had been a tragic chord ever since the time of Orpheus, and still is in operas and movie scores. Discoverers usually took along trumpets, flutes, and violas, and, though only a few musical instruments of the time have come down to us, sixteenth-century manuals give us some idea of how those instruments were tuned and played, while the facial expressions of musicians pictured in contemporary paintings indicate the tempo of their music.

8. Eratosthenes was Apollonius' successor at the Library of Alexandria. He measured the angular altitude of the sun from Alexandria when he knew it was shining vertically into a very deep well at Syene (Aswan). He found that the angular difference between the two places corresponded to one-fiftieth of a full circle. He figured the linear distance between them at 5000 stadia, and this, multiplied by 50, gave him 250,000 stadia as the circumference of the earth. That figure is equivalent to less than 25,000 nautical miles—not a bad approximation to our nearly 22,000.

9. When at the end of his last voyage Columbus timed an eclipse, he placed Jamaica at "nine hours" from Europe. If he was referring to the difference in time, his error was nearly fifty percent.

10. Along with the newer models that Kendall made for Cook and for Bligh, I have examined the famous "Number Four" in the Maritime Museum at Greenwich. It is like a modern pocket watch but three times as large and quite similar to most modern ships' chronometers. These did not change significantly until even wristwatches began to use the pulsations of a quartz crystal to achieve the accuracy of today's marine chronometers, plus or minus two-tenths of a second per day (equivalent to one and one-half nautical miles after sailing for a month along the equator). Atomic clocks are now so accurate that in some years a "leap second" is necessary to keep them in step with the mean sun, just as leap years are necessary to keep the calendar in step with the seasons.

11. The compass needle's magnetism, obtained by hammering a hot iron bar placed in a north-south position, had to be renewed frequently with stone from Jason's Magnesia. A log is a rope knotted every seven fathoms (more exactly, fifty feet) and attached to a sea anchor, which a sailor holds in a loose grip so that he can count the number of actual knots that slide through his grasp in half a minute. This gives him the nautical miles per hour, or "knots," at which the ship is traveling.

12. Ptolemy's *Geography* was not translated into Latin until 1410, the year *Imago Mundi* was published by Pierre d'Ailly, whose undersized globe so deeply influenced Columbus. We have seen that until maps were added by Crivelli for the Bologna edition of 1477 the *Geography* was published without maps.

4

COLUMBUS
AND
VESPUCCI

Columbus: The Atlantic

That the Ocean is not Infinite was finally to be proved by Christopher
Columbus, Admiral of the Ocean Sea. In 1492 he was forty years old and
of good stature in an age when most men were short. His eyes were blue
and his reddish hair prematurely greying. Always courteous, even with
his crew, yet as remote as he was religious, he was an imposing figure. He
signed himself Cristo Ferens (he who bears Christ) because he knew that
God had called him to carry the Cross to the Indies. He insisted vaguely
on his high birth, the first of his three obvious complexes, in spite of the
fact that his grandfather Giovanni, his father Domenico, and his mother
Susana Fontanarossa all came from a long line of weavers. He looked on
the science of the Renaissance with the innocent eyes of the Middle Ages
and strove to explain his navigation scientifically with a jumble of
erroneous figures. In fact he was the greatest intuitive sailor of all time,
and practice, not theory, proved him right. Therein lay his second
complex. Peter Martyr of Angheira said of Columbus' calculations, "All
this is unintelligible to me and I confess that the Admiral's arguments
please me not at all." His third complex, persecution, would catch up
with him later and with better cause. Who can be a genius without
complexes?

Born in Genoa, in the province of Liguria, in 1451, the same year as
Queen Isabella, one year before King Ferdinand, and two years before
the fall of Constantinople to the Turks, Columbus was brought up in
Genoa and in neighboring Savona. Doubts about his birthplace did not
arise until a century after his death. Nevertheless he was not exactly
Italian, for Italy did not become a nation for another four centuries, and
to this day some Ligurians speak a dialect that is almost unintelligible in

Christopher Columbus (*D'Orchi Collection*)

the rest of the peninsula. Genoa was an amphitheatre full of seagulls and sails, and while Christopher worked at his family's looms, his soul began to fill with dreams of far horizons. Around 1471, he set sail for the first time and then signed on to defend a fortified Genoese trading post on the island of Chios. In 1476 he went into the Atlantic with a Genoese convoy that was attacked and sunk by the famous corsair Guillaume de Casenove. Clinging to an oar, Columbus reached the beach at Lagos in Portugal, where he joined his brother Bartholomew, two years his junior, who was working as a mapmaker in Lisbon.

Though Portugal's population had not yet reached two million (Britain's had just passed the one million mark), she was Europe's balcony on the Ocean. Around 1420 Prince Henry the Navigator established his "control center" at Sagres, below Cape Saint Vincent in the Algarve (*Garb* in Arabic means west). Under his orders, Gonçalo Velho Cabral sailed west and discovered the Azores precisely where it was necessary to go in order to catch the wind to return to Portugal from Africa. Then, knowing that it was possible to sail home, several Portuguese dared to round the eastern headlands of Africa: Cape Bojador to the south of the Canaries, Cape Verde where Dakar stands today, and Cape Blanco midway between the two.

When Prince Henry died in 1460, it was still not known whether the equatorial sea boiled, but King Alfonso V, his nephew, sent Fernán Gómez close to the equator and Lope Gonçalvez across it in 1475, and they returned unscalded. Then the king signed a treaty with Castile confirming the papal bull of 1454 which had secured a monopoly of the African coast to Portugal (excepting only the Spanish Canary Islands). Finally Alfonso's son, João II, dispatched Bartholomeu Diaz to round the Cape of Good Hope in 1488, and Vasco da Gama to Calcutta via the Cape in 1497. From there the Portuguese advanced their fortified trading posts like pawns in a chess game against the Muslims, all the way to the Spice Islands, which faced the Ocean from Eurasia's eastern shore.

In the process the Portuguese made great strides in cartography, and Columbus learned from them. I have compared his map of Navidad on the island of Hispaniola, which is in the Duke of Alba's library, with an aerial photograph and found the map almost perfect. His plan was "to make a new navigational chart in which I shall locate . . . the lands of the Ocean Sea in their right places under the wind, by equinoctial latitude and west longitude." In Portugal he also learned to read Latin and to write Castilian, the tongue many cultured Portuguese then used.[1]

In 1477 he sailed with the Portuguese via Ireland to Iceland, where he saw two "oriental" cadavers in a dinghy washed up by the sea. It was said later that in Iceland Columbus heard of the Norsemen's Vinland, but the possibility is irrelevant: He was not interested in looking for Skrellings in northern seas; he wanted to reach the court of the Great Khan in the southern Ocean. Next he captained a vessel that sailed to the Portuguese island of Madeira, where, in 1479, he married the daughter of the captain general of Porto Santo, Felipa de Perestrelo y Moníz, who, about a year later, gave him his first son, Diego. In 1483, sailing again, with the Portuguese, this time down the African shore to the Gold Coast, he noted that while the prevailing winds at the Azores blow toward Portugal, from the Canaries down they blow from Africa out to sea. He also confirmed

Map of Hispaniola by Columbus, and what remains of the accompanying letter (*Duchess of Alba's Library*)

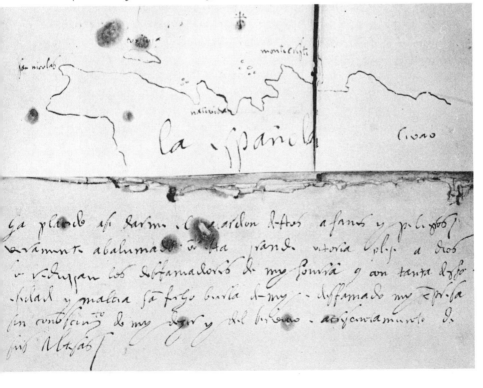

what he had first learned in Chios: that the trade of a vast region can be controlled from one fortified trading post like São Jorge de Mina, where the Portuguese collected the gold that gave the Gold Coast its name. In 1484 Felipa died.

Anyone who has ever seen a sail or a coastline disappear below the horizon knows that the world is round, but until Magellan measured the Pacific, many supposed that Asia was so wide—or the world so small— that no great sea distance separated Asia from Europe. In 1484 the great Florentine geographer Paolo Toscanelli sent João II, king of Portugal, a map (now lost) that was probably similar to Martellus' map of 1488 and to Martin Behaim's globe of 1492. Don João, a cautious king who had refused to have his demons exorcised lest his angels leave with them, studied the map and listened to Columbus' proposal to sail westward to the Indies. Then he referred the project to a scientific committee that soon rejected it, remembering that Greek and Muslim estimates of the circumference of the earth put some ten thousand nautical miles of sea between Portugal and Asia.

Reason prevails little against faith, and Columbus was not convinced by the committee's mathematics. Rejected by Portugal, he sent his brother Bartholomew to talk to Henry VII of England and to Charles VIII of France. When these missions failed, Columbus sailed in 1485 with his son Diego for Palos de Moguer, the first Spanish port south of Portugal. There he made the pilgrimage to the Franciscan monastery of La Rábida, where he met the first of the three men whom fate would place along his way like lighthouses. Friar Antonio de Marchena, the astronomer, not only listened to him but introduced him to the powerful Duke of Medina, who seemed interested in Columbus' request for two caravels. But nothing could be done without the queen's blessing. To obtain it, Columbus went to Córdoba, only to find that the court had moved on to Granada (the Catholic court moved continually, as did the Tudors' in England). While in Córdoba he met warmhearted Beatriz Henriquez, who in 1488 gave birth to his second son, Ferdinand. He never married Beatriz, no doubt because she lacked the class necessary for his high designs, and this may well have cost him his chance of being canonized.[2]

On May 1, 1486, Queen Isabella received Columbus. She was as cultivated as the Portuguese king (her personal library included Aristotle and Boccaccio), and so, like him, she passed Columbus' proposal on to a commission of scholars whose chairman was her confessor, Friar Hernando de Talavera. But the queen did more: She paid Columbus a monthly retainer of a thousand *maravedies*—approximately the wages of an ordinary seaman. For the next two years, Columbus put up with the Spanish *mañana;* then he obtained a new audience with the king of Portugal (who, in passing, forgave him his debts). Columbus arrived in Portugal just in time to see Bartolomeu Diaz drop anchor after rounding the Cape, an act that opened Portugal's route to India via Africa and canceled any interest Portugal might have had in Columbus' plan to reach India by sailing west. When the Spanish commission also rejected his proposal, Columbus returned to the monastery of La Rábida to collect Diego and make for France.

Fortunately, at La Rábida his second lighthouse awaited him: Friar Juan Pérez, who insisted that he stay in touch with the queen. Money soon arrived from the Court for Columbus to buy clothes and a mule so that he might present himself in Santa Fe, near snow-framed Granada, where their Catholic majesties were awaiting the Moors' surrender. "On the second of January [1492], I saw the Royal Standard hoist by force of arms on the towers of the Alhambra," Columbus wrote at the beginning of his diary. A new committee was charged with reviewing the proposal, and this encouraged Columbus, always a good Genoese merchant, to come up with new conditions: He and his heirs were to be not only admirals but viceroys in perpetuity of the lands to be discovered; they would get ten percent of whatever these lands produced (twenty percent would be the royal "fifth"); they would have the right to invest one-eighth in any future expedition and the privilege of proposing candidates for governors and judges.[3]

The second Spanish committee also returned a round negative, but when Columbus retired once again with Friar Juan, the third lighthouse appeared, this time not a friar but a farsighted Jew. Luis de Santángel, King Ferdinand's personal treasurer, convinced the queen that she had nothing to lose by giving the imposing Genoese visionary a chance. She did not even need to pawn her jewels; instead, Santángel would advance a million and a half *maravedies* out of the coffers of Aragon. (The Castilian queen's approval was necessary because Spain's pact with Portugal assigned the Western Ocean to Castile, but the financial backing came from King Ferdinand of Aragon, so Columbus' first Spanish documents are in the Crown Archives of Aragon in Barcelona, not in the archives of Seville.)

In April 1492 Columbus signed the *Capitulaciones*, the agreement that granted him all the rights and titles he had requested plus a passport and three letters of introduction addressed to an anonymous prince. His landfall was evidently still in doubt.

The great adventure which would dispel the mists that still covered half the globe started on May 23 at Palos, in the aptly named Condado de Niebla (Fog County). In front of the church of Saint Francis (when I visited it, a little gypsy, spotting my grey beard, enquired if I were a grandson of Columbus) Friar Juan read the royal decree ordering the city of Palos to cancel its debt to the Crown by providing Columbus with two caravels, and the recruiting of the first ninety adventurers began. A *nao* from Galicia sailed into port and Columbus chartered it from Juan de la Cosa, who was to make half a dozen trips to America and draw the first map of the new world. The total cost of the fleet was some two million *maravedies*, about twenty thousand dollars in today's money—if "today's money" means anything at all.

At dawn on Friday, August 3, 1492, where the rivers Odiel and Tinto meet and form the Saltes, three ships whose names will never be forgotten set out to sea bound for the Canaries. We have no reliable picture of them, but experts have been able to piece together a description from nautical manuals, from pictures on old charts, and also from the "Mataró ship," the only contemporary model in existence, which unfortunately represents neither a *nao* nor a caravel. [4]

The Galician *nao Santa María (La Gallega)* displaced about a hundred *toneles*, rather more than one hundred tons. She measured almost twenty-five meters on the waterline and eight meters on the beam, drew a little more than two meters, and had a hold some four meters deep. She carried a large squaresail on her mainmast that was twenty-seven meters high, a small topsail above the maintop tower, a lateen sail on the mizzenmast on her poop, a small squaresail on the foremast, and a spritsail (like a false jib) under the bowsprit.

The *Pinta* was a caravel of seventy *toneles*, twenty meters long, three meters on the beam, and with a draught of nearly two meters. She carried a square mainsail and a lateen on her poop. The *Niña* (or *Santa Clara*) was a slightly smaller caravel but a better sailor. Columbus' favorite, she was the only one of the original ships to make two more voyages to America after the Discovery. She started with a classic Portuguese lateen rig, but in the Canary Islands she was rerigged like the *Pinta* for faster downwind sailing, which indicates that Columbus may already have been planning to return by the northerly route with a favorable wind. All three ships carried fixed ballast of mortar and also loose stones; all were completely decked and had forcastles and aftercastles, except for the *Niña*, which had a castle only on her stern. Below the castles two thick beams pierced the hulls; their purpose is still unclear even to the experts, but we know that these beams came directly from *Argo*. The traditions of the sea change slowly.

Thanks to the late Alice Bache Gould (the famous Miss Alice), we know the names and biographies of eighty-six of the ninety crew members, forty in the *Santa María*, twenty-six in the *Pinta*, and twenty in the *Niña*.[5] Columbus was commander of the *Santa María*, and her owner, Juan de la Cosa, was shipmaster. Her pilot was Peralonso Niño, and her master-at-arms was Diego de Arana (cousin of Beatriz, the mother of Columbus' second son). On board was an interpreter, Luis de Torres, "who, having been a Jew, knew Hebrew, Chaldean and even Arabic" (he must have converted to Christianity to escape the exile just imposed on his less pliant brethren.) Captain of the *Pinta* was Martín Alonso Pinzón, who would be the first to confirm the sighting of America and the first back to Spain. Her master was Francisco Martín Pinzón; her owner, Cristobal Quintero, sailed as an ordinary seaman. Also on board were Diego Martín Pinzón and Juan Rodriquez Bermejo (Rodrigo de Triana), who would first cry *tierra!* (land ho!). Captain of the *Niña* was Vicente Yañez Pinzón, future discoverer of the Amazon, and her master and owner was Juan Niño. Also on board was Francisco Niño. Thus the two families, the Pinzóns and the Niños, who with Columbus' own would spearhead the discoveries, were well represented. Displaced persons, like Columbus and Jason, are often best at putting together good teams.

Each ship carried a surgeon but no priest, perhaps because Columbus was as good as three clerics and never forgot the Holy Offices. He knew that Christ and the Virgin would guide him to the Indies and bring him back because the riches he would bring home would finance a new Crusade. Nevertheless he made but one vow: to cross the Ocean. On the Canary Island of Gomera he fell in love with Inés Pedraza de Bobadilla, widow of the captain general of San Sebastián (*"tincto d'amore"* is the diagnosis of cheerful Michele de Cuneo, one of the four Genoese who constantly accompanied the Discoverer), but he had more important things to do than marry. All he noted in his diary was that Inés and her son saw "land to the west of the Canaries every year."[6]

On September 6 the wind blew "more lovingly" (Columbus' phrase) and the fleet weighed anchor. But on the northern limit of the trades the wind is variable, and it took three days to lose sight of Hierro, the westernmost of the Canaries, and Teide, the four-thousand-meter volcano that crowns Tenerife with "much fire."

Once in the trades, the first Atlantic crossing was a pure delight—within the limits of the seagoing luxuries of the day. The long tiller creaked constantly under the captain's cabin, which was the only one on board, for the other adventurers slept under the stars, at the mercy of spray and wind. Salt meat, fish, lentils, and chick-peas, cooked by anyone over embers in a sandbox under the forecastle, were swallowed with ship's tack and bread made of salt flour and washed down with red wine while it lasted and then with stale water until fresh rainwater could be collected in a sail. (As far as I know, Sebastian Cabot was the first discoverer to take along a cook.)

With a following wind and the salt flavor of the unknown on his lips, Columbus, like Odysseus, had only to pursue the constellations that followed the latitude he had chosen, 28°N, the latitude of the Canaries, of the legendary Antillia, and of Cipangu (Japan). He probably followed the Pleiades, which in this season sailed through the heavens after midnight in close order at the head of the splendid procession formed by Taurus, the giant Orion, and Canis Major, the constellation that includes Sirius, our brightest star. He checked his latitude by measuring the altitude of the Pole star and also by sighting the sun at midday with a quadrant and comparing its declination with astronomical tables like those compiled in Lisbon a little earlier by Abraham Zacuto.[7]

Time was measured with a half-hour sandglass, turned over eight times by each watch to the chant "Blessed be the hour when God was born, Saint Mary who bore Him, and Saint John who baptized Him." The hour had to be corrected, probably once a week at local noon, for as one sails west, time advances about ten minutes a day.[8]

In the calm sea the fish played in safety. The Spaniards did not fish much, just as for a long time they would not plant much in America; to discover is one thing, to work another. The faithful trade winds sang in the rigging, and the sky, blue as God painted it, was dotted with small white cumuli. Columbus wrote that the taste of the mornings was so delicious that he almost expected to hear a nightingale, and that the weather was like April in Andalusia. Nothing in this life is so sweet, not even final success, as to know that one has embarked on one's chosen course.

On September 16 the expeditionaries entered the Sargasso Sea, where so much flotsam had accumulated (today it is largely plastic bottles) that it looked like an island; the compass needle varied to the northwest; they saw pigeons, dolphin, a whale, and a "fork-tailed bird which makes pelicans disgorge their food in the air in order to eat itself" (an exact description of the frigate bird so common in the Caribbean). Was this Antillia? On September 25, "in a sea like a river [in which] many sailors [took] a swim," Martín Alonso Pinzón thought he saw land.

October came in with rain but no land, and within a week a worried Martín Alonso began to consult with Columbus. On several occasions they had made eight knots downwind, a respectable speed under sail even today, and the total distance run was already much greater than their estimated distance to Asia. But the wind did not encourage them to go about, and Pinzón had seen birds flying to the south-southwest. Columbus gained a breathing space by promising to turn back if no land was sighted in three days. "Forward," he said, for the air was again so sweet "that its perfume [was] a joy to breathe."

Columbus: The American Barrier

At ten o'clock at night on October 11, Columbus saw a light that oscillated on the horizon. Pedro Gutierrez also saw it, but Rodrigo Sánchez de Segovia, the king's inspector and a good bureaucrat, saw nothing. At two in the morning Rodrigo de Triana's cry of *tierra!* was heard from the *Pinta*, and Martín Alonso confirmed that white cliffs were visible under the light of the moon. But it was Columbus who kept the ten thousand *maravedies* promised by the king to the first man to sight land in the Indies, and Rodrigo de Triana was left to sail to his death in the Pacific with Loayza and Elcano, whom we will soon meet.

The Admiral (he was Admiral now by right) was a prudent sailor who would not approach an unknown windward shore before dawn. He had the Salve sung and gave orders to heave to because, says the diary, in all these islands there are "rocks under the sea close to land, and one must keep one's eyes open if one wishes to come to anchor . . . though the waters are very clear, and one can always see the bottom." With the first light of October 12, the squadron sailed round the south end of the island and found a passage through the coral reef to leeward. Under a high sun the Admiral took a launch to the dazzling beach where naked Indians happily received the bearded men who had come from heaven in their winged castles, bringing mirrors, red caps, and hawks' bells which the Indians called "chuc chuc." Their island they called Guanahaní, but Columbus christened it San Salvador and took possession in the name of their Catholic majesties.[9] He remarked that the Indians "would better be freed and converted to our Holy Faith by love than by force . . . for it seems to me that they belong to no particular sect."

The light that Columbus saw "like a wax candle being raised and lowered" was explained to Morison and me by Ruth Bage Malvin, who lived for many years on the island of San Salvador and has pointed out that even today the natives light bonfires on the cliffs to keep off the mosquitos, just as the ancient Egyptians did. It seems that Columbus did earn the ten thousand *maravedies*. Anyone who still doubts that this was the first Caribbean island that dropped its veil to the west should compare it with Columbus' description and then study my map of the courses and times which Columbus notes from here on in the diary. Columbus' route through the Caribbean could not have started from any other island if it was to finish in Cuba and today's Haiti, the first map of which was drawn by Columbus himself.

But San Salvador was not the mainland, and Columbus must press on to the Court of the Great Khan. Island hopping through the beauty of the Bahamas (which he called Lucayas) made his diary positively rhapsodic. "The fish are so different from ours that it is amazing. There are some like roosters, of the most delicate colors in the world, blue, yellow, red . . . and others mottled in a thousand different ways . . . so that . . . it is a great satisfaction to see them." His words will surprise no one who has seen parrotfish in the Caribbean. There were "oaks and evergreens . . . and the song of the birds is so sweet that a man would never wish to leave this place, with its flocks of parrots . . . which darken the sun."

The fleet was guided by half a dozen Indians "the same color as the people of the Canaries, neither black nor white . . . as naked as their mother bore them, and the women too . . . [and] with thick hair [cut] in a fringe down to their eyebrows." Their language was "the same in all these islands." They had "cloth of spun cotton," slept in "beds which are like cotton nets," and sailed in "canoes made from a single tree trunk," some of which carried from forty to fifty men. Above all, they had gold, and to judge by its color, says Columbus intriguingly, "there must be a great deal of it."

The squadron reached Cuba and anchored in Puerto Gibara, where the pointed hill known today as Bariay's Teat reminded Columbus of a mosque. Cuba appeared to be the eastern tip of the Asian continent, but when an embassy headed by Juan de Jerez and the interpreter Luis de Torres explored the nearest settlement, instead of gold and spices they returned with a "firebrand" of herbs that gave off a pleasant smoke. It was tobacco, and has proved even more addictive than gold. After a brief excursion west to today's port of Covarrubias, the Admiral followed the coast eastward and left Cuba at today's Cape Maisi, which he named Alpha and Omega—that is, the beginning and the end of Asia. Crossing the strait to today's Haiti, he arrived on Saint Nicholas' Day, December 6, at the magnificent port that still bears the saint's name. It is one of the five places Columbus located on his Navidad map; the other four are Tortuga Island, Navidad, Montecristi, and the province of Cibao. After naming Puerto Príncipe, today's Port-au-Prince, he explored the northern coastline of the island and christened it La Española (Hispaniola). On November 22 Martín Alonso Pinzón went off on his own in the *Pinta* to

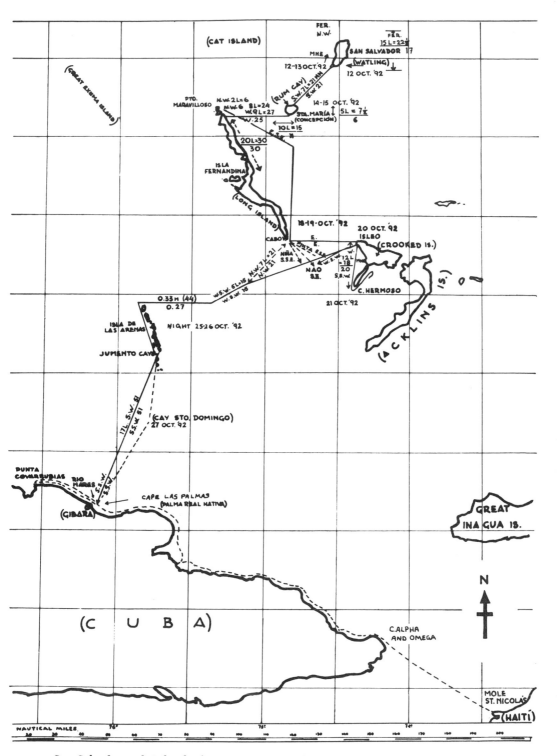

San Salvador and Columbus' route to Hispaniola (*M.O. and M.F.*)

the island of Babeque, where the Indians said there was gold (probably today's Inagua, which produces nothing but salt). "This and much more he [Martín Alonso] has done to me," wrote the foresighted Admiral, "and if he gets safely back to Spain . . . he may well lie to the King and Queen."

On Christmas Eve the *Santa María* and the *Niña* passed through a gap in the reef that protects the broad bay over which the castle of Cap Haitien now presides and anchored in calm off the small bay we know by the relaxing name of Limonade Bord de Mer. The Admiral and his men entertained many Indian ambassadors and their pretty daughters without incident. Columbus, though he noted that the Indians were "so docile that it would be easy to put them to work," treated them kindly and sent them away with presents. It was a night to rest, so calm that a ship's boy was all the watch that would be needed. But the current stirred, the *Santa María* dragged her anchor, and when at eleven o'clock the ship's boy felt the keel scrape on coral, he gave the alarm. Columbus rushed on deck and sent Juan de la Cosa out in the longboat to try to tow the *Santa María* free. Instead, de la Cosa rowed on to the *Niña*, presumably to seek help, and when he got back an onshore breeze was blowing and the *Santa María* was firmly aground. No one could budge her, and she began to take on water. At dawn the Admiral resolved to dismantle her and improvise a fort from her timbers, to be known as Navidad (Nativity) in honor of the day. Diego de Arana would defend it with twenty men, and to make sure that Guacanagari, chief of the friendly Indians, would not waver in his friendship, an artillery demonstration was carried out on what was left of the *Santa María* (it is therefore difficult to take seriously the rediscovery of her hull that someone claims about every five years).

Now it was urgent to get back to Spain with the news of the discovery. Navidad was no more than a month's sail from Spain, and the Admiral, whose imagination always ran ahead, was already planning his next voyage to Hispaniola with everything needed to establish a real colony. On January 2 he sailed east in the *Niña* and, passing Montecristi, noted that it was a good landfall for finding Navidad because it "has the form of a huge tent." On January 6 he saw the *Pinta* approaching and grudgingly accepted Pinzón's explanations. Pinzón had brought gold, and in the Yaque del Norte River there was more gold, so on January 18 the two caravels finally set course for Spain well laden, taking their leave of America from the deep Bay of Samaná at the eastern end of what is today Santo Domingo. Like most of the ports found by Columbus, it is almost untouched today, for progress despises natural ports, preferring to serve rich hinterlands.

Montecristi (*D.C.*)

We have seen that in these latitudes the trades blow out of the east, and since squaresails do not permit a course closer than sixty degrees to the wind, Columbus spent the rest of January tacking to the northeast. By February he was far enough north to catch a westerly, but like a good zephyr it came with a storm. On the night of February 13 the *Niña* lost sight of the *Pinta* in the gale. Striking all sails, Columbus dropped a coffer containing extracts from his diary into the sea, terrified lest his discovery be lost with him. To make the Azores he had to run down latitude 37°N, following, I think, the constellation Auriga, which then shone in the evening and which includes the bright star Capella.

On February 15 he sailed into the port of Santa María in the Portuguese Azores, where it took him a while to convince the governor that the *Niña* had not been poaching in Portugal's African preserves. Impatiently, he began to write his first "American" letter. He finally set sail again on February 24, rode out another gale, and at last, on March 3, running before a strong wind under spritsail alone, he saw the full moon shine on the coast of Portugal. Wisely, he ran down the coast at a safe distance and, on March 5, anchored in the broad mouth of the Tagus, which forms the port of Lisbon. Crew and caravel were at the limit of their endurance.

In regal Lisbon, Columbus insisted on being treated as an admiral. He requested an audience with Don João, not only to ask his help but surely also to show him that he had succeeded in the project the king had rejected years before. It was a risky demonstration, for we have seen that

Don João was a true Renaissance prince; he had just had his brother-in-law murdered for reasons of state, and he would certainly not be pleased to see that his Castilian cousin had succeeded where he had failed even to try. But the king received Columbus kindly and ordered the *Niña* to be repaired so that the Admiral could set sail on March 13 for Palos, after finishing his letter and sending it to Luis de Santángel in gratitude. The bar of the Saltes River was crossed on March 15 and the anchor dropped where it had been weighed seven months before. In all, Columbus had spent about a month reaching the Canaries, another to San Salvador, three in the Antilles, one to the Azores, and one to Lisbon and Palos—seven months for a leap as long as those of Jason and Odysseus, as long as ours to the moon.

The *Pinta* made Palos the same day, after sailing from Hispaniola directly to Bayona in Galicia. There, as Columbus feared he might do, Martín Alonso Pinzón had requested an audience with the king and the queen, but they had refused to receive him without Columbus. Pinzón was ill (some say he brought syphilis from America), and in less than a month he was dead. The expedition could not have been put together without him, and he was the first to see the cliffs of the new world and to bring news of it to Europe; but he tried to go it alone, and Providence did not forgive him.

The Admiral sent off two copies of his Lisbon letter, one to Barcelona and one to Córdoba, and spent two weeks fulfilling his religious duties at La Rábida and at Holy Week in Seville. There, on Easter Sunday, he received their Catholic majesties' reply. Addressed to the "Admiral and Viceroy," the letter already spoke of the next voyage, and Columbus, in his answer, began to expound his ideas as a colonizer. I believe the Navidad map belongs to this second Columbus letter, because a paragraph on the sheet marked X which accompanies it (were there ten?) reads, "So it has pleased you to reward me for my trials and risks and, truly overwhelmed by this great victory, I pray God that the defamers of my honor will be silenced." Columbus' fear of persecution had emerged, and it seems to me characteristic of him not to have sent the map of Navidad before receiving his "reward," that is to say, not with his first letter but with his second.

The Admiral picked up his two sons in Córdoba, where the good Beatriz had been a mother to both, and proceeded to Barcelona accompanied by a triumphal procession of Indians carrying gold ornaments and parrots. On April 20, 1493, he appeared in the great arched hall El Tinell and received from the satisfied sovereigns the privilege of quartering his crest with the arms of the kingdoms of Castile and Aragon on a

field of islands and anchors. He had been proved right and had proved
Castile and Aragon right in supporting him. And he had so changed
contemporary geography that, in order to prevent conflict between the
two discoverer nations, on May 3 and 4 Pope Alexander VI promulgated
papal bulls that divided the globe between Spain and Portugal along the
longitude that passes "a hundred leagues to the west of the Azores and the
Cape Verdes" (approximately 30° W).

The Admiral made three more voyages, but here we can only sketch
them.[10] The second, the triumphal voyage of 1493–1496, set sail from
Cadiz via Gomera with seventeen ships (including the *Niña*), a proud fleet
with pennants snapping in the breeze, headed by the *Mariagalante*, a
flagship of some two hundred *toneles*. The fleet carried seeds, tools,
cattle, twenty horses, and some twelve hundred souls, including Catalán
friars, but no women—nor Jews, heretics, or heathens, for it was the
Church's duty to convert the Indians to the true faith, and it had been
authorized to levy a tax to support itself in the new world. Juan de la Cosa
was on board, as were the father and the uncle of the future Friar
Bartolomé de las Casas; so too were Alonso de Ojeda, who would be the
second discoverer, and Diego Columbus, the Admiral's youngest brother.

Columbus' four voyages and those of his first competitors (*M.O. and M.F.*)

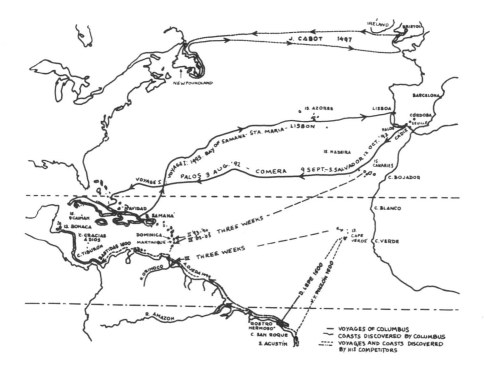

In three weeks, and on a Sunday (hence the name), the fleet sighted the island of Dominica, over the cliffs of which the jungle hangs like a horse's mane. Then the fleet threaded the bright necklace of the Lesser Antilles, beginning with Guadeloupe and pressed on to the island of San Juan (which later switched names with its capital city, Puerto Rico) and thence to Hispaniola and Navidad.[11] There the triumph ended. The fort was gone, and when the surgeon Chanca examined Guacanagarí, who claimed to have been wounded while defending it, not a scratch was visible beneath his bandages. Nevertheless Columbus remained faithful to his policy of getting the Indians on his side and forgave him. Dr. Chanca, also a chronicler, described a white line hanging from the clouds on Guadeloupe, which remained an enigma until we photographed it from the air: it is a high waterfall which forms only when the volcano is in the clouds.

For "Isabella," his new colony, the Admiral chose a site near the Yaque del Norte River, where he had first seen gold panned—an unfortunate choice, for it soon disappeared (even today there is not much there). He dispatched to Spain twelve ships loaded with gold procured from the Indians, and continued west to explore the southern coast of Cuba, whose many islands he named "the Queen's Gardens." As though

Guadeloupe: The vertical waterfall (*D.C.*)

he feared discovering the contrary, a few miles from the island's western extreme he required all his officers to certify that Cuba was the eastern headland of the Asian continent and not an island at all. Then he turned back to explore lofty Jamaica.[12] After riding out his first hurricane in Santo Domingo, the Admiral set sail for home via Guadeloupe in the faithful *Niña,* with the *India,* the first caravel built in America, in company. But he made the mistake of returning by the southern route and spent almost two months beating against the wind to Cadiz to round off the three years of this voyage of triumph and disillusion.

Meanwhile, emissaries had begun to come and go between Spain and America, and they reported at Court that Diego Columbus, whom his brother the Admiral and Viceroy had unwisely left in charge of the growing Spanish colony of Hispaniola, had lost authority. Columbus himself, to please the unruly colonists, was finally obliged to abandon his benevolent policy toward the Indians and to authorize the first *encomiendas,* a form of legal servitude. (The Indians could not simply be enslaved, for, unlike Africans, they were supposed to have souls.)

For his third voyage (1498–1500) the Admiral weighed anchor in Seville and proceeded via Madeira and the Cape Verde Islands. His fleet consisted of two hundred men, and three ships plus another three that sailed directly to Santo Domingo, the new capital of Hispaniola. In three weeks Columbus made his landfall in Trinidad and for the first time explored part of the mainland, the peninsula of Paria in what is today Venezuela. That this "earthly paradise," as he called it, was part of a continent must have been clear to him from the volume of fresh water that here flows from the mouths of the Orinoco. Then, anxious to return to Santo Domingo, his capital, he attempted one of his greatest feats of dead reckoning—and succeeded. He sailed direct from the island of Margarita to Santo Domingo, crossing a whole new sea, the Caribbean, from an unknown point and arriving at a fixed destination (try it!).

In Santo Domingo (where he befriended Bartolomé de las Casas, who would later defend him and his Indians also) what little authority Columbus still had disappeared with the arrival of the new governor, Bobadilla, whose appointment effectively ended the Discoverer's unsuccessful vice-regal role. The new governor's authority had to be recognized by all, even by a "Viceroy" whose two sons had been pages at Court since 1498, and Columbus and his brother were sent back to Cadiz under arrest (if not actually in chains) on the caravel *Gorda.*

Surprisingly, the Admiral had been candid enough to send to Spain from Santo Domingo another map (now lost) and more than a hundred pearls from the island of Margarita. Thanks to that map, I think, he began to lose his monopoly as well as his authority. Before the end of the century several expeditions had set sail for the new world: first the adventurer Alonso de Ojeda, then Peralonso Niño, later the great Vicente Yañez Pinzón, Martin Alonso's brother, and immediately after him Diego de Lepe. With them went Juan de la Cosa and the brothers Guerra, and Amerigo Vespucci, soon to become the "pros" in the discovery of the rest of America. (In Seville the building that now houses the Archive of the Indies became *La Casa de la Contractación,* which until the Council of the Indies moved to Cadiz functioned for the discoverers as Houston Control Center has for the astronauts.) Meanwhile, in 1497 another expatriate Genoese, John Cabot, had planted the standard of Henry VII of England in North America.

The Admiral, no longer really Viceroy, called his fourth and last voyage (1502–1504) the "high voyage." He set sail from Cadiz and Grand Canary with four ships and one hundred forty men, among them Ferdinand Columbus, aged eleven. In three weeks they sighted Martinique and, at Santo Domingo, Columbus recognized the signs of the first hurricane of the season. His warning was ignored by the new governor, Obando, who refused to allow the Admiral ashore and lost his own fleet.[13] Having laid to during the storm, Columbus continued westward along the southern coast of Cuba and crossed to the island of Bonacca in the gulf north of Honduras. There Indians in a luxurious canoe invited him farther west, but he preferred not to sail on downwind, and rightly so, because it took him twenty-eight days to beat back along the coast to Honduras to Cape Gracias a Dios (Cape Thank God), where he finally put the wind on his beam. However, his sailor's prudence cost him the chance of discovering Yucatán and probably Mexico; the wings of destiny sometimes brush even great men too lightly.

Columbus knew by then of the voyages of Ojeda and Niño to Venezuela, of Vicente Yañez Pinzón and Lepe to Brazil, of Rodrigo de Bastidas to Colombia, and of John Cabot to the coasts of Labrador and Newfoundland. So, perhaps hoping to take the lead once more, the Admiral, in his fifties now and ill, began to dream that he heard the roar of another "Sea which would lead to the Ganges" as he put it and insisted on searching for a passage across Central America, which—if this were Asia—might be Marco Polo's Malacca Strait. But though his son Ferdinand noted that the Chagres River in Panama looked like a canal, there was no strait. The wings of destiny once more; if Columbus had sailed up the Chagres, he could have walked to where the Pacific comes into view.

One of Columbus' ships had gone aground on the bar of the Belén River some sixty miles west of Panama, and another in Portobelo.[14] The

Cape Tiburón, Colombia (The white striations of "Marmóreo") (*D.C.*)

Cape Tiburón (The end of the continent) (*D.C.*)

crews, worn out, complained that it was time to turn north for Santo Domingo, but the Admiral knew it was necessary first to sail farther east. His last night on the continent was spent below a cape which, because of its striated appearance, he named Cape Marmóreo (Marble Head), and which according to Ferdinand seemed to be the "end of the continent." This, I feel sure, is the tight little anchorage we Colombians call Zapzurro, below Cape Tiburón, the only high and striated cape on this whole coast, and not Punta Mosquito, its traditional identification, which is a low, sandy point. Heading north at last, the Admiral stopped for water at the Cayman Islands, sailed on to Cuba, and, unable to make Santo Domingo, beached his two remaining ships on the sands of Santa Gloria, which we know as Saint Ann's Bay, in the center of the north coast of Jamaica. There he spent a year, subdued the Indians by foretelling the famous eclipse of February 27, 1503, and finally sent Méndez and Fieschi in a canoe to Santo Domingo, whence he himself later returned to Spain, with his last hundred survivors, in a chartered caravel.[15]

In Spain the queen had died. In 1506, at Valladolid, the Admiral died too, attended by his two sons, his brother Diego, and Méndez. He was not poor, for the Crown had always respected his financial rights, but he was bitter at the loss of the power he had always desired more than riches. During his four voyages he had covered more ocean than if he had circled the globe, had brought twenty-seven ships across the ocean and twenty-two back, and—though he is seldom given credit for it—had discovered not only the Antilles but also a large part of the South American continent. A practical man, he had introduced Europe to the hammock, tobacco, maize, cocoa, rubber, and the sweet potato ("a carrot with a chestnut flavor"). Yet he was a dreamer who created a mystery about himself that was to follow him beyond the grave. His bones, confused with those of his son Diego and those of his brother Bartholomew, were first moved from Seville to Santo Domingo, then (perhaps) to Havana, and (again perhaps) back to Seville. As a result, no one is sure where the remains of the first Admiral rest, though I believe they are in Santo Domingo, the capital that he loved and that was denied him.

With Columbus' first voyage the Infinite Ocean which Odysseus left just beyond Gibraltar ceased to be Infinite, but the world was slow to realize it. News of the letter which the Admiral began to write on February 15, 1492, in the Azores and finished on March 4 in Lisbon, took months to reach Nuremberg or even Paris, where the Admiral's brother Bartholomew did not hear of the discovery until after Columbus' second voyage had begun. The letter was published in April 1493 in Barcelona and later in Rome and Basle (one of the first editions is in the

Amerigo Vespucci (*M.O. Collection*)

New York Public Library). Peter Martyr of Angheira, the Court historian, was soon speaking of a "New World," but the new world still lacked someone to spread the news of its existence throughout the globe.

Vespucci: An Hypothesis

It was Amerigo Vespucci who really made Europe feel that there was a new world between it and Asia. So many legends have been spun around him that it is time to try what I have called informed speculation. Though still unproved, the hypothesis I will propose seems to me to fit the facts better than what historians have accepted up to now.

Born in Florence on March 9, 1454, and therefore only three years younger than Columbus, Vespucci was a fellow citizen of Ghirlandaio, Leonardo, Michelangelo, Machiavelli, and Verrocchio and a relative of Simonetta, Botticelli's model for Venus, Primavera, and the Madonna. He worked first in Florence as a clerk for Pier Francesco de Medici, who sent him in 1491 to collaborate with Juanotto Berardi in Seville. When Berardi died in 1485, Vespucci stayed on as head of the firm, and it was he who supplied the stores for Columbus' third voyage. Unlike Columbus, he was an extrovert and a great storyteller. Columbus was a poet, Vespucci a reporter.

Of Amerigo's famous letters only the Florentine copies have come down to us, but that is no reason to doubt their authenticity (until a century ago it was normal for a collector to throw away hard-to-read originals after having them transcribed). The letters chronicle four voyages along the coasts of the American continent. They describe the ferocity of Indian warriors, the generosity of Indian women, and the splendor of fauna and flora with such zest that, where the Admiral's historic account of his discovery only ran to seventeen rather limited printings, the Florentine's letters were instant best sellers that immediately ran to some forty printings.

Amerigo's letters date his first voyage in 1497, a year before Columbus set foot on the continent (as distinct from the islands), but they never specify who was in command. As a result, historians have formed two irreconcilable camps. Some consider Vespucci a charlatan who invented his first voyage in order to steal Columbus' glory; others believe he did set foot on the continent before Columbus, and explain the fact that the 1497 voyage is not mentioned in any document other than Vespucci's own letters by classifying it with what Navarrete calls "explorations carried out secretly in order to defraud the exchequer" or with those which sailed "under secret orders from the King."

To me, three facts make both these hypotheses unacceptable. First, so little escaped the archives of the insatiable bureaucracy of the growing Spanish empire (all empires are bureaucratic) that I find it unlikely that Vespucci's first voyage, if it occurred, should have remained secret. Second, early in February 1508, at a meeting with the king, Juan de la Cosa, Vicente Yañez Pinzón, and Juan Diaz de Solís, Vespucci was appointed first chief pilot of the realm, effective March 22, a post he took up on August 6, 1508. His letters had been published in 1506, and in 1507 a map by Martin Waldseemüller of Saint-Dié had appeared, which showed the still incomplete continent as "America," and I find it difficult to believe that such a team of discoverers could have accepted a foreigner as chief pilot, knowing that his widely publicized first voyage had been an invention. Third, the extraordinary veracity of Vespucci's descriptions of American lands, customs, plants, and beasts makes me hesitate to dismiss the whole of his first voyage out of hand.[16]

In his letters Vespucci says that his first two voyages were made "by order of Ferdinand, illustrious King of Castile" and the last two "under mandate from King Manuel of Portugal, toward the South." His description of these last two voyages along the whole coast of Brazil confirms the tradition that he made them under the command of Gonçalo Coelho, who had been present when Caminha arrived at the Cape Verde Islands with the news that Pedro Alvarez Cabral had discovered Brazil.[17] That Vespucci does not mention Coelho presents no problem; we will see when we come to Magellan that chroniclers often omitted commanders' names.

It is therefore the first two voyages that must be explained, and

Vespucci's second voyage has traditionally been identified with the first voyage of Alonso de Ojeda, the cheerful filibusterer who declared in the *Pleitos* of 1499 that he "brought with him Juan de la Cosa, pilot, Emerigo Vespuche and other pilots." The *Pleitos* were contemporary enquiries into the behavior of the discoverers—interminable, but containing a mine of information.

Tired of libraries and archives, I decided to follow in both directions the ten thousand kilometers of Atlantic coast that stretch from Colombia to Argentina, and, having enjoyed doing so, I propose what follows.

Vespucci's first voyage was not necessarily either false or secret. Only one date and one latitude need be revised to make it fit Ojeda's voyage with which Vespucci's second has usually been identified. Amerigo himself is inconsistent about the date of his first voyage, first saying that he sailed on May 20, 1497, and later that "after eighteen months of voyaging" he got back to Cadiz on October 15, 1499—which would mean he had sailed in April 1498. If an error was made (perhaps by the copyist) in the date of the voyage, another may well have been made with respect to Vespucci's landfall at latitude 16°N, which could easily be a misprint for 6°N. It seems to me more realistic to accept these two corrections than to deny the entire trip and assign to Ojeda Vespucci's second voyage rather than his first—which in any case requires reading latitude 5°N instead of 5°S.

With my two proposed revisions, Amerigo's account of his first voyage reads like this: He set sail from Cadiz on May 20, 1499, and put in at Grand Canary. He sailed west by west-southwest and arrived in twenty-six days "at a land we [believed] to be a continent," dropping anchor off a beach in latitude 6°N. He followed a long coastline with an "onshore wind," visited Paria, and discovered "a village built over the water like Venice." He says that "all of [the Indian] men and women alike go completely naked" and that the women, whose "long, black hair suits them well . . . have beautifully elegant and well-proportioned bodies, though I will not refer to their way of satisfying their insatiable concupiscence in order not to outrage modesty . . . [but] they were certainly most affectionate to us. These people live in freedom, obey no one, and have no law or lord," he continues. "When they speak they appear to be very simple, but in reality they are most astute and wise. . . . Their daily bread is made from the root of a tree which they grind and make into quite good flour; some call it *yuca,* other *cambi* and others *ñame.* . . . In wartime the enemies they kill or take prisoner . . . they devour with indescribable brutality." They also eat "snakes with long strong legs armed with sharp claws [and] skin of the most varied colors." From "Little Venice," Vespucci came to "the best port in the whole globe," although scourged by "manhunting cannibals" (the same word as Caribs or Caribals). In the port, his men built "a small ship out of the remains of other boats and barrels," then sailed until they were "below the Tropic of Cancer." Heading east-northeast, he sighted numerous islands and on one of them captured "many slaves." He returned to Cadiz on October 15, 1499.

Apart from the marvelous description of Indians, cassava bread, and iguanas, it seems to me that the courses and details of this voyage, as far as the Greater Antilles, correspond to Ojeda's first expedition much better than do the details of Vespucci's second voyage. Ojeda made his landfall in the Guianas, about 6°N, then followed the Venezuelan coast east, where the prevailing wind is in fact "onshore." In Lake Maracaibo, he saw a "little Venice" and baptized Venezuela, where Santa Rosa de Aguas still stands on stilts over the water (as do several other villages on Lake Maracaibo and in neighboring Colombia). He entered Bahía Honda in the Guajira peninsula, still an excellent natural port for vessels of low draft and well within range of Caribs from Aruba and Curaçao. He continued on to Santo Domingo, where (no doubt taking advantage of the first uprising against Columbus to play some of his own tricks) he stayed from September 5, 1499, until June 1500, when he returned to Cadiz. Thus far Ojeda's first voyage agrees well with Vespucci's and from here on it makes sense that Vespucci, unwilling to get involved in Santo Domingo, should proceed on his own to the Virgin Islands and from there sail back to Cadiz on October 15, 1499.

If we are going to identify Vespucci's first voyage with that of Ojeda, we must then find a place for Vespucci's second voyage. Here is a summary of the Florentine's account: He sailed from Cadiz in November or December 1499 (the letters say May, an obvious error since they also say that he did not return from his first voyage until September). He sailed to Fogo in the Cape Verde Islands, and from there southwest in nineteen days to latitude 5°S, to a "very swampy coast, watered by huge rivers . . . where it was difficult to find a place which was not flooded." "Weighing anchors," he continues, "we tried to sail east by southeast . . . but all our efforts were in vain, for the current flowed so violently from southeast to northwest that it was quite impossible to sail against it." So, "turning to the northwest, we ran along the same coast" and reached a large anchorage with an island, where the cannibals fattened their captives like capons by "cutting off their genitals." From "that beach" he sailed on to a "peaceful people" who sell pearls to "an enemy nation . . . to the West." Finally, "along the same coastline," he entered a good anchorage to repair his ships, then sailed to an island inhabited by people who have "no water or . . . any kind of spring . . . or any of the food one finds on the continent . . . and live off fish and turtles they catch from the sea. . . . [They] shelter under big leaves from the heat of the sun. . . . They also wear two dried gourds round their necks, one full of an herb they keep in their mouth and the other of a whitish flour like ground chalk." Next came the island of the giants, then a land where "the inhabitants greeted us with the greatest friendliness . . . large quantities of pearls . . . and many of the little oysters in which they are formed. . . . They sleep in a kind of big net made of cotton and hung in the air." At last, "we arrived at the island of Antillia, discovered a few years ago by Columbus, where we stayed two months and two days repairing our rigging." He left there on June 22, arriving in Cadiz on September 8, 1500, after "twice crossing the Equator." Such was Vespucci's account of his second voyage.

In 1499 Niño, Pinzón, and Lepe set sail one after the other for the new world. Niño, Las Casas tells us, followed Ojeda in a single vessel, explored from Paria and Margarita westward as far as Canchiete (between today's Puerto Cabello and Coro), and then returned by the southern route in sixty-two days from Curiana (Coro) to Bayona in Galicia with sixty-two pounds of pearls. This therefore cannot have been Vespucci's second voyage. Pinzón's route is more like Vespucci's, but the complete list of his crew, which we have, does not contain one name that could be the Florentine's, even taking into account that men may be listed in the archives by their Christian name, surname, nickname, or birthplace. That leaves Lepe, and the names of only nineteen of the men who sailed with him have been established, which means that at least eighty names from his two *naos* are still missing. One of them could be Amerigo's.

According to the archives, Diego de Lepe's two *naos* (with perhaps another in reserve) set sail from Seville in December 1499, only a month after his kinsman Vicente Yañez Pinzón. According to testimony in the *Pleitos*, he touched at Fogo in the Cape Verde Islands and sailed again on February 28, 1500. While the great Pinzón seems to have made his landfall at Cape San Agustín (near today's Recife) and then followed the coast with wind and current first to the north and then to the northwest, Lepe sighted land at the end of January at Rostro Hermoso, which Las Casas' map places near today's Fortaleza on the northern coast of Brazil, at about 5° S. Thus Lepe gained some ground on Pinzón but lost it trying to sail east against wind and current. The attempt is understandable, however, for his purpose was to discover, not to explore what might already have been discovered by Pinzón. Yet I know from experience how difficult it is to round Cape San Roque (the northeastern corner of Brazil) to the south under sail. Lepe gave up the attempt (again according to testimony in the *Pleitos*) and veered westward in the wake of Pinzón, overtaking him in the Amazon delta. Then, says the testimony, "the said Diego de Lepe, sailing on to discover alone, passed by the Great River, and this witness knows it because he was in the Great River with said bicente añez [sic] and saw it with his own eyes."[18] West of the Amazon Lepe truly went on to "discover alone," for he was the first to run along the coast that separates the Amazon from Ojeda's landfall in the Guianas. He continued along the Venezuelan coast (his servant Harnán Pérez says in the *Pleitos* that he visited Paria), crossed to Puerto Rico, and returned to Cadiz in the second half of 1500 (in June, says Navarrete).

We have seen that in his second voyage Vespucci arrived at a coast watered by huge rivers on latitude 5°S, which fits the northern coast of Brazil; tried without success to continue east and turned back, just like Lepe; passed in front of a large anchorage with an island, which fits the Amazon delta; came to a peaceful people who sold pearls to an enemy nation to the west, surely Columbus' Margarita; arrived at a good port, probably Niño's Canchiete; discovered a very dry island, probably Bonaire, which is dry as a bone; saw another that was peopled by giants, a tradition that fits Curaçao; and finally found friendly people who gave him oysters and pearls and slept in hammocks. I once made a forced landing on the Guajira peninsula, where the Indians brought up oysters from the seabed, which, after removing their pearls, the women boiled slowly into a delicious soup; there were large hammocks for married couples, small ones for children, and medium-sized ones for bachelors—like the one they slung for me under the wing of my plane (which the Indians called Uchí, meaning bird). All of this agrees with Vespucci's descriptions, so what we know of Lepe's voyage fits Vespucci's second. The coincidence that both set sail from the same Cape Verde island, Fogo, is important, and their return dates match too: Lepe got back in July, while Vespucci says he delayed in Antillia and sailed home at the beginning of September.

There is something even more intriguing. In February 1501 Juan de la Cosa sailed for today's Colombia with Rodrigo de Bastidas, leaving in Spain the first complete map of the coasts and western islands of America, dated "Puerto de Santa Maria in the year 1500." Today it hangs behind a curtain in the Naval Museum of Madrid (the director of which is involved in the argument as to whether there were two Juan de la Cosas or one, which fortunately does not affect our hypothesis). The map shows that the northern coast of Brazil, as it runs east, turns abruptly southward and then again to the southwest, thereby forming two Atlantic headlands that clearly correspond to Cape San Roque (near today's Natal) and Cape San Agustín (near today's Recife). From the sea they now seem conspicuous only because at each the coast changes direction, but for many years they remained the principal reference points on this coast. Between them on his map, Juan de la Cosa writes, "This Cape was discovered in the year one thousand four hundred ninety-nine for Castile, the discoverer being Vicente Yañez."

But as Captain Max Justo Gedes, the Brazilian Navy's historian, has observed, the curious thing is that other names on the map start only from Cape San Roque to the west. In 1500 the names on this section of the coast could have been provided only by Pinzón or Lepe, and they apparently are not Pinzón's, for there are no names on the part of the coast between capes San Agustín and San Roque, where he alone sailed. The first two names are Rio Fermoso and Puerto Fermoso near the Fortaleza of today—which must refer to Lepe's landfall, Rostro Hermoso. Moreover, further west the map says, "River where a cross was found," and the cross must have been found by the second who passed that point (Lepe) after the first (Pinzón) put it up.

Consequently, La Cosa must have obtained his information about the north coast of Brazil from someone who was with Lepe, and to me it seems probable that this informant was Vespucci, who had been La Cosa's shipmate under Ojeda. We have seen that Amerigo returned to Cadiz from his second voyage on September 8, 1500, and thus had five months in which to pass on his information to La Cosa, who sailed with Bastidas in February 1501. The map was to become the first of the series of royal *padrones* (official maps) that would be kept up to date by chief pilots, the first of whom was Vespucci himself.

Juan de la Cosa's map explains another Vespuccian problem that has caused a lot of argument. We have seen that in his first voyage Amerigo claims to have seen land under the Tropic of Cancer, the latitude that passes between Cuba and Florida. Once again historians have taken sides, some maintaining that this is added proof that Vespucci invented the voyage, others crediting Vespucci with the discovery of Yucatán and even Florida. But in Juan de la Cosa's map the Tropic of Cancer is clearly drawn well to the south of its true position, passing through Puerto Rico and the Virgin Islands. If, as I propose, Vespucci helped to make the map, his account of his first voyage takes him only far enough north to catch a favorable wind for his return (probably from the Virgin Islands) and shows

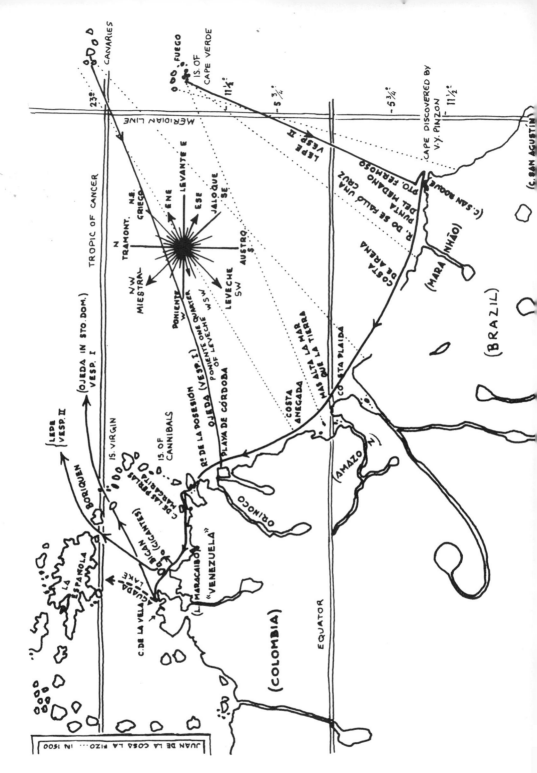

Amerigo's first two voyages superimposed on Juan de la Cosa's map of 1500
(M.O. and M.F.)

The beaches of Northern Brazil *(M.O.)*

again that the latitudes he gives should not be taken too literally.

Reading Vespucci's letter carefully, studying Juan de la Cosa's map, and following the coast as I have followed it, one cannot avoid being struck by their agreement. Where Vespucci speaks of beaches, La Cosa writes "dunes" or "sand," and there are in fact enormous sand dunes, sculpted by wind and sea, that recall the undulating ornamentation of Rio's pavements. Where Vespucci says that it was difficult to find a place that was not flooded, La Cosa writes "submerged coastline" and "sea higher than the land," and this part of Brazil is so watery that I have seen people wait patiently on schooners beached at the side of the street for the tide to set them afloat and allow them to spread their triangular brown sails.

My proposal, then, is that Vespucci may well have made the four voyages he describes in his letters. The first requires only the correction of one date and one latitude to fit Ojeda's first; the second, so faithful to La Cosa's map, requires only the correction of an obvious mistake in the sailing date to fit Lepe's, the incomplete list of whose crew leaves plenty of room for Vespucci (see table). This seems more reasonable than to deny or to hide the whole of Vespucci's first voyage and still have to correct a latitude in the second. There is no argument about the third and fourth, for although the Florentine exaggerates the furthest southern limit of the third, they both agree perfectly with Coelho's voyages.

Having placed my modest wreath at the grave of the Admiral of the Ocean Sea, I must wait for the record to prove or disprove my Vespuccian

VESPUCCI'S FIRST TWO VOYAGES AND THE VOYAGES OF OJEDA AND LEPE

	Starting Point in Spain	Starting Point for Atlantic Crossing	American Landfall	Return	Area of Information for La Cosa Map of 1500
Ojeda and De la Cosa	Puerto de Santa Mariá May 18, 1499	Gomera (Canaries)	Guianas, approximately 6°N. Wind onto coast	From Santo Domingo September 5, 1499 to Cadiz June 1500	Guianas to Cabo de la Vela
Vespucci (first voyage)	Cadiz May 1499	Grand Canary (Canaries)	6°N. Wind onto coast	From "numerous islands" to Cadiz October 15, 1499	Guianas to Cabo de la Vela
Lepe	Seville December 1499	Fogo (Cape Verdes) February 28, 1500	Rostro Hermoso near Fortaleza, approximately 5°S. Many rivers	From Puerto Rico to Cadiz June 1500	Fortaleza (Brazil) to Guianas
Vespucci (second voyage)	Cadiz December 1499	Fugo (Cape Verde Islands)	5°S. Coast watered by great rivers	From "Antillia" July 22, 1500 to Cadiz September 8, 1500	Fortaleza (Brazil) to Guianas

hypothesis. In the meantime I can let Amerigo die in 1512, a braggart but not a liar. The Admiral himself seems to agree with me, for in his letter of February 5, 1505, to his son Diego he says that Vespucci was an excellent purveyor for his third voyage, and makes the Florentine one of his executors (he owes Vespucci eighty thousand *maravedies*). The name America is certainly an injustice; there is no doubt that it ought to be Colombia, but there is nothing to show that Vespucci himself had any part in this misnomer. History teaches us that legend sometimes garlands not only the discoverer but also the one who makes the world value what has been discovered, perhaps because he speaks a more contemporary tongue, and Vespucci's colorful prose was more to Renaissance taste than Columbus' poetry, still shrouded in the discrete beauty of the Middle Ages.

A thoughtful Genoese discovered the new world, and a loquacious Florentine made it known. Yet beyond America another third of the world still lay in restless sleep, an Ocean endlessly chanting the infinite rosary of its waves, waiting to be unveiled by a stubborn Portuguese in the service of Spain and by a weather-beaten Basque.

NOTES

1. Don Ramón Menéndez Pidal has pointed out that Columbus' Portuguese training shows quite clearly through his Castilian.

2. The friar who opened the door for me at the convent of La Rábida would not let me in until he had finished trying to convince me that the Discoverer did indeed marry Beatriz and should therefore be canonized. He did not succeed, though the idea of Saint Christopher Columbus appeals to me.

Beatriz Henriquez' son, Ferdinand Columbus, grew up to be a bibliophile, a scientist, and a historian who bequeathed his library to the Cathedral of Seville. It includes books inherited from the Discoverer, among them Pierre d'Ailly's *Imago Mundi* (Louvain, 1480), Peter Martyr's *History*, and an annotated edition of Pliny. I have spent many hours in Ferdinand's library, and when once I asked the canon for permission to photograph a map, his answer was, "Out of the question! Don't you know that every time a document is copied it loses value?" Later he suddenly asked, "This map—do you really need it?" and when I answered that I needed nothing since mine was a labor of love, he said, "I will have it photographed for you." Spaniards have to be convinced, as Columbus soon found with the queen.

3. All we have is Las Casas' transcription of Columbus' diary, for the original is lost. Perhaps it may one day be found in the still unclassified "Indiferente General" files at the Archive of the Indies. They contain documents, such as Elcano's *Paces*, which we will rediscover when we come to Magellan, not easily classified under any particular jurisdiction. Why not Columbus' diary, which was mostly written at sea?

It is a pity that among so many privileges Columbus forgot to demand that the new lands should bear his name and to correct the phrase in his *Capitulaciones* (agreement) which speaks of what Columbus "has discovered." Arguments about this phrase have lasted for five centuries; to me it clearly refers to the lands Columbus "has discovered" to his sovereigns in "a navigational chart which he carried, in which he had drawn the Indies and isles," as Las Casas says. Furthermore, the second paragraph of the agreement, which those who argue seem to ignore, says "will discover or win"—so the doubt is dispelled. No time should be wasted on "prediscoveries."

4. The Mataró ship represents a carrack. It is a beautiful Catalan votive offering, more than a meter long, which hung until the first half of this century in the church of Mataró. Sold first to the United States, it is now in the Prinz Hendrik Naval Museum of Rotterdam, having reversed the usual route of antiquities.

5. Most of Alice Gould's detailed findings were published by Editorial Viuda de Estanislao Maestre, Madrid, 1940–1945. Her intellectual executor, Don José Peña, has yet to publish the rest of her invaluable work.

6. *La Pinta*'s tiller had to be repaired in Las Palmas. Columbus suspected it had been disconnected by Quintero "because he was loth to join the voyage."

7. Anyone who thinks it is easy to navigate under sail with a quadrant should try it and see if his error is less than the five degrees by which Columbus erred.

8. Change in time with longitude might help explain Columbus' errors in distance run, though Las Casas was convinced that Columbus purposely reduced daily runs by about twenty percent so as not to frighten the crew. We have seen that, because longitude could not yet be determined accurately, position had to be established by dead reckoning (distance, course, and speed). In the end what really mattered was the Discoverer's uncanny instinct.

9. Off "Saint Sal," long known as Watlings in honor of an English pirate, Morison and I nearly lost our manuscript when we capsized a rowboat. There are three monuments to Columbus on the island, a misplaced cross on the high windward shore, a well-placed cross on the leeward beach, and, perhaps best, a satellite tracking station.

I photographed a Russian missile base on Cuba's Cape Maisí before Kennedy and Khrushchev had the bases removed. Then I approached Guantánamo on a very precise course, for antiaircraft practice was going on to both sides of our aircraft.

10. For details and identifications, see Morison and Obregón, *The Caribbean as Columbus Saw It*, Atlantic-Little, Brown, Boston, 1964.

11. On top of Dominica the last remaining Caribs live today in a reservation, climbing down every day to work on the dugout canoes at which they still excel. Once I had climbed up and then down to see them, my "interpreter," a young Carib girl, spoke up for the first time. "Now you carry me up again," said she.

12. Jamaica became the Columbus family's estate, probably the loveliest any family ever owned. After bickering for years with the Crown over their rights,

they exchanged it for the Dukedom of Veragua, today's Mosquito Coast, where there was supposed to be plenty of gold but where, even today, there is nothing but jungle.

13. Despite Columbus' warning, the governor's twenty-four treasure ships, with former governor Bobadilla on the *Capitana*, sailed and were sunk by the hurricane in Mona Passage. For anyone who can work at a depth of more than one kilometer, this is the treasure fleet to find. Only three ships escaped, among them the *Aguja* with Rodrigo de Bastidas, future discoverer of the Colombian coast, on board. Columbus' "tenth" (four thousand pesos in gold) was also saved on the *Aguja*, and in his *Life of the Admiral* Ferdinand says that this gave rise to rumors that Columbus was a sorcerer. Sorcerer or not, he was a good seaman; his own fleet was not lost.

14. Now that Portobelo's fortifications are being restored, it would be worthwhile looking for the remains of Columbus' caravel, the *Vízcaína*.

15. Admiral Diego Colón, the first Admiral's son, founded a town in Santa Gloria called New Seville, and Peter Martyr became its bishop. Its remains, located by M. Cotter, enabled Morison to identify it with St. Ann's Bay.

Rafael Obregón and I sailed into the bay in the *Tarena*, comparable in size to a caravel, and beached her where it seemed to us Columbus would have done so. Then we went over the stern in search of the underwater buoys that diver Bob Marx had left where he had found what he hoped might be the remains of Columbus' last caravels. At first we could not find them, but when we got hungry and returned to the schooner we saw the buoys right under our keel. The place, at least, was right.

With the help of Victor Najar and the Government of Jamaica, I brought in Frederic Dumas, Commander Jacques Cousteau's underwater expert, and spent days diving with him while his assistant scared off the sharks. Finally, Dumas came up onto the beach and with a Gallic sense of drama slowly pulled off his mask and gloves. "*Monsieur Obregón, vous avez raison: elles sont là!,*" said he, referring to the caravels. Then he handed me a hambone just like the one Obando sent to Columbus when he left him stranded here for a full year. Nevertheless, the ships' remains we were able to recover were not sufficient to identify the *Bermuda* (*Santiago*) and the *Capitana*, the last of Columbus' ships. A Rastafarian, seeing me leave the water with my beard dripping, said, "Sir, yo' is either an archaeologist or a Holy Man."

16. The fact is that in Vespucci's "Vaglienti" letter of 1500 he speaks for the first time of a continent that separates Asia from Europe. If he later seems to go back to the belief that America is an appendix of Asia, it was he who first publicized its size.

17. Vespucci's calculations placed most of Brazil within the Spanish hemisphere (he was the first to try to measure longitude by opposition between planets and moon), but however much this might have pleased the Spaniards, it could never have silenced all comment had the first chief pilot of the realm been a public liar.

Pedro Alvarez Cabral discovered Brazil (he thought it was an island) in

1500 when he sailed even further southwest than Da Gama had recommended in order to catch the wind for rounding the Cape of Good Hope. We already saw that the Azores were found by the Portuguese precisely as far northwest as it was necessary to sail in order to catch the wind to return to Portugal from the African coast. The practical Portuguese seem to have made their greatest discoveries in seeking the wind they needed to sail south and east around Africa to the Indies, while the Spaniards sailed west to discovery pretty much on faith alone.

18. The testimonies in the *Pleitos* to which I refer were given by Cristobal Garcia, Luis del Valle, and Juan Calvo respectively. Historians Herrera and Navarette both refer to Lepe's attempt and failure to sail east.

5

MAGELLAN
AND
ELCANO

Magellan: The Strait

History distinguishes truly great men by translating their names from
tongue to tongue, and Fernando de Magalhaes, or Magallanes, has long
been known in English as Ferdinand Magellan. The son of Ruy de
Magalhaes and Alda de Mesquita, he was born into the local nobility
around 1480 in the rugged Portuguese province of Tras os Montes (Behind
the Mountains). Black-bearded and with prominent eyes, he was a short,
tough, taciturn, and astute highlander, but the sea got into his blood
when, still young, he moved to Oporto. In the service of King Manuel and
Alfonso de Albuquerque, first viceroy of India, he sailed in 1510 for the
Spice Islands. There he began to show his mettle: His ship went aground
on the "Padre Banks" in the Indian Ocean (probably near the Maldives),
and when all her officers decided to seek help in the longboat, Magellan
stayed, took command, and saved the *nao*. Subsequently he visited
Ambon just south of the main Spice Islands.

   Back in Portugal, he asked Don Manuel for a raise of half a ducat in
his *vivencia* or *moradía*, a courtier's regular allowance. More important,
he asked the king's support for his dream of finding a way through
the American barrier in order to return westward to the Spice Islands.
Don Manuel refused him on both counts but granted him permission to
transfer his loyalty to Charles I of Spain, soon to be Emperor Charles V.
Some Portuguese still consider Magellan a traitor to his country, but
there was then an accepted procedure for transferring from one court (or
city) to another, and no Genoese ever accused Columbus of treason.

   Seville was then the capital of American discovery (later it would be
Cadiz), and in bustling Seville Magellan stayed with Diego Barbosa,
another Portuguese who served Spain, and married Diego's daughter

Ferdinand Magellan, a modern portrait by Antonio Menendez (*Courtesy Museu de Marinha, Lisbon, copyright reserved*)

Sixteenth-century Seville (*Centro Iberoamericano de Cooperción, Madrid*)

Beatriz, who bore him a son. The boy died while Magellan was at sea, and Beatriz herself was to die shortly after hearing of Magellan's own tragic death.

In 1518 King Charles received Magellan in Barcelona along with his navigator Ruy Faleiro. The king liked what the two Portuguese had to say. We have seen that in 1493 Pope Alexander VI had divided the globe between Spain and Portugal at approximately 30°W longitude, and in 1494 the Treaty of Tordesillas had moved the line three hundred leagues farther west, to approximately 50°W. Before the sixteenth century no one had worried much about the effect of this division on the Antipodes; now Magellan and Faleiro pointed out that if the treaty had given Brazil to Portugal, it might well have given the Spice Islands to Spain, for the prolongation of 50° longitude in the western hemisphere is 130° longitude in the eastern hemisphere. Though Portugal regarded the Spice Islands as hers, in fact they lie at 127°E and could therefore quite reasonably be disputed—especially at a time when longitude was still so difficult to measure. Magellan and Faleiro demonstrated all this on a globe, and Charles did not hesitate long before signing the *Capitulación* authorizing

The division of the globe. Brazil and the Spice Islands (*M.O. and M.F.*)

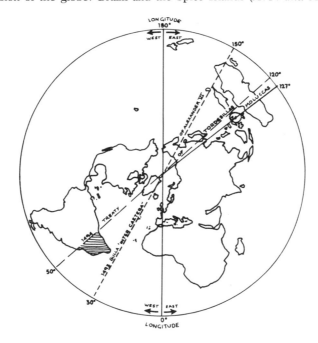

the second project that Portugal would regret having ignored (the first was Columbus').

In so doing, Charles followed in the footsteps of his grandparents, the Catholic sovereigns, who had steered Spain to the west just as Prince Henry the Navigator had steered Portugal south and east around the Cape of Good Hope. East is east and west is west, but the twain do in fact meet on the other side of the globe; and the Pacific, the new Spanish sea that Magellan's Strait and the westerly trades would protect for two generations, was destined to become the first theatre in a war of global agreements and disagreements which would last from Tordesillas on the threshold of the sixteenth century, through the Congress of Vienna in the nineteenth, to Yalta in our day.

To clear port was therefore, for Magellan, a much longer and more complicated matter than obtaining the emperor's approval. Today both the Sevillian river port of Las Muelas (in Triana) and whitewalled Sanlúcar at the mouth of the Guadalquivir River are quiet places; in 1519 they teemed with nautical, commercial, and political activity. Emissaries of Don Manuel of Portugal did everything possible to make the expedition miscarry, and the local people, confusing Magellan's standard with that of Portugal, rioted. Purveyors cheated Magellan as much as they could, and Ruy Faleiro went mad and had to be replaced as soon as he had handed over his "secret formula for measuring longitude." To take his place the emperor appointed Juan de Cartagena *conjunta persona* with Magellan and captain of the *San Antonio*. He also appointed Luis de Mendoza captain of the *Victoria*, Gaspar de Quesada captain of the *Concepción*, and Antonio de Coca purser. I have found nothing in the archives about this quartet of courtiers turned mariners; yet we shall see that the meaning of *conjunta persona*, which might be translated as "partner," caused a great deal of trouble.

Magellan dedicated his voyage to the Virgin of La Victoria, ordered that 12,500 *maravedies* be paid yearly out of his salary for Masses in her honor, and received at her feet the emperor's standard and his captains' oaths of loyalty.

La Victoria is hard to find in Seville. I began by knocking on the door of the old Franciscan convent of Los Remedios in Las Muelas, which was built in 1516 to commemorate the victory of Christians over Moors at Málaga. Soon a young girl smiled out at me over the carnations adorning the convent's only window in its whitewashed frame and told me that the Virgin had long ago been transferred to another convent, La Consolación. I found that from there she had moved to a church in Triana dedicated to Saint Anne in 1266 by King Alfonso "in gratitude for the miracle that saved his eye even though it had been gouged out of its socket." In front of Saint Anne's, children played in a little square that could hardly have changed in five centuries, and a matron in mourning, her hair up in a bun, looked out of her balcony and cried, "Why photograph the church? Take a picture of me: I am old but beautiful."

Finally, a deaf and dumb sacristan showed me La Victoria next to a side altar, a handsome and smiling Virgin with a plump Child in her lap, sitting unadorned on a pedestal marked with a ceramic ship. Next to her

The Virgin of La Victoria *(M.O.)*

is the grave of a black saint (one of Magellan's men?) to whom, the
sacristan explained in graphic sign language, childless *Sevillanas* pray.

On August 10, 1519, Magellan's five ships went down the Quadal-
quivir from Seville to Sanlúcar, where the river makes a wide curve as if
straining to hear the voice of the sea. After Confession and Communion,
some three hundred men embarked. They were mostly Andalusians and
Basques, but included also were some thirty Portuguese, a dozen
Genoese, several Greeks, some Flemish and German gunners, a couple
of Frenchmen and Englishmen, and five blacks. Apart from the two
pilots, one from Genoa and the other Portuguese, who wrote reports on
the voyage, there were four indispensable chroniclers on board: Antonio
Pigafetta, listed as *sobresaliente* (tourist), a gentleman from Vicenza who
arrived at the Spanish Court with the papal legate just in time to learn of
the voyage and join it; Francisco Albo of Rhodes, navigator; Diego
Gallego (the Galician), sailor; and Martín Méndez, king's accountant.

The diary of cheerful Pigafetta, full of anecdotes and tall stories and
including an "Indian" dictionary, is today the best known chronicle of the
expedition (Maximiliano Transilvano's is an edited version of survivors'
stories). Albo's log, which is in the Archives of the Indies, is less well
known because it consists mostly of courses and latitudes, beginning at
Cape San Agustín in Brazil. The log of El Gallego, now in Leyden,
Holland, received little attention until Morison reread it. But Martín
Méndez' *Paces* (peace agreements) had apparently disappeared.

Elcano in his final report to the emperor referred to a complete book
of *Paces* signed with the sultans of the Spice Islands, and I persisted in
searching for it and enquiring about it. One day Katherine Romoli, who
had been looking for quite a different document, mentioned that she had
seen something like the *Paces* in Indiferente General, the catch-all where
documents not subject to any specific jurisdiction were filed when the
"Indian" part of the archives was moved by Charles III from Simancas to
Seville. Following up this tip, I discovered the lost *Paces*, thirty pages of
them, notarized by Martín Méndez. We will use them here for the first
time.[1]

On September 20, 1519, having prayed to "Our Lady of the Safe
Voyage" in the Franciscan chapel of Sanlúcar, the five captains boarded
their vessels: Magellan, the *Trinidad*, one hundred ten tons; Cartagena,
the *San Antonio*, one hundred twenty tons; Quesada, the *Concepción*,
ninety tons; Mendoza, the *Victoria*, eighty-five tons; and Serrano, the
Santiago, seventy-five tons. On board were twenty-three maps by Nuño
García, six pairs of dividers, six wooden astrolabes plus one of brass,

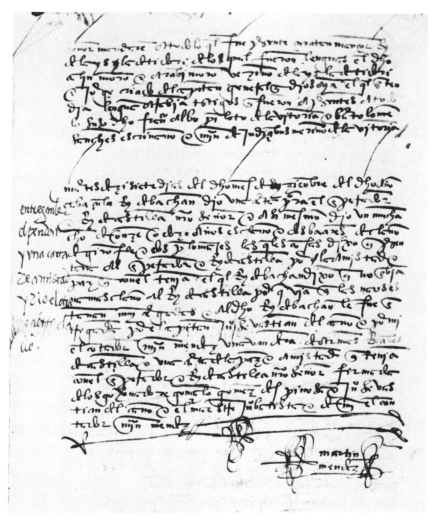

The last page of the *Paces (Archives of the Indies, Seville)*

twenty-one wooden quadrants, thirty-five compass needles, and eighteen half-hour hourglasses.

Firing a farewell salvo, the five sailed south with the Portuguese trades, the crystal clear Boreas that *Sevillanos*, like the Romans, call Solana. In a week they raised the beautiful Canary Islands, where water, wood, and salted fish were taken on. Leaving the Canaries with a fair wind, they passed between Portugal's Cape Verde Islands and the African cape of the same name, but instead of setting a direct course for Brazil, the Captain General decided to follow the coast southward to Sierra Leone. Juan de Cartagena immediately objected on the ground that

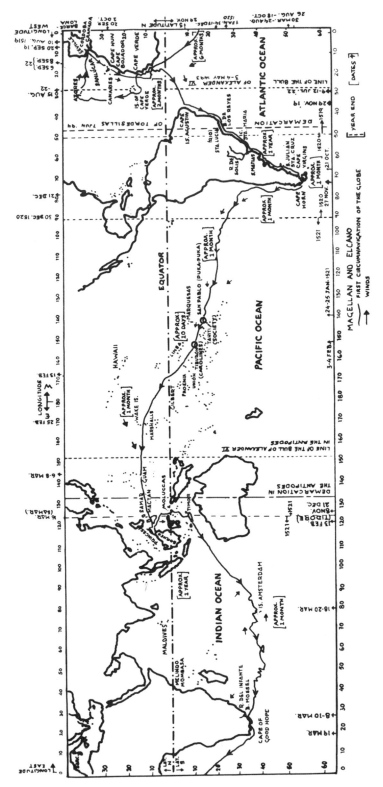

Route of the first circumnavigation (*M.O. and M.F.*)

sailing directions could not be changed without his approval, but Magellan, never one to share his command, replied that his captains should not bother their heads with such matters but should concentrate instead on following the Captain General's flag by day and his lantern by night. For the moment, Cartagena made no reply, but when a storm followed by a great calm interrupted their progress, he blamed Magellan, addressing him simply as captain. Magellan demanded that he be called Captain General, and Cartagena stopped talking to him altogether. A few days later Magellan called a meeting of his captains to try the case of a sailor who had "sinned against nature" with a ship's boy, for which the penalty in those far-off days was death. Cartagena became impertinent again and sought the support of the other captains, at which point the taciturn Magellan simply said, "Be under arrest," and, turning Cartagena over to Mendoza, put the *San Antonio* under Coca's command. The courtiers would have to be cut down to size one by one.

The wind made up again and the five ships crossed the South Atlantic without further trouble, raised Cape San Agustín on November 29, and entered Rio de Janeiro on December 13. Magellan christened it Santa Lucía because it was her day.

For two weeks the crews rested, surrounded by the serene beauty of Rio's great bay with its islands and sky-seeking mountains. Here the naked Indians willingly handed over their sisters and daughters in exchange for penknives—but not their wives, probably because the wives did the hard work. Life was easy and cheap: half a dozen fowl for a fishhook, a basket of potatoes for a hawk's bell, and free tapir meat, sugar cane, and brazilwood (valuable for making dyes). Each Indian hut, swarming with children, monkeys, and parrots, housed one hundred adults. Forty Indians paddled one canoe (almost as many as rowed *Argo*), but the Spanish ships seemed so huge to them that they wondered if the *naos* suckled their longboats. Juan Carvallo, who had been here earlier with Coelho and Vespucci, and who now picked up the *mestizo* son he had left behind, warned that in wartime the good-natured Indians became cannibals, but no conflict marred these two weeks. Magellan took advantage of the general good humor to remove Coca from command of the *San Antonio* and replace him with his own nephew, Alvaro de Mezquita, thus demoting the second courtier.

Its crews refreshed, the fleet visited the island-dotted Bahia del Rey, between Rio and Santos. Then, proceeding south, Magellan eventually rounded a low cape that he called Santa María, today's Punta del Este, to the south of which he saw a "hat-shaped" hill he named Monte Vidi, near today's Montevidéo. The little Santiago explored the River Plate to see if it was a strait, but it turned out to be the convoluted delta of two enormous rivers. Here one of the Indians who had devoured Juan de Solís, the discoverer of the River Plate, dared to board the *Trinidad*. His news of abundant silver gave the river, and later the whole of the Argentine, their name, though what silver there was came from Potosí, across the Paraguayan lowpoint of the Andes.

Further south the weather deteriorated, but the fleet found good anchorages such as Puerto Deseado, where, Albo says, the green country comes to an end. This change is still obvious even from the air, for the fertile pampa gives way here to the varied ochers of the Patagonian desert. Albo notes further that south of Deseado "the *Victoria* often hit its arse on the bottom," and the shallows too are visible from the air.

The southern autumn came early, and Magellan decided to spend the winter in a Patagonian anchorage which he entered from the north on March 31, 1520, through a very narrow mouth, and which he christened San Julián in honor of the date. He sent the *Santiago* to explore to the south, then invited the three remaining captains to lunch on board the *Trinidad* after Mass on Palm Sunday. Only his nephew Mezquita came. That very night Quesada freed Cartagena, and with Coca and thirty men boarded the *San Antonio*, mortally wounded her master, and put Mezquita in irons, leaving Juan Sebastián de Elcano aboard as master. Three courtiers, Cartagena in the *Concepción*, Quesada in the *San Antonio*, and Mendoza in the *Victoria*, now stood against Magellan, alone in the *Trinidad* under Elcano's guns. Elcano on his return to Spain would explain in the *Pleitos* that he had intended only to force the Captain General to divulge his plans, but this was a lame explanation in view of the accusations against Magellan in the same *Pleitos*.

Believing they had won, the mutineers sent a longboat to parley with the Captain General. He, like Odysseus at Telepylus, had anchored the *Trinidad* right in the mouth of the port, so that to put to sea his enemies would have to pass under his broadside. Detaining the longboat, Magellan sent Gonzalo Gómez de Espinosa over to the *Victoria* with a letter for Mendoza. When Mendoza laughed at it, Espinosa stabbed him in the throat and a sailor finished him off. Barbosa, Magellan's brother-in-law, then boarded the *Victoria* without resistance. With Mendoza dead and the *Victoria* recaptured, Quesada was not seadog enough to fight Magellan man to man. Weighing two of the *San Antonio*'s three anchors, he let the other drag, and the current carried him alongside the *Trinidad*, from which Magellan swept his deck with shot. And when Cartagena shouted his last orders from the bridge of the *Concepción*, no one obeyed him and he surrendered. Magellan's justice was as swift as his victory:

San Julián, Patagonia. The narrow mouth (*M.O.*)

Quesada was beheaded by his own servant and his body and that of Mendoza were quartered on the beach. Cartagena was put ashore in Patagonia and stranded there with his chaplain. Wisely, the other mutineers, including Elcano, were pardoned.

Meanwhile, to the south, Serrano, commanding the *Santiago*, had discovered the great river mouth at Santa Cruz, the high banks of which make it more hospitable than San Julián. But the *Santiago* ran aground, and although no hands were lost other than one black who would not abandon ship, Serrano had to send his men the sixty miles back to San Julián on foot, with supplies and rigging on their backs. As a result, the fleet remained in San Julián, and the first two winter months were spent exploring the interior, collecting shellfish, and hunting ostriches, foxes, parrots, and "rabbits" (probably the two-toned Patagonian maras which, as they lope away, look like rabbits in miniskirts). Soon Indians showed up with their hideous wives, "all as tall as Germans," says El Gallego (six foot to six foot nine, said Wallis in 1776). Their invaluable "guanacos," which look exactly as Pigafetta described them, half donkey and half camel, provided meat, skins, and gut for stringing bows. (I think the Indians were called Patagones—bigfeet—because of the bulky guanaco skins they wrapped around their feet; otherwise they went naked, only occasionally throwing another skin over their shoulders.) They gulped "enough soup for twenty," ran like greyhounds, danced with painted faces and ashes in their hair, and for entertainment put arrows down their throats. Magellan captured two by filling their hands with presents and then offering them pretty irons for their ankles. One agreed to go with the fleet if he were allowed to bring his wife, but when a patrol went to his guanacoskin tent to fetch her, Diego Barrasa died with an arrow in his side. Another Patagonian, baptized John the Giant, was permitted to hunt rats on board, but he soon tired and went back to his people, invoking his devil Setebos, a name that turns up next in *The Tempest*.

On the beach, Andrés de San Martín determined their longitude with great care according to Faleiro's secret method, and the result was as poor as was to be expected. His latitude, on the other hand, was remarkably precise: 49°08'S (it is in fact 49°11'S).

At last, on August 24, the fleet sailed south, leaving Cartagena and his chaplain on the shore with a few biscuits and wine, never to be heard from again. Another two months were spent in Santa Cruz sheltering from a fierce gale, doing a lot of fishing, and observing an eclipse of the sun. Four Portuguese (Magellan, Mezquita, Barbosa, and Serrano) were captains now, and the crews had been warned that Magellan would not stop above the 57°S line (the chronicles say 75°, but I suggest they inverted the figures) and that if he did turn back even then, it would not be to Spain but east to the Cape of Good Hope and, by the Portuguese route, to the Spice Islands.

Fortunately, such a heroic solution did not prove necessary. Two days south of Santa Cruz the contrary winds became favorable, and on October 21, the day of the Eleven Thousand Virgins, the armada rounded a high sandy point which Magellan named Cape Virgins. A broad saltwater bay, which he named Posesión, lay behind it, and here Magellan anchored, convinced that he had found the strait almost exactly where he had seen it on Schöner's globe (not Behaim's, as Pigafetta would have it). The latitude, actually 52°20'S, was determined by Albo as 52° (not bad).

Riding out a storm in Bahia Posesión, Magellan sent the *San Antonio* and the *Concepción* to reconnoiter. They returned under full sail, pennants streaming in the breeze, crews cheering, and guns ablaze, says Pigafetta. Immediately the armada passed through two sandy narrows (Las Angosturas) and dropped anchor in a bay even larger than Posesión. On a low island, which was christened Isabella for the empress, the first Mass was said in the Strait, and after it Magellan asked his officers to confirm what he had already decided. All agreed to sail on except Esteban Gómez, chief pilot of the *San Antonio,* the only Portuguese who had not received a command after the San Julián executions. Perhaps he bore a grudge, but his proposal was not unreasonable: Having discovered the Strait, why not return to Spain in triumph and commission another

The Strait of Magellan *(Bill Ray, Life Magazine © 1972 Time Inc.)*

fleet before venturing into "such a huge gulf"? The reply was given by Andrés de San Martín: "Why not press on at once, with summer flowering around us?" Satisfied, Magellan swore once again to do what he had promised the emperor even if he had to eat leather off the yards, which, little did he suspect, he would later have to do. So the fleet sailed on, and, rounding Punta Arenas (Sandy Point), entered a narrowing channel. Here Magellan decided to drop the hook in the mouth of the "River of Sardines" and dispatch the *San Antonio* to look into another passage to the southeast, today's Admiralty Bay. The *San Antonio* never returned; once out of sight, Gómez and Gerónimo Guerra clapped the unfortunate Mezquita into irons again and made off for Spain, where, after the usual *Pleitos*, Gómez was given a new command to seek the Northwest Passage.

The exact location of the "River of Sardines" has caused some discussion. The chroniclers say that it flowed into the Strait right next to another river and near several islands, and that from there Magellan's longboat reached the Pacific and returned in three days. Today's Fortescue Bay affords the best anchorage in these waters; it has its own river, there is another on its far side, and it is within sight of Carlos III Island with its two cays. But the Pacific is far off, and, what is worse, the bay is situated just before the Strait divides again—to port, toward the Pacific; to starboard, into the San Gerónimo channel, which leads to an endless series of saltwater lakes. How could the longboat have chosen correctly between the two channels and then have gone so far in so short a time against the prevailing northwester?

Having seen at San Julián how it was possible for Magellan to have bottled up the mutineers (and having overcome engine trouble as we flew low around Cape Virgins), we sailed through Magellan's Strait in the Chilean Navy's LSM *Orompello.* As we anchored at night in Fortescue Bay, the Southern Cross and the Magellanic Clouds stood above us, surrounded by clouds that the light of the moon transformed into a baroque frame. The snows looked down on us from peaks three thousand meters high, and the bay slept as if no one had disturbed it since Magellan wept tears of joy when his longboat brought him news of the Pacific. "Steady as she goes, three hundred and twenty, bottom at five cables," called the officer of the watch, and the anchor chain shattered the frozen silence of the bay.

At dawn we rowed ashore just as Magellan must have done, and beside the bottle-green river we walked through peat bogs, sometimes sinking to our knees in moss *(Sphagnum Magellanicum)* and wild flowers *(Senecio)* and surrounded by dwarf trees *(Drimys Winteri).* According to the Patagonian Institute at Punta Arenas, it was the bark of these trees (together with wild celery) that for the time being saved the discoverers from scurvy.

Continuing northwest through the Strait, we were able to answer all the questions about the "River of Sardines." Three days in the southern summer, where it gets dark for only a few hours every night, is a long time; and the northwester does not prevail over the Strait all the time, for in "Orompello" we had several days of a south wind that blew steadily up the Strait to the Pacific. So, with a bit of luck, it is quite possible to sail a longboat with a small lateen from Fortescue to the Pacific and back in three days. And, seen close up, the choice between the real Strait and the San Gerónimo channel is not so difficult for a sailor, for the dark waters of the Strait are rippled by the surge of the distant Pacific, while the green and glassy waters of the San Gerónimo channel are marked by eddies characteristic of a river.

Clearly it was at Fortescue that Magellan finally learned that the Pacific was within reach of his sails, then waited in vain for the *San Antonio*'s return. The Strait he named "All Saints," but posterity for once did justice by renaming it in his honor. The small continent of islands to the south of the Strait he christened Tierra del Fuego because of the fires he saw (I wonder if they were fueled by escaping natural gas, which

The Glaciers (*M.O.*)

abounds there today). The *Victoria* sailed back to the Atlantic in search of the *San Antonio* and thereby became the first ship to pass through the Straits twice as well as the first to sail around the globe. (Some ships carry a special blessing, just as in Spanish we say that certain women "have an angel.") Not finding the *San Antonio,* she left two messages marked by flags.

Magellan sailed on with his three remaining ships and passed, surely in silence, below the solemn cantata of green glaciers, black cliffs, and snowclad peaks of the Western Strait, the loveliest in the world for Pigafetta and for me too. On November 28, 1520, he rounded rocky Cape Fermoso (or Deseado) and entered the South Sea, the slow rhythm of whose rollers spoke to him of distances yet unknown.

Magellan: The Pacific

The first crossing of the Pacific Ocean is best summarized, I think, by my table based on Albo's log. Questions come up at once. Why did Magellan follow the coast of today's Chile so slowly, without ever going ashore? How did he manage to sail across the Pacific without raising any inhabited islands when on our charts there is hardly room for all their names? Between the two uninhabited islands that he did see, why did he make only half his ordinary average speed? How was it that Magellan, Elcano, Pigafetta, Albo, and Martín Méndez all escaped the scurvy that decimated their crews? And once across the Pacific, why did Magellan sail all the way up to latitude 12°N when he knew full well that the Spice Islands were on the equator? To answer these questions we must follow the accounts of our chroniclers.

THE FIRST CROSSING OF THE PACIFIC

Albo's Log (my identifications in brackets)	Average Track (from Albo)	Approximate Distance (nautical miles)	Average Speed (knots)
November 31 to December 21, 1520 From Magellan's Strait to latitude 30°S	North	1300	2.5
January 24, 1521 San Pablo Island, uninhabited [Puka-Puka] latitude 16°S	West-northwest	3700	4
February 4 Tiburones Island, uninhabited [Caroline] latitude 11°S	West-northwest	600	2.5
February 13 Equator crossed, 12 die of scurvy	West-northwest		5
February 25 latitude 12°N	West	1900	5
March 6 Ladrones Island (Guam) latitude 13°N	West	1200	6
March 15 San Lazaro Islands [Samar, Philippines] latitude 10°N	West-southwest	1100	6.5

The armada sailed slowly up the Chilean coast, keeping well out to sea; their only landfall was Cape Tres Montes, where they did not go ashore. Having spoken to Chilean sailors and twice flown low over the coast in a light plane, this course does not surprise me. Up to Cape Tres Montes the sea shreds the slopes of the Andes into thousands of islands that are covered with an almost permanent layer of low cloud formed by the meeting of maritime and Andean air currents. Thus it was prudent on the part of the Captain General not to close the coast, and equally prudent, with so many islands in view, to sail only by day—which explains his low average speed. North of Cape Tres Montes, I suggest,

Magellan sailed even further off the coast in order to test the wind as it began to turn fair for the crossing, and so missed the ports that today are called Valdivia, Concepción, and Valparaiso. Finding the wind uncertain, he closed the coast again at latitude 30°S, precisely where the Chilean desert begins and where it was therefore no use going ashore. Finally, on December 21, 1520, he headed (from off today's La Serena) into the South Sea, a sea which he still thought far narrower than it really was.

A month of almost perfect sailing gave the Pacific its name. Full sail in a following wind through a sea as blue as the sky, small white clouds led the ships and flying fish pursued them through the spray. Every half hour a ship's boy sang out as he turned the hourglass. Every evening all sang the Salve Regina after Serrano and Barbosa, commanding the *Concepción* and the *Victoria*, came alongside the *Trinidad* and hailed Magellan, "God save the Captain General, the Master, and their good company."

Little by little the balmy nights adorned themselves again with known stars. Earlier, Pigafetta had seen "two clouds of tiny stars [and]

Meterological chart of Pacific winds (February) (*U.S. Navy*)

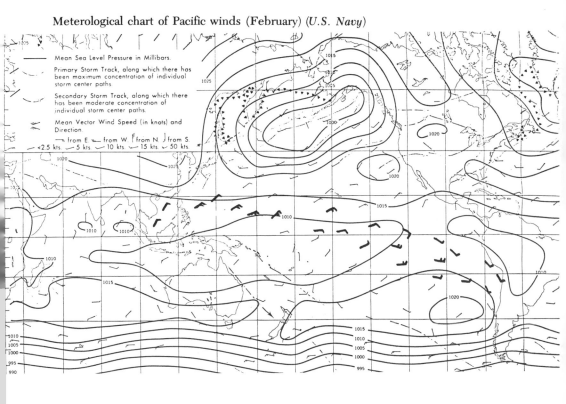

two stars of low magnitude that hardly move around the [South] Pole."
Now he saw "a cross of five very bright stars equidistant one from another
exactly in the west of the open sea." The Magellanic Clouds are
unmistakable, and the stars Beta and Gamma in Hydra do stay close to
the south pole; but I believe the cross cannot be the Southern Cross, as
traditionally supposed, because it would have been well to the south of
due west. I suggest instead that it was the constellation Grus (the Crane).
At noon Albo measured the altitude of the sun with his astrolabe and at
night that of the pole star, and calculated the latitude. In these conditions
it is easy to average four knots or more day and night.

On January 24, the Day of the Conversion of Saint Paul, an island
appeared on the horizon, but Magellan saw no anchorage or sign of life
other than a few trees. He called it San Pablo and held to his course. I
believe that, knowing he might now be surrounded by islands, he went
back to sailing only by day, which explains why for eleven days and nights
he again averaged only two and a half knots, as he had off the Chilean
coast. On February 4 another island was sighted, also uninhabited except
by birds, its waters infested with sharks, of which the sailors caught as
many as they wished. Magellan called this second island Tiburones, the
Isle of Sharks, and Pigafetta called both isles the Unfortunate Isles. San
Pablo and Tiburones have since been identified with all sorts of places
from the air, and the story serves to demonstrate once more my method
none of which agrees with Albo's data. The solution is to search for them
from the air, and the story serves to demonstrate once more my method
of "airborne experimental history."

The head of Air Tahiti fixed me with the astonished eyes of a
Frenchman threatened by bureaucracy. "You want me to rent you our
only light plane," he said, "you want me to install an extra gasoline tank
in the cabin and to hook it up with this mass of tubing and valves you
have brought with you, and you want me to let you fly all day over the
Pacific without first consulting the aeronautical authorities in Paris.
Impossible!" But when I told him that we were on our way to meet
Admiral Laure, things began to look up. The admiral in command of the
French South Pacific had been one of Morison's most enthusiastic
admirers since he was a midshipman, and he was a flyer to boot. He
made some calls, and Jim Nields, Special Installation, which permits
carrying an ordinary barrel in a light plane's cabin as an extra fuel tank,
was authorized. In a test flight I proved its safety to an inspector, and
the flight was cleared. But rain had blanketed Tahiti since our arrival,
and while we waited, I looked around.

Everywhere, barefoot and singing to themselves, the leisurely Tahitian women ambled or cycled by, their smiles always ready, flowers in their hair, a few shells around their necks, gaily colored cloth wrapped around their generous bodies; Gauguin's brush did not lie. Nor did Darwin when he said Tahitians must be amphibious, for the rain would not let up, and beyond the beach the neighboring island of Mooréa appeared and disappeared in the mist, while from the two-thousand-meter crest of Mount Orohena three steep waterfalls cascaded into streams that giggled just like the naked boys who romped in them. Everyone lounged under the breadfruit trees. Captain Bligh of the *Bounty* transplanted some from here to the Caribbean. Earlier, Wallis, Bougainville, and Cook in turn had explored this paradise two centuries after Magellan sailed by it and sighted only the two solitary cays we now had to identify.

Puka in Polynesian means tree, the only sign of life Magellan saw on "San Pablo," and tradition places that island in the Tuamotú group, where the island of Puka-Puka closely fits Albo's courses and latitudes as well as the winds prevailing at the end of the year. Heyerdahl's *Kon-Tiki,* at the mercy of winds and current similar to Magellan's, fetched up at Puka-Puka, as did the Dutchmen Schouten and Le Maire in 1616 after they discovered Cape Horn. This left "Tiburones" for us to find, and we figured that the distance and course that Albo gives place it in the wide channel which runs between the Marquesas and the Line Islands to starboard and the Society, Union, Phoenix, and Marshall Islands to port. On a modern chart filled with names, this channel looks quite busy; but having flown through it at low altitude, I know that it contains many hundreds of square miles of solitary sea. Fortunately, in the middle of this void and at the right distance and heading from Puka-Puka, there are three small islands: Caroline, Flint, and Vostok. I maintained that sharks and birds have habits so constant that they amount to traditions; and that therefore we must look for an atoll whose coral reefs, inhospitable even to the ubiquitous Polynesians, could enclose a lagoon whose mouth opened only at high tide, the ideal hunting ground for sharks. I checked this with a Tahitian fisherman at the Café Vaima and he agreed with my Caribbean reasoning. Morison too was convinced, and so we had one more factor to aid our identification.

Waiting for the island of Mooréa to appear once again on our rainy horizon, we took off dawn in Aztec F-OCIT, known for its last two letters as *India Tango.* It had repeatedly been explained to us that our flight was risky and useless, and hours of empty sea soon began to dim our faith. The nearest radio beacon (on Christmas Island) was too distant for us to take a bearing, and Flint and Vostok, surrounded by storm clouds, are high islands and have no lagoons. Then, suddenly, the weather cleared and ahead lay Caroline, like a mirage. The first thing we saw were Pigafetta's birds, then ten miles of narrow beaches and coral reefs enclosing a multicolored, mile-wide lagoon with only two small openings to the sea, one now dry and the other barely awash. As little visited by man today as she was four centuries ago, and just as attractive to sharks, Caroline suns her turquoise, ocher, and coral body where Albo left Tiburones, ten degrees plus one minute south of the equator and as far from the Marquesas as from the Union group.

We knew we had found Tiburones (and later, in the Vatican Library, old maps confirmed our findings). Well pleased, we checked our cabin tank with a dipstick and, finding it almost dry, set our course for Ranguiróa. There, while gasoline was being pumped aboard by hand, we waded through the lagoon to a *parc á poissons* enclosed in corals, where one could catch fish to one's heart's content, just like Caroline's sharks.

When I finally landed *India Tango* on Tahiti, it was evening and Faaa airport was getting dark. Faaa is written with three a's, not surprising in this isle where even the vowels let time run by.

For the Armada of the Moluccas the sea turned lonely again beyond the Unfortunate Isles, and as soon as the last salted shark had been eaten food began to run short. Hardtack, according to Pigafetta, crawled with worms and smelled of rat's urine; and the rats themselves became delicacies worth half a ducat each. Drinking water turned yellow and putrid. Soon the crews pulled the leather off the yards, soaked it for four or five days in brine, then breaded it with sawdust and cooked it over the embers. Worse than hunger was scurvy and also, I suspect, pellagra, both of which cause the gums to swell and make it impossible to eat what little food there is. A dozen men died, but the officers survived, and it took us a while to discover the reason in the Archives of the Indies: Magellan, like Columbus, had a sweet tooth, and the flagship carried several barrels of quince, a good source of vitamin C, though the Captain General could not have known it.

The fleet sailed day and night at an average of five knots and on February 13 crossed the Line. But instead of making straight for the Moluccas, Magellan maintained his west-northwest course up to latitude 12°N. After I had flown over the Philippines and Indonesia and studied wind and current charts, the explanation was clear to me: It was the season for the monsoons to blow hard out of the north, and Magellan knew this from personal experience and also from correspondence with his friend Francisco Serrao, who had lived for years on the Spice Islands. (Pigafetta says it was Serrao who first gave Magellan the idea of returning via America.) Magellan also knew that the eastern approach to the Moluccas was blocked by the large island of Gilolo, today's Halmahera, whose capital is still called Djailolo, and that only to the north of the Spice Islands were there no Portuguese *factorías*, or trading posts. The Captain General therefore set his course so as to avoid all risk of being caught by the Portuguese and, worse, downwind. He must have steered in early

Umatac (Humata), Guam (Ladrones) *(S.O.)*

evening for the latitude of Aldebaran, the brightest star in the horns of the constellation Taurus, or at midnight for the latitude of Regulus in Leo. Sailing between the Marshall Islands and Wake, he finally set a westerly course not far from Bikini Atoll, and on March 6 he sighted two high islands, known today as Rota and Guam. Almost one hundred days after leaving his strait, he sailed between them and turned south. Then he ran down the western coast of the larger island, Guam, until he found anchorage at Humata (Smoke), today called Umatac.

Magellan called Rota and Guam the Ladrones, the Isles of Thieves, because the friendly natives, known as *Chamorros* (shaven-headed), laid hands on everything not nailed down—cutlery, china, belaying pins, lines.[2] The only way to get rid of them was to shoot them, and when a Chamorro pulled a crossbow bolt from his side and stared in amazement at his own blood, the rest fled in the flagship's longboat. The Spaniards were too weakened by hunger to stop them; all they could do, out of frustration or out of medical superstition, was to beg for "the guts of their enemies."

The next day Magellan sent two armed boats to recover the stolen property, and, after taking on water, fruit, and vegetables, his men burned down the Chamorros' village. Despite their seven dead, in the morning the Chamorros ran a hundred *praus* down the beach. *Praus,* says Albo, are canoes "with outriggers and sails of triangular matting [which] sail either way, making the bow the stern, and the stern the bow whenever they wish." As the great Spanish ships set sail, the Chamorros sailed around them, laughing, shouting, and offering fish to the Spaniards; but whenever the expeditionaries let them come close, the Chamorros rewarded them with a shower of stones.

Once free of "the thieves," the fleet sped west by southwest toward the Spice Islands, and the sick recovered, except for one English gunner who died. Running with the wind at six and a half knots, it took only seven days to raise the "white cliffs" of the San Lazaro Islands, later christened the Philippines in honor of Philip II of Spain. We searched for these white cliffs down to the southern tip of Samar, and there white limestone finally shone out at us from under the jungle. Thus Magellan must have entered Leyte Gulf by the Strait of Surrigao, still the best approach to the Philippines, via the thickly wooded islands of Homonhón and Limasawa ("island of the five wives"—which serves to remind us that, step by step, the Muslims had reached the Moluccas almost five centuries before their kinsmen from the Iberian peninsula, and that here the Portuguese, and the Spaniards after them, had to deal with sultans).

Enrique de Malacca, the servant Magellan had brought home from his first voyage to the East Indies, was able to speak with the natives in their own language, and today's Filipinos still maintain that he was the first to circumnavigate the globe and return to his point of linguistic origin. What most impressed Pigafetta was *palang*, a sexual practice in which the men adorned their penises with "golden spurs" (in Java it was rattles). Nonetheless, says the modest Pigafetta, the ladies of Limasawa preferred the expeditionaries. (According to islanders, *palang* has not entirely disappeared.)

The sultan of Limasawa received the Europeans kindly, even listening respectfully on Easter Sunday to the first Philippine Mass. On April 7, 1521, he accompanied the squadron to the big island of Cebú, where welcome was even warmer. Humabón, sultan of Cebú, with his women and all his retinue, allowed himself to be baptized and declared himself a subject of the emperor. To commemorate the occasion a cross was raised in the main square; one still stands there today, in the center of a big modern city.

But the cross without the sword did not satisfy Magellan, for the Achilles' heel of the great has always been pride. The chieftain of the small nearby island of Mactán, Lapu Lapu (the name means sea bass), refused to acknowledge the emperor's sovereignty. Thereupon, in spite of the sultan of Cebú's warning, the Captain General resolved to demonstrate that fifty Spaniards were capable of keeping a thousand Indians in line.

In a single ship Magellan came as close as possible to Mactan's shallow bay, then ordered himself and the landing party rowed to the beach in longboats. Lapu Lapu's village was burned without resistance, but when the Indians counterattacked from behind the rocks that bracket both ends of the beach, the expeditionaries had to fight their way down to the water. Magellan, with seven men including Pigafetta, covered the withdrawal, fighting in water up to their waists. On April 27, 1521, at the age of forty-one, Magellan paid with his life for having left his ship's guns out of range. He fell, and a horde of Lapu Lapu's men finished him off. Pigafetta and the others, several of them wounded, just made it to the last longboat that dared approach the beach.

We approached Mactán over the bay where Magellan died and landed at the airport which today occupies a large part of the island. Below the monument which on one side honors the Captain General and on the other Lapu Lapu, "the first Filipino who resisted foreign invasion," we walked down to the beach and, wading into the water, saw for ourselves how a tactical error could have cost the life of the greatest of all navigators. Later we crossed by launch to Cebú, where the day after

Magellan's death the newly baptized sultan invited all the expeditionaries to a banquet, ostensibly to reaffirm his friendship. Fortunately, only twenty-seven attended, for all who did perished, including Magellan's brother-in-law, Barbosa. Serrano barely managed to fight his way down to the beach, and Carvallo, shouting from the ship, unsuccessfully tried to negotiate his ransom. Magellan's servant, Enrique de Malacca, whom Carvallo had ill-treated, stayed behind and was probably the sole survivor. Christianity was thus extinguished in the Philippines, but in Cebú today the statue of the Christ Child, which tradition says belonged to Magellan, is venerated with fervor.

In the midst of his figures the good Albo has nothing to say about the Captain General's death, but Pigafetta provides Magellan's epitaph: "We lost our example, our light, and our consolation. More constant than any of us in adversity, he bore privations like the best. He understood the art of navigation better than anyone, and no one else would have had the determination or the talent to circumnavigate the globe!"

Elcano: The Spice Islands and Home

Juan Sebastián de Elcano was born around 1486 in the village of Elcano near Guetaria in the Basque province of Guipúzcoa. A professional sailor, he was over thirty-five when he joined Magellan's armada as master of the *Concepción*. According to the payroll, he took command of the *Victoria* on September 21, 1521. Despite his part in the mutiny at San Julián in Patagonia, during the eight months of the return voyage from the Moluccas to Spain he showed the highest qualities as commander and navigator.

After Magellan's death and the massacre at Cebú, the survivors set sail to the southwest with Juan Carvallo as "pilot" (no one seems to have dared take the title of captain general). They visited the island of Panglao, peopled by natives "as black as Ethiopians" (they still are on neighboring Negros Island). On the south cape of the island of Bohol, the *Concepción*'s hull was put to the torch because she was in poor repair. Then the *Trinidad* and the *Victoria*, refitted with the *Concepción*'s tackle, and with the hundred or so survivors on board, embarked on a leisurely cruise of the sapphire Sulu Sea, its little coral beaches framed by rocks and its golden rivers flowing out of the dark green jungle. It has been asked why they did not sail directly south to the Moluccas, but the fact is that they could not because the summer monsoons were already blowing out of the south. They put in first at Quipit, near today's Zamboanga, on the tip of the southwestern peninsula of the island of Mindanao. Here Pigafetta was

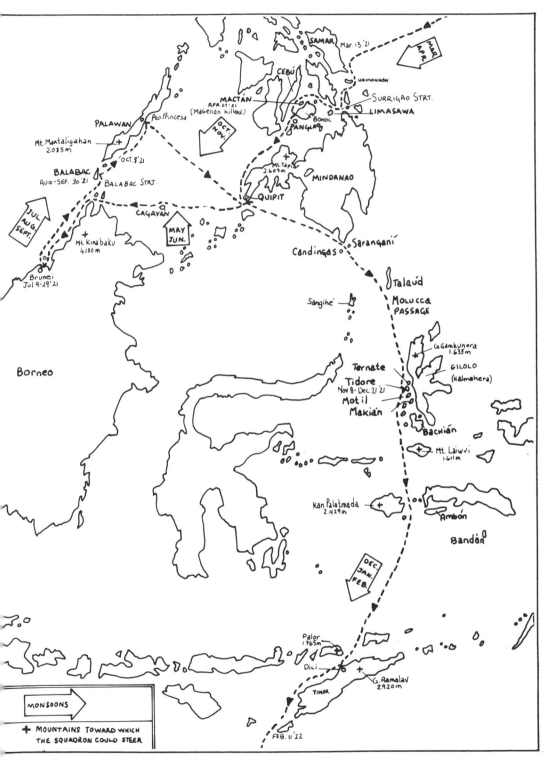

The Sea of Spice *(M.O. and J.O.)*

entertained by Raja Calamao and his two wives, who between them "drank up a large jar of palm wine without eating anything" and, the gentleman chronicler notes with disgust, offered their guests nothing but smelly fish and rice. Then, by way of Cagayán, an island peopled by savages who used poisoned arrows, they sailed to Borneo.

On July 9, 1521, they anchored "in the Brunei Channel." A gilded *prau* flying a blue pennant adorned with peacock feathers brought an exotic band to welcome them, and Pigafetta and his embassy of six rode to the palace on elephants draped in silk and saddled with "castles." They probably thought the Thousand and One Nights were about to begin, but once the splendidly armed guard had escorted them into the palace, they were allowed to see Raja Siripada, sultan of Borneo, only through a window, and to talk to him through a tube, while he continued to chew betel nut and to play with one of his numerous children among the cushions of his harem. Nevertheless an agreement was signed, presents exchanged, and a banquet of thirty courses served. Yet the Spaniards never trusted Siripada, and on July 29, seeing a fleet of armed canoes and *praus* approaching, they sailed in such a hurry that Carvallo's Brazilian son was left behind.

At this point our newly recovered *Paces*, despite its dry language, must take precedence over all other documents when there is any discrepancy, for it is the only one "notarized" and witnessed in the full Spanish sense. According to the *Paces*, then, the expeditionaries were too weak to fight in Brunei harbor, but on the way out they did capture a *prau* and two junks (which Pigafetta describes as ships with high wooden decks, bamboo masts, and sails of tree bark). Carvallo was apparently relieved of command, and Elcano began to share the responsibilities of captain general with Gonzalo Gómez de Espinosa, who took command of the *Trinidad*, and with Juan Bautista de Ponsorón. The *Paces* says that all three were "governors," which differs from what has hitherto been understood.

In the Balabac Strait, which separates Borneo from Palawan, two months were spent careening the ships, probably on the island of Balabac, where the expeditionaries saw crocodiles and giant oysters. I imagine they used the same materials as I have seen used by today's Muslims in Singapore: lemon, shark oil, and goat fat.

On September 30, heading toward Palawan, Elcano had the good fortune to capture the *prau* of Tuan Mahmúd, Borneo's governor of Palawan, and in the negotiations that ensued, as described in the *Paces*, three things are especially worthy of note. First, the interpreter was Paseculán, "a Moor who spoke some Castilian." Unless what Paseculán spoke was Portuguese, here was Moorish Spain in the Antipodes. Second, the Spaniards took from Tuan Mahmúd a small bronze gun *(lombardete)*, confirming that the Moors were well equipped on all these islands, and not only on luxurious Borneo. And third, the *Paces* makes a clear distinction between *Cafres* (Pagans) and *Moros* (Muslims), in other words, between the natives and their Moorish overlords. The Spaniards were therefore no longer really discovering or building an empire as we understand it; they were visiting Moorish colonies for long standing, where all they could do was wrest from the Portuguese the right to establish trading posts through which the priceless crop of spices could be brought to Spain to finance European wars.

An agreement of friendship was signed with Tuan Mahmúd. He swore on the Koran to supply all future Spanish expeditions, and the Spaniards swore on a crucifix to do no harm on Palawan. (The *Paces* calls this part of the agreement a "letter of insurance.") Then the eighty-eight captives were set free, all but Mahmúd himself and his son, who remained on the *Trinidad* until four hundred measures of rice, twenty goats, twenty pigs, and one hundred fifty chickens had been delivered. (The chroniclers must have been very hungry, for on this one statistic Pigafetta and the *Paces* agree exactly.)

The *Paces* is careful to point out that Mahmúd was not held for ransom ("we would not have given him up for twenty thousand ducats") and that he was sent home loaded with cloth of silk and wool "and other Castilian things." His *lombardete* was returned to him because he said the *Cafres* might attack him if he arrived unarmed. Palawan itself, peopled by pagans though ruled by Moors, turned out to be very pleasant, its crops plentiful, its rice wine *(arrack)* much better than the palm wine of Quipit, and its cockfights entertaining. Pigafetta, who gives an enthusiastic description of the island, seems to indicate that the fleet visited it twice, once before and once after Borneo, but the *Paces* says that it did so only after Borneo.

According to the *Paces,* on October 7 the *Trinidad* and the *Victoria* were still in Palawan. Shortly thereafter the winter monsoons must have come in out of the north, and the squadron finally set sail to the southeast and passed through the Basilán Strait off Mindanao, where they had been told they would find a pilot. At Quipit they captured twenty men, one of whom volunteered to be pilot but proved ignorant. They also captured three women and lost two Spaniards. Still searching for a good pilot along the coast of Mindanao, "a great storm overtook them," says Pigafetta, "and the three holy bodies appeared" (the spooky corposants whose static electricity lights up the mast tops). Saved by their prayers, Pigafetta says, they sailed along an endless string of islands (the *Paces,* however, always more conservative, mentions only four). Passing between the twin islands of Candingas and Carraganí (today's Sanganí), the expeditionaries saw people whose "houses are boats, and they do not live on anything else"—a common sight still all over southeast Asia—and here they finally grabbed two real pilots, one of whom escaped to San Gil (today's Sangihe). But with the guidance of the other they made the difficult crossing of the wide Molucca passage, passing Talút, today's Talaúd.

At last, on November 6, 1521, "after a voyage of twenty-seven months less two day," writes Pigafetta, there appeared on the horizon a graceful succession of conical islands which the Moorish pilot at once identified as the Moluccas (Maluku), the legendary archipelago of the Spice Islands: Ternate, Tidore, Motil, Makián, and Bachián, a rosary of precious jewels with legendary names, set in the equatorial sea by ancient volcanic eruptions. Long occupied by the Moors who had come eastward across Asia, sought by Columbus in the west, and reached by the Portuguese around the African cape, these were the islands whose treasures Magellan had come to claim in the name of the emperor. Their immensely valuable crops of cloves, nutmeg, cinnamon, ginger, and sandalwood had first been brought to Europe by Muslim coastal navigators and by camel train; Portugal had then monopolized them; and Spain now planned to dominate them. Pigafetta says that cloves grew only

The Spice Islands (*S.O.*)

on these islands because here a cloud descended almost every day to envelop the trees. No wonder the Spanish flotilla sailed into the port of Tidore firing salvos to give thanks to God.

We approached the Moluccas flying at mast-top height, and the Fortunate Isles appeared one by one on the silent sea, like the notes of a Balinese *barong*. I flew around Ternate and, spotting an abandoned but serviceable landing field, decided to come on in. The Albatross amphibian that Philippine President Marcos had insisted we take along as escort followed suit. While we were still taxiing, the runway filled with laughing and cheering children, and according to Morison, only my grey beard restored enough order for us to begin the procession to town.

Ternate's dream of wealth is now over, and today the capital sleeps in such tranquility that, though an old Portuguese fort still stands, spice seems to have been forgotten and nobody understood us when we asked for cloves. Fortunately, it occurred to me to draw a picture of a clove, and the hotel boy, delighted, found a tree for us to photograph. Later, flying down the necklace of Spice Islands, we landed in Ambón, the headquarters of the Chinese middlemen who in our own day have managed to raise the price of cloves more than fivefold, thereby awakening new hopes for the spice trade. Here the Philippine Albatross was stopped by the Indonesian authorities, and we flew on alone.

The Isles of Spice gave the Spanish fleet a much more splendid welcome. The sultan of Tidore, Raja Mansúr, sent two servants to the *Trinidad*, and they reported to him that the squadron brought promises of friendship and trade from the emperor. Demanding that no arms be carried in his presence, Mansúr himself then came on board with a large retinue. Dreams and astrological calculations had warned him two years earlier of the fleet's arrival, so he willingly swore by Allah eternal friendship to the emperor. He was given clothes, silks, and "other Castilian things" (the phrase is continually repeated in the *Paces*), as well as the three captive women and all the men taken at Quipit (except for two "who went to Castile"). He promised to return the men to Mindanao "so that the Sultan would welcome future Spanish visitors," but the women he kept, according to the *Paces*.

Surprisingly, though Mansúr had his own interpreter ("a resident of Tidore who understood some Castilian"), the interpreter all this time was the pilot Juan Carvallo, "who understood a little of the language of the land" and who now recapitulated for the sultan the squadron's itinerary from Cebú to Tidore. One would like to know more of Carvallo, with his

Brazilian son and his smattering of Arabic. He has been accused of abandoning Serrano on the beach at Cebú, but the records show that he did everything possible to ransom him; tradition says he died on board the *Trinidad* in Tidore, but the *Paces* does not mention it.

Mansúr apologized for the lack of cloves on Tidore and undertook to go to Makián and Motil to buy spice for the Spaniards, but on his return he was shocked to find the squadron preparing to sail without waiting for its precious cargo. The crews had grown impatient. "It is getting late in the year for our return to Castile," they said, as quoted in the *Paces*, "and it is better that the Emperor should know all we have discovered than that we wait to fill the ships. By the grace of God, other ships will come from Castile, and meanwhile the Emperor's merchandise can be stored in the Portuguese *factoría*." For the conquerors of the Pacific, discovery—which depended on getting home—was more important than commerce.

Mansúr insisted that they stay, for if not, he said, "those who did not love him" would whisper that he had done something to displease the emperor. He had a Koran brought on board so that he could renew his oath, and he talked the Spaniards into renewing theirs on a crucifix and waiting another two weeks. Eventually he even got from them a flag with the arms of Castile, a letter signed by the emperor, and six small bronze cannon. In exchange, Mansúr sent the emperor two coffers richly ornamented with sea shells from the island of Bandán to the south, ten birds of paradise, four parrots, and some of the "tree cloth that they make in the Spice Islands" (it is still made from bark in the Chocó region of Colombia). A banquet was laid on at which every man had at his side a girl swathed in silk from waist to knees—to Pigafetta's delight, of course.

Mansúr also arranged meetings between the Spaniards and Yosopót, Quichiluma, and Aboyát, the sultans of Gilolo, Makián, and Ternate, with all of whom the visitors signed *Paces* and exchanged the usual presents. All sent the emperor letters "signed by their own hand" but relatively little spice, most of which, they said, was still green. They did offer to plant more trees "which would take seven or eight years to bear fruit," and also offered "armed men to make war on other islands," but the Spaniards politely refused. Finally, Mansur announced that Subasubu, sultan of Bachián, awaited the Spaniards in the port of Ternate on his *prau*, which carried one hundred twenty oarsmen. Subasubu wanted to explain personally how it had happened that a Portuguese delegation headed by Captain Ximón Correa had been massacred just over a year before on his island. The Moors were apparently unsure as to which of the two Iberian powers would end up on top, just as they were not too certain of each other. At any rate, Mansúr advised the Spaniards to meet Subasubu in his (Mansúr's) palace rather than on Subasubu's *prau*.

According to Subasubu, Captain Correa had arrived from Malacca in a junk with seven Portuguese to buy cloves, and having bought all there was, he began to insult the *Cafres* and to steal their chickens and goats. The Moluccans complained twice to their sultan, and when Subasubu did nothing, they surrounded Correa's house and massacred the eight Portuguese. The sultan insisted to the Spaniards that he had arrived on the scene too late; even so, he said, he was afraid that if the Portuguese returned, they would "lay waste his island." Subasubu's story was confirmed by "Calín, a Moor who had come from Malacca on Ximón Correa's junk . . . and the interpreter was Jorge, the servant of the Captain General, whom God keep in his glory." So the *Paces* gives us another Malaysian (the first was Enrique) who had come with Magellan round the world.

The Spaniards replied that the Portuguese must now know that the Spice Islands lay in the emperor's half of the world and that they would surely not dare to return. All Portuguese property was forfeit, including Correa's junk and five hundred *bahares* of his cloves (each equivalent to four or five hundredweight), because they were now "within the limits of the demarcation." Just in case the Portuguese did try to return, four Spaniards (one of them an accountant!) were to remain on Tidore to watch the merchandise that was to be stored in the Portuguese *factoría*. On hearing this, Subasubu sent the emperor a special present: "a slave eleven or twelve years old."

Between feasts, agreements, and haggling about whether new clove trees would have to be planted, the ships were gradually loaded with spices, but when the *Trinidad* was laden, she sprang a leak the Moluccan divers could not repair without unloading her. So Gómez de Espinosa and Elcano made a sort of Antipodal Treaty of Tordesillas: Elcano in the *Victoria* would proceed at once to Spain, westward across the Portuguese hemisphere while Gómez de Espinosa, once the *Trinidad* was repaired, would try to return eastward across the new Spanish sea, the Pacific, to America. Her cargo of spices would then cross the Isthmus of Panamá by mule and be shipped on the regular Treasure Fleet from Cartagena to Spain. But Gómez de Espinosa soon found out that in order to cross the North Pacific eastward it is necessary to sail far north to catch the wind (our clockwise winds again). So the *Trinidad* was forced to go back to Tidore, where the Portuguese had indeed returned, and Gómez de Espinosa was obliged to surrender to Portuguese Admiral Antonio de Brito. We can imagine what had happened in the meantime to the four Spaniards who had been left behind to guard the emperor's stores and, worse still, to poor Subasubu. Of the *Trinidad*'s crew of fifty-three, only four, including Gómez de Espinosa, managed eventually to get back to

Spain. Meanwhile, the *Victoria* under Elcano completed the first circumnavigation.

Elcano spent six weeks exploring the islands to the south of Tidore, as far as Timor. The western half of this island was until recently the last Portuguese possession in the Seas of Spice; its name means east, as in Timur Khan.

On February 11, 1522, Elcano rounded southwest Timor and sailed into the Indian Ocean, and in three months he made the crossing to the Cape of Good Hope. He sailed first to the southwest, probably seeking the latitude of Pi Puppis in the constellation Argo, then visible before midnight, and that of Menkent in Centaurus after midnight, for both marked the latitude of the Cape. On the way he made a landfall in latitude 30°S on the mid-ocean islands known today as Amsterdam Islands (Los Romeros in old maps), where he remained from March 8 to March 20 without finding much in the way of provisions. Then he followed an irregular course through the infamous "Roaring Forties" and beat with great difficulty up to latitude 34°S. Prudently, he made his landfall northeast of the Cape of Good Hope in order not to miss it by passing to the south. From May 8 to May 10 he rested at the mouth of the river he named Fish River or Rio del Infante (probably in today's Mossel Bay). On May 22 he rounded the Cape under the two-hundred-seventy-meter-high rock which today bears the name of Da Gama, against the wind but with the Agulhas Current, where the warm waters of the Indian Ocean meet those of the frigid Atlantic.

From there he set his course directly for Cape Verde in order to avoid the numerous Portuguese *factorías* dotted along the African coast. After almost two months of privations there remained nothing on board to eat but wheat and rice, and worse, "no wine" (Elcano's words). Twenty-two men died, and once overboard, according to Pigafetta, the bodies of the Christians floated mouth up while those of the Indians floated mouth down. On July 8 Elcano had to enter Santiago, the capital of the Portuguese Cape Verde Islands, whose one-thousand-five-hundred-meter peak is easy to spot. Only thirty-one Europeans and three Indians remained on board, all exhausted. Fortunately, the crew of the first longboat managed to convince the Portuguese that the *Victoria* came from the Spanish Indies, and so obtained provisions. But on July 13 some fool offered the Portuguese Moluccan cloves in exchange for supplies. Impounding the longboat, the Portuguese went after the *Victoria*, and Elcano was forced to weigh anchor with only eighteen men on board.

Setting his course for the Azores to catch a fair wind for Sanlúcar, he spent another frightful month with scarcely anything to eat, probably seeking the latitude of Vega in the constellation Lyra (the Harp) which,

Juan Sebastián de Elcano and survivors   *Cafre* guard at Timor (*S.O.*)
(*Salavería, Beladiez Collection, Madrid*)

followed by the Swan, passed over the Azores before midnight in Elcano's time. On August 15, knowing that he could not go ashore, he sailed around the Portuguese Azores and at last put the *Victoria*'s stern to the wind. The final month was spent working every pump and even bailing with pots and pans until at last the famished survivors sighted their home peninsula. "It was Cape Saint Vincent," says Albo, "and we were to the northeast of it."

In round figures the first circumnavigation of the globe went as follows: two months from Spain to Cape San Agustín; a year to follow the eastern coast of South America; a month to pass through the Strait; a month to sail up the western coast of South America; a month to reach the Unfortunate Isles and another to Guam and the Philippines; a year in the Spice Islands; three months to the Cape of Good Hope; two months to the Cape Verdes; and another two to return to Spain. A total of over three years.

On September 6, 1522, the *Victoria* dropped anchor at Sanlúcar and had to be towed to Seville. There she disappeared, like so many other historic vessels. Elcano, amazed at having lost a complete day on the other side of the world, set foot on the wharf at Las Muelas on September 8, the day of the Virgin of La Victoria. On September 9 he led his men in penitents' garb, candles in hand, to give thanks to the Virgin, who received them smiling, as she had bid the splendid Armada of the Moluccas farewell three years earlier.

Five ships and three hundred men were now reduced to the lonely *Victoria*'s crew of eighteen Christians (no record of "Indians"). Navarette and Herrera list their names, and I have marked with asterisks those who have figured personally in our account (Martín Méndez, author of the *Paces*, does not seem to have survived).

> *Juan Sebastián de Elcano, captain
> *Francisco Albo, pilot
> Miguel Rodas, master
> Juan de Acurio, boatswain
> *Martin de Yudícibus, sailmaker
> *Hernando de Bustamante, barber
> Aires, master gunner
> *Antonio Lombardo, Pigafetta, tourist
> Juan de Zubileta, page
> *Diego Gallego, sailor
> Nicholás de Nápoles, sailor
> Miguel Sánchez de Rodas, sailor
> Francisco Rodriguez, sailor
> Juan Rodriguez Huelva, sailor
> Antón Hernandez Colmenero, sailor
> Juan de Arrantía, ship's boy
> Juan de Santander, ship's boy
> Vasco Gómez Gallego, ship's boy

In their diaries neither Pigafetta nor Albo ever mentions Elcano's name, though he brought them both home halfway around the world. But then Elcano, who signed Méndez' *Paces* as a witness, was not bothered by the fact that the Captain General's death is mentioned but not his name. It seems that such omissions were customary in those days.

Elcano's report to the emperor is brief and to the point. It mentions Magellan's death and prays that God keep him in his glory; it announces "the promises of peace and friendship [*Paces*] of the Kings and Lords of the [Spice] Islands, signed by their own hand"; it begs the emperor to negotiate the release of the thirteen men captured by the Portuguese on the Cape Verde Islands. It ends thus: "We have discovered and made a course around the entire rotundity of the world . . . I pray Your Majesty that, for the trials, sweat, hunger and thirst, cold and heat that these people have suffered in Your Majesty's service, you grant them your fourth part, plus the twentieth of the goods they have brought with them. And with this I close, kissing the hands and feet of Your High Majesty. Written on board the vessel *Victoria* at Sanlúcar, on the sixth of September, 1522. The Captain, Juan Sebastián Elcano."[3]

Gratefully, the emperor granted Elcano's requests and, further, bestowed on him arms bearing the motto *Primus circumdedisti me*, for he was the first captain to bring a ship home around the globe (Drake would do it sixty-eight years later). Elcano went home, made a will in favor of his two children and his two ladies (he was a real sailor), then sailed with Friar García Jofre de Loayza in 1525 to circle the globe for the second time. Trying to cure himself of scurvy by eating roast rat, he died in mid Pacific in 1526, at the same time as Loayza. He was certainly one of the most modest and most stubborn captains of all time.

Meanwhile, the correct longitude of the Moluccas remained in such doubt that Charles V set up the Committee of Badajoz to clear up the matter. A truly honest scientist, Columbus' illegitimate son Ferdinand, proved that with the instruments of the time it was impossible to determine longitude with any accuracy, and the day "lost" by Elcano was clearly explained by Jesuit Father Giuseppe de Acosta. In 1529 all rights to the Moluccas were sold by Charles V to the king of Portugal, and eventually they passed from Portugal to Holland, one of whose governors, the well-named M. Poivre, transplanted the spices to Mauritius, whence they were taken to Madagascar and to Africa. The legendary daily cloud that Pigafetta thought responsible for the Moluccas' monopoly of spices was no longer necessary.

So ended Magellan's and Elcano's circumnavigation, probably the greatest of all naval feats. While they sailed, the High Renaissance flowered. Maximilian I died, and Charles V and his bankers began building the greatest of all empires. Fox-faced Francis I prepared an alliance with Suleiman the Magnificent in order to prevent Charles from uniting Europe (the French always prefer presiding over the European table to sharing it). Henry VIII was given the title of Defender of the Faith by Pope Leo X; he had not yet begun to switch wives, churches, and enemies. After a lifetime *provando e riprovando*, Leonardo died, leaving a complete "flight plan" for the next four centuries. Copernicus had already confirmed but dared not publish what Pythagoras had proposed in the sixth century B.C., that the earth revolves about the sun. Raphael died, but Michelangelo, Titian, Dürer, and Holbein continued to illuminate Europe. Machiavelli extolled the art of war. Luther nailed his theses to the Church's door, Erasmus cracked it open so that the wind could scatter dogmas, and Loyola began his *Spiritual Exercises*. Cortés entered Mexico, and Pizarro made ready to sail for Peru down the coast of the South Sea.

All this and much more happened while the Armada of the Spice Islands circumnavigated the globe, and it is difficult to judge if it was the Renaissance that demanded the circumnavigation or the circumnavigation that characterized the Renaissance by presenting it with a complete globe washed by a single sea. This is the globe we have inherited; in it the

Infinite Ocean of the Greeks is just another of the gulfs which a series of straits string together from continent to continent. We no longer live on a solitary island. To be alone again we must launch ourselves into space.

NOTES

1. The *Paces* is also signed by witnesses Francisco Albo, pilot; Bartolomé Sánchez, notary; Martin de Yudícibus, sailor and sailmaker; Juan Sebastián de Elcano, captain; Gonzalo Gómez de Espinosa, captain; and Juan Bautista de Ponsorón, master.

2. In 1565 Miguel López de Legaspi took possession of the Ladrones Islands and renamed them the Marianas in honor of Queen Anne Marie of Austria. Humata, Magellan's port, remained the Spanish capital until the end of the nineteenth century, when the governor surrendered it to the captain of a United States cruiser with a good phrase: "Sir, I have no shells with which to return your bombardment; please come in, and I will sell you the island." The United States did not then want Guam or Rota, and the Germans eventually bought them from Spain only to lose them in World War I. In the end the United States got Guam, Puerto Rico, and the Philippines for twenty million dollars. (It doubled its territory for a little over a hundred million dollars, including what it paid for Louisiana, Florida, Alaska, the Virgin Islands, and the Canal Zone.)

3. In his report to the emperor, Elcano says that Magellan's Strait is three hundred leagues long. Its length is some 100 nautical miles, which allows us to interpret contemporary information concerning the first circumnavigation at three leagues per nautical mile.

Part Three
THE SEA OF AIR AND THE OCEAN OF SPACE

Cape Canaveral (Cape Kennedy) from space (*NASA*)

6

THE
MONTGOLFIERS
AND THE
WRIGHTS

On July 16, 1969, I watched Apollo 11 blast off for man's first landing on the Moon. It was as if a thirty-six-story building, suddenly conscious of a new mission and spewing smoke from its basement, had risen slowly from the ground and accelerated into the sky with a roar that shattered the air.

As soon as the scared wildfowl had returned to earth, my host, Colonel Cannon, suggested that before flying to Houston Control Center, I sail with him down the Indian River and out into the sea. There, boarding one of two roofed barges loaded with compressors and other equipment, we donned aqualungs and dropped to the shallow, sandy bottom where a ghostly procession of divers worked among the remains of the Spanish Treasure Fleet of 1715.

Thus, on the same day that I saw the first men set off for the Moon, I was able to pluck from the sea bottom pieces of eight belonging to their Spanish predecessors. (I have the replicas on my desk.) *La Flota de Tierra Firme,* the Continental Armada, used to sail every year from Spain to Cartagena, the most splendidly fortified port in the Caribbean, where gold, emeralds, and pearls from the coasts of today's Colombia and Venezuela were put on board together with Peruvian silver shipped up the Pacific coast, and carried across the Isthmus of Panamá by mule train to Portobelo. In the meantime, spice, silk, and porcelain from the Far East came to Acapulco on the Manila galleon and then crossed the Isthmus of Tehuantepec via the second "mule canal" to Veracruz, where, together with Mexican silver and dyes, they were shipped to Havana on the Armada of New Spain. In Havana the two armadas met, and the combined Treasure Fleet set sail in spring, following wind and current up the Bahama Channel and along the flat Florida coast as far as its first recognizable cape, Cape Canaveral. There the armada finally veered east with the wind that circulates clockwise around the North Atlantic—the same wind that brought Columbus home from the Azores after his first voyage.

In 1714 the armada never left Spain because the War of the Spanish Succession had ended only the year before. And in 1715 the combined Treasure Fleet, with fifteen million pesos of treasure in the holds of eleven ships, started its homeward voyage late, just in time for the first of the hurricanes that the Caribbean likes to brew up in summer. South of Cape Canaveral, a thousand men went to the bottom and only two ships survived: the *Griffon,* a captured French privateer that was caught by the hurricane far enough off shore to ride out the storm, and the *Nuesta Señora del Carmen* (or *Holandesa*), which was washed up onto the rock-strewn beach without the loss of a single hand. Her captain sent word to San Agustín, the capital of Spanish Florida, and the captain general of Havana soon organized a rescue fleet. Naked Indians, working under diving bells, recovered four million pesos of sunken treasure but lost half a million pieces of "Real Eight" to Henry Jennings' five pirate ships out of Jamaica.

My little expedition into the past completed, I flew to Houston Manned Spacecraft Control Center, a sort of western university campus complete with flowered shirts and ten-gallon hats. There I watched Cap. Com.(Capsule Communicator) transmit instructions and reports between the specialized desks and Apollo 11, until, after the actual Moon landing, and during a "routine" stretch of the return voyage, Chris Kraft, the flight director, invited me to lunch outside the center with a group of scientists and astronauts. He owed his name, he told us at table, to his parents' lifelong interest in Christopher Columbus, and having seen the book I had written with Samuel Eliot Morison, he now wanted to ask me what, in my opinion, was the most important difference between the discovery of America and that of the Moon, which we had just "witnessed."

I suggested that while Columbus' "flight plan" was pretty imprecise, his purpose seemed clear: to carry the Cross and the Crown across the Atlantic and to return loaded with treasure for a Crusade, and glory for his sovereigns and for himself. Apollo 11, on the other hand, followed an absolutely precise flight plan, but the real purpose of its flight had perhaps not yet been properly defined in public. After some discussion, Kraft defined NASA's purpose: to keep the United States at the head of the world's technical and scientific progress (a good answer, for discovery needs transcendent motives, such as patriotism, as much as it needs material ones). I then proposed another difference between the two voyages of discovery: The first was the work of an individual hero whose name would always be remembered, the second the work of a great and anonymous team the name of whose first representative on the Moon might soon be forgotten. My NASA friends maintained that the television image of the moon landing would stick in the memory of history, and I maintained that it would be buried like a sunken galleon under the surf of a million other television images.

Our world overflows with people who tend to forget the continuity of history, and our souls, which, with the Renaissance, started asking how instead of why, seem now to be changing again. There are few heroes or villains worthy of immortality, for few dare to attempt the great intuitive leaps which used to be the vocation of mystics, poets, and leaders. The young seem more interested in denouncing injustice than in continuing the ancient search for justice. Women pay for equality with impersonal labor, which, having been a necessary evil, became first a virtue and then a new form of slavery. Without tradition to steady the tiller, values and laws run before the wind of propaganda. Magic, superstition, and naiveté—not to mention inflation and drugs—are all more rampant now than in the sixteenth century (the New York Telephone Company offers Horoscopes-By-Phone as a public service). In a world hungry for prophets, Religion, whose very name used to mean the union of the natural with the supernatural, concerns itself more with the stomach than with the soul, and the churches surrender myth and the sense of wonder to Hollywood and television. Fifty percent of Americans believe in flying saucers, yet Catholics no longer have to believe in angels.

God, in whose presence every desire was a prayer and every adventure a hymn of praise, seems now to waste the Earth's fragrance, the sea's tang, and the wind's caress on men whose senses are overridden by their brains. It is as though the Trinity took turns in revealing Creation: God the Father reigned in ancient times, a feudal overlord; then came the Son, to found His Church; and today, with both feudal family and sacred Church in apparent decline, we seem to be waiting for the Holy Spirit. Let Him come soon, for the presence of God is as necessary to our sense of reality as the presence of the Earth is to our sense of motion; astronauts know it, and Malraux may well be right when he says that "the twenty-first century will be religious or it will not be."

Perhaps there is time. Prophets are thundering again, and the "big bang" theory of the origin of the Universe now seems to point to a real Creation some twenty billion years ago. The globe we thought we had possessed and exhausted is now shown to us from space, and it looks as if it were the only green planet in black Infinity. It is again the Island of the Argonauts within whose solitude gods, men, and nature may all once more be part of the same brave family, capable of great adventure in a new Infinite Ocean whose gods wait to be challenged—and therefore believed.

But the Ocean of Space lies beyond the Sea of Air, and to conquer the air is a dream at least as old as the Golden Fleece. Some time between the Argonauts and Odysseus, an Athenian architect, Daedalus, and his son, Icarus, built for King Minos of Crete a labyrinth in which to hide the Minotaur, the bull-headed son of his unfaithful queen. Then, when their work was done, the king imprisoned the designers in their own invention. Seeing how vultures and gulls soared on the northeast wind over the cliffs at Knossos, they decided to escape on wings of cloth fixed with wax onto a bamboo skeleton, and since the birds used about one-tenth of a square meter of wing for each pound of weight, they knew that they themselves would each need a little more than ten square meters of wing (I have watched my son Sancho build and fly a hang-glider with a wing area of about ten square meters). Ovid in his *Metamorphoses* tells us that when Icarus tried to outfly his father by riding the wind too steeply toward the sun, he crashed into the Aegean "because the sun melted the wax in his wings." It seems clear then that the first aviators took off correctly by jumping from the labyrinth's wall above the cliffs, facing northward out to sea, that is, into the prevailing wind, and that one of them suffered the classic "stall" accident while trying to climb too steeply and lost his wings on recovery.

The Japanese have a legend as likely as the Athenians' and roughly contemporary: In the second millennium B.C., a monk who had painted on his kite the words "when she soars my soul goes with her" disappeared into the sky, entangled in his line. In less legendary times, a twelfth-century Saracen dived off the top of Galata tower in Constantinople, frantically beating the air with a wooden frame sewn under his cape. The Chinese flew balloons to celebrate the coronation of Emperor Fokien (and Marco Polo says he saw flying machines in Cathay). Finally, man was preceded into the air, as into space, by animals: On September 19, 1783, the brothers Joseph and Etienne Montgolfier, papermakers, sent a duck, a rooster, and a lamb up to an altitude of some five hundred meters in a hot-air balloon which stayed up for eight minutes. Louis XVI and Marie Antoinette, who had witnessed the miracle, knighted the Montgolfiers and took the lamb home to the queen's zoo. In a land of gourmets and gourmands it is not difficult to guess what happened to the other animal aeronauts.

The first human incursion into the new sea, the first in our history (for we have no record of anyone's having ridden those Chinese balloons), occurred on October 15, 1783. Jean-François Pilâtre de Rozier ascended twenty meters into the air in a tethered *Montgolfière* made of linen and paper and carrying its own fire of straw and wool; on October 19 he came close to one hundred meters altitude with Girond de Villette as passenger. Louis XVI suggested that condemned prisoners be the next test pilots, but on November 21, standing under his balloon in a wicker gallery with the Marquis d'Arlanges, Pilâtre rose to some three hundred fifty meters and flew nine kilometers in twenty-five minutes. While one aeronaut stoked the fire, the other extinguished spark holes in their ornate twenty-one-meter-high balloon. Pilâtre failed to do so two years later and died in flames.

On December 1, 1783, Jacques Charles filled his balloon with hydrogen produced by pouring sulphuric acid onto a pile of iron filings, and his *Charlière*, which could stay in the air for hours, rose to a thousand meters. On January 7, 1785, Jean Pierre Blanchard and Dr. John Jeffries, a Bostonian, made it across the English Channel by throwing even their trousers overboard. Blanchard took his balloon to the United States and, with no less an audience than Washington, Adams, Jefferson, Madison, and Monroe, made the first flight there in 1793, just twelve days before Louis XVI went to the guillotine. In 1808, after Blanchard died of a heart attack, his diminutive wife, Marie, succeeded him, became the first woman flyer, and was killed when her balloon burned. By 1797, people were parachuting from balloons for fun. In 1870, besieged in Paris by the Germans, the French launched sixty-four balloons that transported eighty-eight people and four million letters. The sea of air was becoming a thoroughfare.

Some twenty meters of colored nylon stretched away from me on the ground as I grasped the wicker gondola and anxiously watched hot air being blown into the balloon with a fan. As the great bag filled, a light wind began to drag it across the ground, but when I tried to jump into the basket, it stopped. We tried again and the balloon took off. In the gondola, I bumped along behind it as if riding in a Roman chariot which had lost its wheels. Then the gondola left the ground, suddenly transformed into a sickening pendulum, until at last the swinging stopped and there was silence.

As long as there remained gas in the cylinder that occupied the corner of the gondola opposite me, I could choose my altitude by controlling the temperature of the air in my balloon with the burner at the center of the ring that held together the cables from which I was suspended. If I was lucky and skillful (which I am not), by picking the right altitudes I might even find a wind which would take me where I wanted to go—and an opposite one to bring me home. With the dignity of two tons of inertia (which fortunately displaces more than two tons of air) I passed over the outskirts of town unnoticed by the earthbound people who puttered around in their patios, but their dogs sensed my presence and howled at me as though I were an artificial moon.

The ground crew tried to follow me in a jeep, bouncing out into the California desert, but they seemed to be nowhere in sight when my solitary indicator told me that gas was running low. My flight path was about to cross a high-tension line that followed a highway across the sand, so I let the balloon cool off, and when it finally started its ponderous descent, I gave it one more blast of hot air to break our fall. The gondola and I hit the ground, and as I dove for the balloon's lower lip to let out air lest we drag across the sand, I heard a dreadful crash and wondered if I had cracked up. A police siren brought me back to reality. The crash had come from the bumpers of several cars that had become entangled on the highway while watching the "nut" come down in his balloon. The ground crew turned up with a couple of *botas* of wine and all was forgotten. All but the beauty of feeling lighter than air, alone, silent, and with nothing much to do.

During the nineteenth century the exploration of the air followed two divergent paths. Count Ferdinand von Zeppelin insisted on craft lighter than air, and by 1900 he had perfected his dirigible, a long, aerodynamic balloon driven by propellers and steered with a rudder. (By the time of the first World War it carried a total of more than ten thousand passengers, and by the time of the second it crossed both the Atlantic and the Pacific Oceans.) Meanwhile, Otto Lilienthal had begun to use the lift produced by air flowing past an inclined plane, and by the turn of the century he had made two thousand controlled glides. But just when he was ready to put an engine in his wings, he crashed; "sacrifices must be made" were his last words.

Success belonged to Wilbur and Orville Wright, whose three-hundred-forty-kilo motorized glider ran along a rail on December 7, 1903—more than a century after the Montgolfiers—and was dragged up into the wind for twelve seconds by a twelve-horsepower engine put together by the Wrights in their bicycle shop. Four times they repeated the experiment; the rail is still on the sandy spit at Kitty Hawk, a rock marks the point of takeoff, and four red posts the four first points of

Lighter-than-air, gravity-powered, engine-driven

Paris Air Show 1909

Lilienthal 1891

Wright Brothers' "Flyer" 1903, taking off

landing, the farthest one two hundred sixty meters away (the Wrights' Flyer 120 is at the Smithsonian). Some still dispute their "first," but if anyone flew before under his own power, his flight evidently had no consequence, whereas the Wrights were soon describing full circles in the air.

Records began to be set and then broken. In 1906 Alberto Santos Dumont, a Brazilian, maintained a horizontal airspeed of forty-one kilometers per hour for seventy-five meters, the first before official witnesses. In 1909 Louis Blériot landed on the golf course at Dover after having flown the English Channel in twenty-seven minutes.[1] Sixty years later a Boeing 747 was large enough to enclose Santos Dumont's entire flight. I was president of the International Aviation Federation (FAI), which sanctioned the first flights, and its treasurer was Blériot's son.

The first World War gave aviation its final push, and out of it came the first two airlines, which survive today: KLM in Holland and SCADTA (now AVIANCA) in Colombia. In 1919 Commander Read of the U.S. Navy leapfrogged across the North Atlantic in eleven days in a four-engine seaplane; one month later the British team of Alcock and Brown did it nonstop in just over sixteen hours. The South Atlantic was conquered in 1922 by Cabral and Coutinho, two Portuguese (those old discoverers), but it took their two seaplanes six weeks to do it. The aerial circumnavigation of the globe was achieved in 1924 by three U.S. Army single-engine amphibians, which covered 42,000 kilometers in six months (including stops) at an average speed of 114 kilometers per hour and used up twenty engines. On the way they met an Englishman, a Frenchman, and an Italian who were also trying to fly around the world but did not make it. In 1929 the Graf Zeppelin made it in three weeks, at 100 kph, with sixty people cruising in luxury on board. The 55-ton dirigible was 237 meters long and 32 meters in diameter, about four times as big as a Boeing 747 "Jumbo." In 1978 three Arizonans made it without power in a gas balloon.

We have seen that it is not necessarily those who were first who become legendary; sometimes it is those who make the rest of the world pay attention. In the air, Charles Lindbergh did it in 1927 by flying alone from New York to Paris in thirty-three and a half hours in a single-engine land-plane whose gas tank blocked the pilot's forward view—a small matter since Lindbergh in the end had to fly low and shout at some astonished fishermen to ask the way to Ireland. His plane, the *Spirit of St. Louis*, hangs today from the ceiling of the Smithsonian, not much bigger than what is for us an ordinary light plane. Legend also embraced Antoine de Saint-Exupéry, airline pioneer and poet laureate of the air, and Amelia Earhart, who crossed the Atlantic alone in 1932 and five years later disappeared mysteriously over the Pacific.

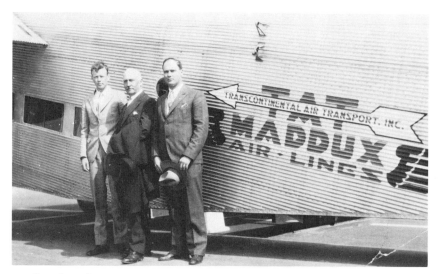

Lindbergh with F.A.I. Authorities

All these fliers found their way around like sailors, with a magnetic compass, a speed indicator, a clock, and perhaps a sextant. Soon radio navigation with reference to ground stations became necessary, and then, for jets, inertial navigation (INS), which continually computes position without external reference by measuring and adding up acceleration and deceleration. This method will work anywhere, even away from the Earth, so when the last aerial frontier, the "sound barrier," was broken in 1947 by Chuck Yaeger in the X-1-A (I "cracked up" in his X-15 simulator), the air was in the palm of our hand and we were ready to leap into space.

NOTE

1. In 1979 an American pedaled the first man-powered plane, a giant insect made of carbon-filament tubing and transparent plastic, across the English Channel.

7
GAGARIN AND NASA

The first to leave the biosphere was a Russian, Yuri Gagarin. "We're off," he said, "is my heart beating?" And Zarya, the Soviet ground controller replied, "Your pulse rate is sixty-four and your respiration is twenty-four." The rocket that boosted him out of the atmosphere on April 12, 1961, was 38 meters high, and his capsule, the first of the manned Vostok series, orbited the Earth once in 108 minutes at 27,000 kph and an altitude of 320 kilometers. To land, Gagarin parachuted out of his capsule—which caused quite an argument at the International Aviation Federation (FAI), which had to sanction his performance as it had sanctioned Santos Dumont's fifty-five years earlier. The rules say that to establish a record the pilot must land in his aircraft; but faced with such a historic achievement, the FAI simply changed its rules retroactively. In the second half of the twentieth century, what cannot be fixed by technicians or by magicians is arranged by small revolutions.

Four months later Gherman Titov completed seventeen orbits, and on February 20, 1962, ten months after Gagarin, the first American, John Glenn, orbited the Earth in Mercury 1. By the time Gagarin was killed in an "ordinary" jet plane in 1968, six Vostoks (the last carrying rosily round-faced Valentina Tereshkova) and six Mercurys had made successful manned orbits.

On October 12, 1964, Voskhod 1, the first of a new series of Russian spaceships, carried three men (Commander Vladimir Komarov, physician Boris Yegorov, and scientist Konstantin Feoktistov) into orbit in a pressurized cabin so that they could work without spacesuits. On March 18, 1965, Alexei Leonov left Voskhod 2 through a double pneumatic lock for the first space-walk (he acted like a cheerful peasant in a haystack). That same year the United States launched Gemini, its second series of spaceships, and Edward White floated out of Gemini 4, leaving its pilot, James McDivitt, exposed to the vacuum. Already adapted to the sea and to the air, we were getting familiar with space.

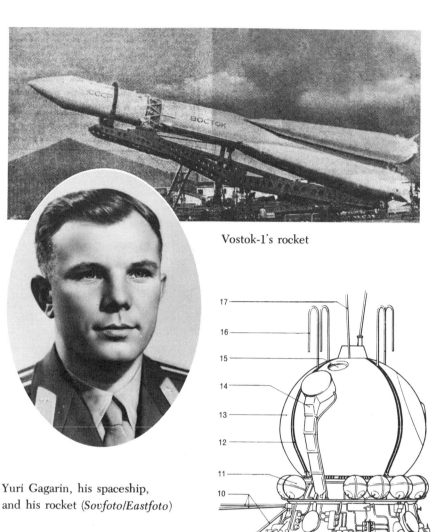

Vostok-1's rocket

Yuri Gagarin, his spaceship,
and his rocket (*Sovfoto/Eastfoto*)

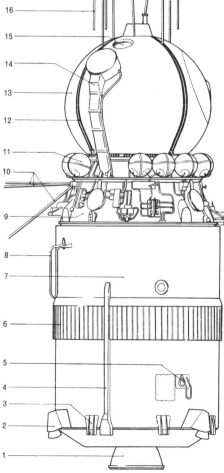

Vostok-1

1-9
Rocket's last stage and service module
11
Oxygen tanks
13
Gagarin's capsule
15
Port

The first space walk

Two Vostoks flew in loose formation in 1962, two Geminis did it in 1965, and on March 16, 1966, Neil Armstrong and David Scott docked their Gemini 8 with an unmanned Agena in orbit, an essential maneuver for putting together in space ships which would be difficult to launch complete. I was in Control Center as the coupled capsules went out of control just before entering a zone of no communication, and I will not easily forget the faces of the astronauts' wives when they came in to talk to them as soon as communication was reestablished, without knowing if they would be able to return to Earth. They made it, and it took the Russians three more years to join Soyuz 4 and 5 in space, though they had been the first to achieve unmanned docking.

The year 1967 was disastrous for both space programs. Two new series of spaceships, Soyuz and Apollo, started with fatal accidents. On January 27 Virgil (Gus) Grissom, Ed White, and Roger Chaffee were burned to death in an earthbound test of Apollo 1, and, on April 23 Vladimir Komarov was killed in the crash of Soyuz 1 when its parachutes became entangled. (I had enjoyed chatting with him in Moscow, even about politics, for seamen, airmen, and spacemen can always talk.)

On December 21, 1968, the United States took a commanding lead when Apollo 8 with Frank Borman, James Lovell, and William Anders on board left Earth-orbit, crossed the space-gulf that separates us from the Moon, orbited our satellite ten times, and returned to Earth.[1] Besides the ability to dock in space, a rapid increase in rocket power was responsible for the feat. The first satellites were boosted by existing military rockets (the Russian RD 107 came directly from the German V-2), and although their total power had increased, the rockets that propelled Vostok, Voskhod, and Soyuz remained constant in size. The Mercury-Redstone, on the other hand, was two-thirds the size of its Russian counterpart, the Titan Mercury was about the same size as the Russian, Apollo-Saturn 1 was twice as big, and Apollo-Saturn 5 three times as big. Payload is about five percent of rocket weight, so the first manned spaceships all weighed between five thousand and six thousand kilos. The Russian space labs (Salyut) weighed up to twenty-five tons (without attachments), Apollo fifty tons, and Skylab nearly one hundred tons.

The rockets (M.O. and S.F.)

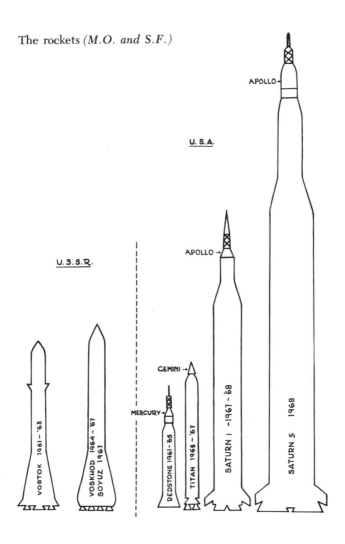

On July 20, 1969, eight years after the first manned orbit, twelve years after the unmanned Sputnik, and fifty years after the first crossing of the Atlantic by air, Neil Armstrong and Edwin (Buzz) Aldrin stepped onto the surface of the Moon while Michael Collins awaited them in Apollo 11 (*Columbia*) in lunar orbit. From Cape Canaveral they had been boosted by a Saturn 5 into Earth-orbit and then out of it and to the Moon at the 40,000 kph required to escape Earth's gravity. The rocket was more than 100 meters high and 10 meters wide at its base, weighed 3,000 tons (including Apollo), and put out 167 million horsepower while consuming each second almost twice the 2,000 gallons of fuel that it takes a Boeing 707 one hour to burn. Sections of the rocket had been built in several parts of the United States and then assembled at the Cape, three rockets at a time, in VAB, the largest building in the world, in whose five-million-cubic-meter interior clouds sometimes form—and it rains indoors. Finally, Saturn had been transported in a vertical position (it will not hold together on Earth in any other) on a caterpillared platform 2,000 meters wide at about one kilometer an hour, to Cape Canaveral's Pad 39. Most successful starts are slow.

Charles "Pete" Conrad is the only astronaut I know who is no taller than I am. He is always in good humor; stepping onto the moon from Apollo 12, he parodied Armstrong's rather solemn first words by quipping that if the step was a small one for tall Armstrong, it was a pretty big one for him. Amused by my having flown a light plane all the way from Colombia to Houston, he offered to show me the simulator on which one learns to "drive" the Lunar Landing Module (LEM). Poised on streams of air, it reacts to control jets with almost as little resistance as if it were in space.

He also took me into the great round hall which houses the Centrifuge. Its long circulatory arm can spin its victims at high speeds and various angles in order to subject them in a variety of artificial "gravitational" forces, often greater than those produced by the accelerations which astronauts are likely to experience in space. It can also "walk" an astronaut lying in a sling, with his feet horizontally against the wall that surrounds it, and, by reducing the angle from the vertical at which he is suspended, let him feel the reduced gravity on the wall, which acts as his floor. Next we sat for about ten minutes in a Gemini spaceship so that Conrad could explain the instruments and controls to me, and when I remarked that I was getting claustrophobia, he pointed out that in weightless orbit there is no such thing. Just in case, there is a red "panic button" on the panel—which does nothing.

NASA has observed that introverts like Armstrong work better in the morning while extroverts like Conrad are happier at night, so I surmise that the astronaut who took a nice juicy sandwich into space and the cosmonaut who took a bouquet of flowers must both have been night people. Certainly the astronauts with whom I sailed through the Panama Canal after they had finished their jungle training were extroverts and night owls, for to oblige a Panamanian girl who challenged them to prove the value of their training by swimming the Canal, they dived into its pitch black waters one by one. It was wonderful to watch two fast patrol boats trying to pick such valuable swimmers out of the dark with searchlights.

Perhaps the astronauts' general good humor is to blame for the cowboy image that television at first assigned them; despite their pranks, or perhaps because of them, they struck me as serious scientists always intent on formulating new questions and seeking new answers, even in the most casual conversations. I wonder whether they do not instinctively adopt a "jock" style and a wry slang in order to be able to live with such a monstrous enterprise without becoming pompous. Many of them have returned from space quite changed, and some of them have turned to careers in public service, ecology, or religion. Perhaps earthmen will in time be as affected by the discovery of space as Europeans were by the discovery of America.

Apollo 11 had covered the 386,000 kilometers that separate us from the Moon, the distance that Hipparchus of Rhodes (and of Nicaea) calculated in the second century B.C. by observing the duration of an eclipse. Now eighty hours from the Earth (about three days, compared to Columbus' three-week voyage of discovery), the expeditionaries were about to enter lunar orbit, so we all returned to our "balcony" at Houston Control Center. Seventy-five guests watched a similar number of technicians huddle over desks full of instruments, screens, and microphones, all connected to a whole building of labs and computers capable of simulating almost any situation likely to occur in space. At 13:10 hours on July 20, 1969, *Eagle*, the Lunar Module or LEM, separated from *Columbia* and started its one-hour descent to the surface of the Moon. (It pleases me that the LEM was built by Grumman, where I worked as engineer and testflight captain on F-6 and F-7 fighters during the second World War, so long ago!) NASA's complete communications transcript is available to anyone with the patience to read it, but for our purposes the following résumé of what I remember will do.

FLIGHT PROFILE

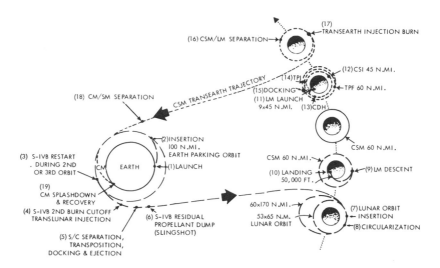

Route to the Moon (*NASA*)

Houston Control Center (*NASA*)

Lunar Module (LEM) and Earthrise (*NASA*)

ARMSTRONG Here we go down U.S. 1. There's a slight vibration, but it doesn't seem to be serious. Well, we've rounded the Cape.

CONTROL You are doing OK.

ARMSTRONG This thing is easier to drive than the simulator. We have a red light; onboard computer is overloaded.

CONTROL (internally) To land or not to land. (Rapid check of the different control desks.) Thirty seconds of fuel . . . Land!

ARMSTRONG We're raising some moon dust . . . skidding a little to the right . . . Eagle has landed! This is Tranquility Base. We had to change course at the last moment to avoid some man-high boulders. We only have twenty seconds of retro-fuel left on board, but we are here.

CONTROL Plenty of smiling faces here at Control Center.

COLLINS (orbiting the Moon in *Columbia*) One more smile here . . . I see something white near a small crater, but I guess it is not the base.

CONTROL Here is some news: Luna 15, a Russian unmanned probe, has landed on the Sea of Crisis, about 500 miles from Tranquility.

ARMSTRONG Congratulations. Eagle stands about 4.5° from the vertical. We seem to adapting to lunar gravity without difficulty. We can't see the horizon; hill in the way. Our retro-rockets have split open some rocks. Looks like basalt.

CONTROL (internally) Watch it! Eagle's fuel and ox. pressures are increasing. The heat-exchanger vent must be blocked, maybe frozen. Do we alert Armstrong? . . . It's going off the scale . . . The line might blow! (He tells Armstrong.)

ARMSTRONG Understand . . . OK, pressure seems to be escaping without blowing the line . . . I guess the vent was frozen. We're going to make everything ready for takeoff before resting. (Three hours later.) Ready for our four-hour rest, but we can't wait to get out. Can we skip the siesta?

CONTROL We've thought about that. Let's see what Flight Surgeon thinks.

FLIGHT SURGEON Astronauts' pulse is normal, around eighty, and so are the other readings. They are no more excited than my kids, who wouldn't even watch this on TV.

CONTROL OK. Go ahead!

ARMSTRONG Hatch open. I'm going to climb out onto the porch with the TV camera. (He steps down.) Very fine powder, some places one-eighth of an inch deep, other places six inches deep; sticks together as if it were wet. (Hesitantly, as if reciting a lesson.) *This is one small step for me but a giant step for mankind.* No problem walking, easier than in simulation. Picked up some rocks but forgot to count them. Remind me . . . Hello, what's this at the bottom of a small crater?

The big screens at Control Center that had been showing trajectories and figures now showed the televised picture of the astronauts on the Moon. Aldrin was also out of the LEM, and the two of them went loping about the Moon like vacationing kangaroos.

At 12:27 hours on July 21 we were ready for blastoff from the Moon. Armstrong and Aldrin were back aboard *Eagle*, waiting to loft her sixteen tons from the Moon to *Columbia's* orbit at nearly 9000 kph. This was the most critical maneuver in the entire voyage, for *Eagle* could carry only one small rocket engine, and if it failed, there was no backup, nor oxygen for prolonged survival on Tranquility Base. Two minutes before blastoff there was complete silence at the Center. Next to me sat the representative of the company that had built the rocket motor. He was tense. Jason and Columbus also fretted most about getting home.

CONTROL Time, T minus two. Tranquility Base cleared for takeoff.

ARMSTRONG Understand there is no traffic, and we are number one for the runway.

CONTROL Five, four, three, two, one . . . We have a perfect takeoff!
ARMSTRONG This is smooth. Rocks a little.
CONTROL OK Eagle, you're back on U.S. 1.

At 13:01 hours *Eagle's* rocket engine was extinguished and she coasted toward her rendezvous with *Columbia*, with only minor corrections. In Control Center everyone stood and applauded, but several minutes went by before normal conversation was restored. Docking and the return to Earth now seemed routine.

For the first time we had set foot on another heavenly body and were safely on our way home. We had seen the Earth from the Moon, and the sense of Infinity was gradually going to return to us. Meanwhile, we discovered how pleasant it is to walk on the Moon as if it were a springboard, leaning forward or back to start or to stop, for though our weight is reduced to one-sixth of what it is on Earth, our inertia has not changed. To stumble is not dangerous, for in such light gravity our falls are no worse than the ones we suffered when we first learned to walk on Earth. Silence is complete, if anything underlined by the "tip . . . tip" that frames our communications and by the faithful whirring of the servomotors that maintain the pressure in our spacesuits. At our feet the dominant hue is silver, turning gradually to gold at the horizon, which is visibly curved. Over the horizon the Earth "hangs from a thread," in the phrase most used by the astronauts (Milton used it as Satan fell). Collins remarked that we should send up a poet who could describe to our statesmen how beautiful, how unique, and how fragile our earth looks from space—four times more luminous than the Moon.

Five more lunar landings followed the first, the last one between mountains 2500 meters high. Apollo 13, commanded by Jim Lovell, lost two fuel cells and two oxygen tanks in an explosion in space that forced the astronauts to cancel their Moon landing and to whip around the back of the Moon, using its gravity as a sling to return to Earth in the Lunar Module in order to conserve Apollo's power for reentry. Lovell told me that, apart from fear (pioneers always confess to that), what "bugged" them most was lack of sleep because of the cold.

Americans are at least as interested in comfort as they are in safety, and, starting with Apollo 15 in July 1971, the astronauts took jeeps to the Moon. I sat in one—carefully, for it is designed for lunar gravity. It has a single control stick that serves to accelerate, to brake, and to steer by individually controlling a quarter-horsepower electric motor at each wheel (for a total of one horse, the unit of power that served to conquer America). On Earth the lunar jeep weighs 250 kilos; on the Moon it

Lunar jeep (*NASA*)

weighs only 42 kilos, and it can carry its own weight at 16 kph over 90 kilometers. It has to be directed by an inertial navigation system because the Moon's magnetic field is not sufficient to move a compass.

Having invaded space, the next step is to colonize it, beginning with semipermanent orbiting stations. On April 19, 1971, Salyut 1, the first Russian space station, was placed in an orbit about 200 kilometers high. Once put together in space, it weighed 80 tons and was 20 meters long (including its own rocket) with a maximum diameter of 4 meters. It is still the only spacecraft with two docking ports. It was designed to support up to four men, each of whom consumes 700 liters of air, two liters of water, and 600 grams of food daily. After Salyut 1 had been tested by the crew of Soyuz 10, Soyuz 11 brought up three cosmonauts who remained on the space station for 23 days but were killed by decompression when a hatch failed on reentry (no one has yet died in space). The second space station, Salyut 2, failed in space in 1973, unmanned, but Salyut 3 supported a crew for two weeks, and in 1975-1976 Salyut 4 and 5 progressively increased manned space time and also tried out unmanned supply docking. Salyut 6 was launched on September 29, 1977, and in January 1978, its crew was joined by the crew of Soyuz 27, so that for several days there were four men on board, as there would be again with the arrival of

Salyut, the first space station *(Sovfoto/Eastfoto)*

Skylab, U.S. apartment in the sky *(NASA)*

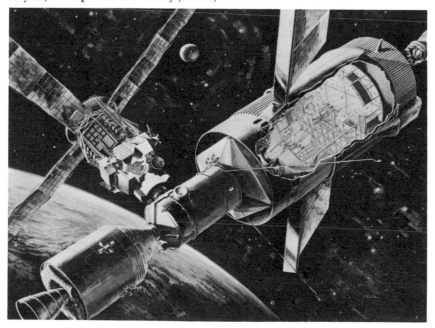

four more visiting teams, including Czech, Polish, and East German copilots (a Bulgarian failed to dock). As I write, Salyut 6 has been operating aloft for over two years, manned more than half the time. It has supported seven crews who have carried out experiments in collaboration with four hundred Soviet institutions and several foreign ones, mostly from socialist countries, but including France. It has been refueled and supplied by seven unmanned Capsules (fresh food!). Its latest crew, Vladimir Lyajov and Valeri Ryumin, has just returned from space in Soyuz 34 after remaining aloft for almost six months. On arrival they had difficulty forming words, and feather mattresses seemed to them as hard as boards; it will take them about a month to readapt to Earth. But they have remained in good spirits and in close contact with Earth, even watching Soviet T.V. The Russians have pioneered again by demonstrating the possibility of keeping a space station occupied almost indefinitely, and Salyut 6 has already traveled a distance far greater than that which separates us from Mars.

The American space station, Skylab, was the third stage of a Saturn 5 rocket that, after serving as fuel tank on the way to the Moon, was remodeled into a three-and-a-half-room apartment plus observatory, fifty-five times bigger than Apollo. It weighed almost 100 tons (as much as Columbus' *Santa Maria*) and was more than 30 meters long and 6.5 meters in diameter, so that while its orbit was almost twice as high as Salyut's, it was just visible to the naked eye from Earth. Circumnavigating the globe approximately every hour and a half, it overflew three quarters of the Earth's surface between latitudes 50°N and 50°S, where ninety percent of the world's population lives.

On May 14, 1973, ten days after Skylab was launched, an Apollo delivered Skylab's first crew: Pete Conrad, his copilot Paul Weitz, and physician Joe Kerwin. As time passed, they "floated" without gravity through an atmosphere (seventy percent oxygen, thirty percent nitrogen) one-third as dense as Earth's, through which they had to shout to be heard and could not whistle. They "walked" by hooking their cleated shoes into the aluminum grills that separate Skylab's "floors," always careful to pass from one floor to the other in the same position in order not to become disoriented. Using ordinary cutlery, they ate reasonable meals chosen from one ton of precooked food (and three tons of water, but no wine—how unhappy Elcano would have been!). They slept like bats, hanging on the wall in their sleeping bags, if one can speak of "hanging" where there is neither "up" nor "down." They showered once a week in a folding tube that recycled each man's liter of water, then changed their suits (underclothes were changed every two days). They used the first true space W.C., which collected and froze wastes to be analyzed back on Earth. And even though much medical information was automatically telemetered from Earth; the ship's doctor gave them periodic physicals during which he "weighed" them by having them oscillate on a spring (where there is no weight, mass can still be measured by its inertia).

A second and then a third crew replaced the first, and when the last one returned to Earth on February 8, 1974, Skylab had been operational for nearly nine months and had been manned more than half that time. In space, the crew's hearts lost about three percent in size, their red blood cell count dropped about fourteen percent, and about half of them suffered vertigo at the beginning of their flights, but these and other physical changes stopped after some forty days. The astronauts adapted quickly to space, provided they kept up their exercises, and Joe Kerwin remarked that what he missed most was the company of the opposite sex and an occasional cold beer. They had more trouble readapting when they returned to Earth, where they again felt vertigo, dragged their feet, and found it difficult to return to the circadian (daily) rhythm of twenty-four hours that they had easily changed to thirty-six hours in space. Does mankind retain some biological memory of an ancient sojourn in space?

Skylab's crews worked constantly, resting only every seventh thirty-six-hour day. Monitoring Earth from space, they located ocean currents, fishing banks, mineral deposits, and water in drought-stricken areas; they even took infrared photographs of the bottom of the sea. They measured the conditions of crops, carried out biological and industrial experiments that are possible only away from gravity, and observed the sun and the sky from outside our atmospheric screen. They cooperated with more than a hundred earthbound scientific teams to prepare maps, measure Alpine snows, find flowers in the desert, and track the birth of hurricanes, and their observations will keep a thousand scientists busy all over the world for some five years. But despite this global cooperation, NASA says Skylab's automatic cameras stopped every time they passed over China or the USSR, the only two countries that refused to cooperate, though spy satellites from both sides continue to monitor the whole world and may already have prevented a war from being hatched in secrecy.

From the beginning the Skylab program had its problems: one of its 15-meter-long "wings," which transform sunlight into electric power, broke off, and another jammed and had to be opened during a space walk; a sunscreen failed and had to be replaced by a white sheet (all space repairs are rehearsed on Earth in the "weightlessness" of a huge water tank). Finally, the lonely station's orbit declined much more than was expected, due largely to the great solar magnetic storms that have expanded our atmosphere, increasing the drag at Skylab's altitude. Efforts to save it were abandoned, and, more than six years after its launching, the fragments which did not burn up on reentry fell in the Indian Ocean and onto the Australian desert, thanks to a last minute maneuver which prevented them from falling over populated areas. The lesson is clear: Our calculations, which may seem almost perfect, are not infallible.

In 1975 Apollo 18 docked with Soyuz 19 over the Atlantic and, for the next forty-four hours, Tom Stafford and his two crewmen exchanged protocol visits and conducted experiments with Alexei Leonov and his copilot (I was present at FAI when the project was first discussed). There was a mosquito on board Apollo-Soyuz, Stafford had to take Lomotil to digest the borscht, and when the Americans forgot their retro-rocket and parachute circuit breakers on their way back to Earth, gas seeped into the cabin. But the mission ended well, and it reminded us that no one can monopolize space and opened up the possibility of international rescue missions. It also had an interesting side effect: Though Star City training center outside Moscow had been visited by many Westerners, the Russian Space Control Center near Leninsk had not (its location was not even marked on Soviet maps). Before the flight the American astronauts insisted on visiting it. It turned out to be a city of some 50,000 inhabitants known as Baikonur or Tyuratam, 2,250 kilometers from Moscow on the railroad to Tashkent.

There are still important differences in style between the Russian space effort and the American. Americans are not comfortable with secrets. Once when I flew out of the clouds by mistake near Cape Canaveral and called Control, I was told not to worry and to look west if I wanted to see a launching that was just about to take place. American equipment is more sophisticated; it is designed to allow astronauts to make their own decisions, based on miniaturized onboard computers, inertial navigation systems, and so on. Russian equipment tends to be as economical as possible and is designed mainly for control from the ground, yet the Russians have spent twice as much money on their space program as the Americans, who give it only one percent of their budget. We have seen that the Russians did much of the pioneering, yet the Americans took the lead with their Moon landings and may take it again with the Space Shuttle. The reason for this, I think, is that the economic system of the USSR does not permit plowing back the commercial benefits of the program, while the economy of the United States has already received about twice what it has spent on its space programs from commercial applications of space techniques. The development of the most powerful computers, half of which are in the United States; the spread of pocket calculators and "chips"; the commercial use of satellites for communications, weather forecasting, and navigation; telemetering for medical and other purposes—these and a multitude of other offshoots of the space program are all economically productive if the system permits it.

Even so, the Russians continue to send up manned missions and to keep their Salyut active, while no Americans have been in space for five years, and no further American manned space flights are planned other than the Space Shuttle, scheduled to be launched in 1980.

The first space vehicle that can be landed like an aircraft and be launched again two weeks later, the Shuttle will open the way for regularly scheduled space service. With a gross weight of 200 tons and a cargo capacity of 32 tons, the shuttle is 40 meters long and has a wing span of 26 meters (comparable in size to a DC-9 passenger jet). It will probably carry a crew of seven, and candidates (including several West Europeans and some women) have already been selected for training. Therefore, according to Kerwin's diagnosis, the only thing that will be missed on board during the thirty days the Shuttle can remain in space will be cold beer.

In the meantime, both the United States and the USSR have continued the exploration of space with "robot" capsules, which do not require rockets as big as Saturn.[2] The planet Mars, which comes as close as 54.3 million kilometers to Earth and seems to be geologically similar, has been visited by four Russian Mars and five American Mariner and Viking robots (the trip is always roundabout, and it can cover ten times the minimum distance). In 1971 the first Martian landing was made by Mars 3, which managed to transmit some information from the Martian surface before going silent; in 1972 Mariner 9 settled into Martian orbit and transmitted more than 7000 photographs; and in 1974 Mars 6 also transmitted photographs from Martian orbit.

In 1976 two U.S. Vikings reached Mars in eleven months, less than twenty seconds behind schedule and less than one hundred kilometers off course. They sent down to the Martian surface two one-ton Landing Modules, each about the size of a jeep, equipped to transmit photographs and information and to detect any trace of life. They did not find any living organisms, but earthly microorganisms have been revived in lab cultures after "hibernating" 10,000 years in Antarctic ice and up to 300 million years in blocks of salt, so hasty conclusions must not be drawn.

The Viking landers have greatly increased our knowledge of the red planet, whose total surface is about equivalent to the sum of all Earth's landmasses even though its diameter is half of ours. Mars seems to be the least inhospitable of solar planets, though it is cold by our standards, with an average temperature of $-40°C$. Its atmosphere is a hundred times thinner than ours, but it contains enough moisture to produce mist in the morning, and its composition indicates that it may once have been similar to the atmosphere of the Earth. Mars' south polar cap appears to contain only dry ice (CO_2), but its north polar cap apparently contains frozen water which before the Martian ice age may have flowed through the clearly visible watercourses and canyons of Mars (which have nothing to do with the mythical "Martian Canals"). Water vapor has also been observed near the Martian Equator, where temperatures are sometimes quite Earth-like. Martian gravity, one-fourth that of the Earth, would be sufficient for us to walk there more naturally than on the Moon but low enough to help us climb Mars' Olympus Mons, which is three times as high as Everest, and Valles Marineris, four times as wide and twice as deep as the Grand Canyon and as long as the United States is broad, or to cross its sand dunes, greater than the Sahara.

Venus, the planet most like Earth in size and density, appears to have evolved quite differently. It gets even closer to us than Mars (37.2 million kilometers), and it has been visited by five American Mariner and Pioneer robots and twelve Russian Venera robots (nine of them successful). Venera 3 put a Soviet State Seal on Venus, and Venera 9 and 10 descended in 1975 to the Venusian surface and managed to transmit photographs before burning up in less than an hour. In 1978 two robots from each nation sent landers toward the surface of Venus. Those sent down by Venera 11 and 12 transmitted information for 110 minutes after parachuting to the surface. Pioneer 1 is still in orbit, radar-mapping the Venusian surface. Pioneer 2 split into five probes that transmitted successfully while they plunged into the Venusian atmosphere and then burned up 100 kilometers from the surface.

Venus is less hospitable than Mars. Its average temperature is almost 500°C (hot enough to melt lead), and its carbon dioxide atmosphere is almost one hundred times denser than ours and is clouded by sulphuric acid droplets.[3] Radar observation from Earth has revealed near Venus' equator a depression and a mountain comparable to those on Mars, neither of which had been spotted through telescopes; and Pioneer has found a similar depression on the planet's far side.

On April 5, 1985, Earth, Venus, and Mars will be in position to allow us to use Venus' gravity to "sling" a manned spaceship toward Mars. The round trip will take a year and a half, and the project could be made ready in time if started now. To survive on Venus we would perhaps have to begin by cultivating algae there that could consume carbon dioxide and produce oxygen until the passionate planet's fever has subsided; on Mars we could live by using techniques we have already mastered.

Twenty years after Sputnik there are adults who cannot remember a world without space vehicles, of which several thousand (about three-fourths of them Russian) have been sent up by the half dozen nations that are exploring beyond our atmosphere. There is even a spatial garbage heap, more than 1500 kilometers up, where used nuclear satellite engines have been placed in orbit in the hope that future generations will know what to do with them. More than fifty manned spacecraft, half of them American, have left the Earth and returned; sixty capsules, manned or not, have flown by or landed on the Moon, which is only eighty times as far away as America was for Columbus—and much more visible. The Moon, like Everest, "is there" and could be used as a base for manned voyages to Mars, Venus, and beyond. On the Moon Apollo 11 discovered a new mineral, containing iron, magnesium, and titanium (it was christened Armacolite in honor of Armstrong, Aldrin, and Collins). Together with lunar aluminum, it could be used to build a permanent base.

Even if we find no sign of life on Mars, the search will certainly continue. We know we can survive almost indefinitely beyond our atmosphere, using solar energy by day and combining oxygen with hydrogen to produce both water and energy at night. Recent experiments with electrons and protons at more than six million volts suggest the possibility of reversing the familiar process and producing matter from energy—and therefore supplies from sunlight. Future deep-space ships, whether launched from the Moon or from artificial bases put together in space, need therefore recognize no limits.[4] It took us two hundred years to be sure that the microorganisms that Van Leeuwenhoek first saw through his microscope in 1674 were alive, and sixty years have not yet passed since we discovered that the Universe extends beyond the Milky Way, today our friendly neighborhood galaxy of one hundred billion stars.

Mariner 10 has already flown by Mercury, the planet closest to our sun, transmitting photographs and then going into solar orbit. Pioneer 11 has covered almost one billion kilometers to Jupiter in less than two years and has gone on to Saturn in less than another five years. Voyager 2 has passed by Jupiter and will visit Saturn in 1981 and Uranus in 1986. It may even visit Neptune in 1989. This would leave only Pluto to be explored, so distant that the sun from there will be just one of the bright stars.

We have already sent several messages beyond the solar system, some written in a "universal language" based on the oscillation frequency of hydrogen, the most common molecule (1.420MH or 21m) and others carrying diagrams of human anatomy, recordings of earth sounds, and maps of our continents as they would have looked from space millions of years ago and as they will probably look millions of years hence—in case anyone is watching us from out there. For more than thirty years our radio and television broadcasts have been reaching out into space at the speed of light (almost 300,000 kilometers per second), and they may already have reached stars with planets capable of supporting life as we know it.

Ours is no longer the orb complete unto itself that Magellan bequeathed us. The Earth is once again an island surrounded by Infinite Space, not unlike the Infinite Ocean of Jason and Odysseus. If they went to its extremes, so can we. We will surely try it, if only in order to emigrate when Earth freezes over like Mars or burns up like Venus, and even if we have to reach velocities comparable to the speed of light in order to leave the solar system. (We have already observed celestial objects that appear to move much faster than light.) What if at that speed time slows its pace and Earth communications cease; didn't Columbus lose contact from the moment he weighed anchor?

So, even though there are as many stars in the sky as separate grains of sand on the strands of our seven seas . . .

Earth, the Space Island (NASA)

NOTES

1. Russian cosmonauts call the speed necessary to escape the Earth's gravity (11.2 km per second) "the second cosmic velocity," the first being the speed necessary to enter orbit (7.5 km per second).

2. The USSR's small Sputnik started it all on Octber 4, 1957, followed four months later by Explorer 1 (U.S.). In 1959 Luna 1 (USSR) and Pioneer 4 (U.S.) escaped Earth's gravity and passed close to the Moon, Luna 1 becoming the first artificial solar satellite. In the same year Luna 2 was the first earthborn object to hit our satellite (on the Sea of Serenity) and Luna 3 the first to enter lunar orbit and transmit photographs of the side of the Moon that is invisible from Earth. Sputnik 2 was the first spaceship to carry animals into space, and space dog Laika (Barker) was as feted as the Montgolfiers' lamb almost two centuries earlier.

In 1965 Luna 5 made the first soft landing on the Moon, followed in 1966 by Surveyor 1 (U.S.). In 1967 two Sputniks, Kosmos 86 and 88, docked automatically in orbit. While the United States moved on to manned lunar discovery, the USSR sent six more unmanned missions to the Moon, and Luna 17 took along a telecontrolled Lunokod Mooncar that rambled about the Sea of Rains for seven months. Three Russian robot missions sent samples from the lunar surface back to Earth, some of which the Russians passed on to their American colleagues for analysis (the Americans eventually brought home a total of 380 kilos of lunar rocks).

In the meantime, American Comsats and Russian Molnyas and Orbits continue to serve long-range communications, and Metsats, Kosmos, and Meteors serve meteorologists. Since the mid 1960s both the U.S. Navy and the Russian Navy have been using High Earth Orbit Satellites for navigation with a sextant (how Magellan's Albo would have loved that!). Interplanetary probes are referred to in our text when speaking of Mars and Venus, but I insist that unmanned capsules can only explore; discovery as we have defined it requires the presence of man.

3. Atmospheric pressure on the surface of Venus is roughly equivalent to water pressure at one kilometer below sea level, where one would have to work to recover the treasure fleet that sank off Santo Domingo when it sailed in disregard of Columbus' hurricane warning.

4. Future long-range spaceships could be monitored and controlled virtually without effort by encephalographic communication with onboard computers. The crew's ills could be diagnosed telemetrically by microtransmitters that would course continually through the crew's bodies and communicate symptoms to shipboard diagnostic computers so that minor problems could be treated immediately. Major ones would have to be solved by the ship's doctor, mostly with human or artificial "spares."

EPILOGUE: ALPHA CENTAURI

It is almost unthinkable that life similar to ours should have evolved only on Earth, and if it exists anywhere else, we are most likely to find it on a planet whose size and mass are in the same proportion as ours, for climate appears to be the result of a delicate balance between gravity (which depends on mass) and radiation (which depends on size). About one-fifth of the stars in our galaxy, the Milky Way, have planets, and of the many hundreds of millions of them, the nearest are those that revolve around Alpha Centauri, the second of the two sentinels which follow the Southern Cross around the skies. A double sun, it is only some forty thousand million kilometers away from us, or 4.3 light years. Of its three planets, the most hospitable seems to be the third. So on to Alpha Centauri B-3.

ARGO 2 Alpha Centauri B-3, do you read me? This is Argo, first manned interstellar ship out of Sun-3, the solar planet we call Earth. Our robot capsules that have been orbiting you for years tell us that you have learned our language. Please say how you read me. Over!

ALPHA CENTAURI B-3 Argo, this . . . Alpha Centauri B-3 . . . read you loud and clear . . . you read me? . . . understand? . . . please give long call to accustom us your language . . . Over!

ARGO Loud and clear, Alpha Centauri! We understand you perfectly! It has taken us nine Earth years to get here. Half that time we have been out of contact with our base, where much more time has gone by. But the voyage has not seemed too long because we have learned to hibernate, to adjust our circadian rhythms, and to play speed against time and mass. Still, to talk to you is like being born again. We are entering orbit. Apogee nine hundred kilometers, perigee five hundred fifty. Say if you are tracking us.

ALPHA CENTAURI Tracking you perfectly. Intentions?

ARGO We plan to land as soon as you clear us. We can do so on any flat area of one kilometer square without affecting the surroundings. Our mapping satellites have picked out several good locations, but we await your instructions.

ALPHA CENTAURI Thank you. First we wish to talk. You are from the third planet of the star you call sun, which we see as the fifth star in the constellation you call Cassiopeia. Our knowledge of you is limited to basic language and data obtained from your unmanned capsules. How long can you remain in orbit?

ARGO Our range is sufficient to return to Earth. Our NERVA reactor can produce its hydrogen jet almost indefinitely. We are ready to maintain orbit as long as necessary to carry out our mission, which is to establish personal and friendly relations with you. How did you learn our language? Our computers only managed to learn a few phrases of yours, although they easily manage this ship—and for that matter almost everything else on Earth since manual labor was eliminated.

ALPHA CENTAURI Computers . . . our ancestors used computers until we found that the easiest one to develop was our own brain. Genetic control of evolution and implants of microcircuits have produced for us a brain capable of learning any language once we have heard enough of it. Our brain even produces its own music, whereas we understand you still listen to old-time electronic music. But it is you who have explored the Universe and come here. Why have you made such an effort?

ARGO To answer your question . . . the earliest of our forebears whose legends we have been able to reconstruct dared only to visit known lands and seas; the rest they considered an Infinite Ocean peopled by beings superior but related to them whom they called gods, and with whom it was necessary to establish covenants. Curiosity and our taste for adventure soon led us to push back the frontiers of that Ocean until we found that all of our seas were one, and that even Ocean could be unveiled. So we launched ourselves into Space . . .

ALPHA CENTAURI And the gods?

ARGO Our gods also became One, who soon retired into the Beyond, and there was a time when He seemed to have abandoned us altogether. But when we explored first the Moon and then Mars, we realized that our world, seen from afar, was like that of our early ancestors, a small island surrounded by the Infinite. The time when we thought we possessed everything had passed, and in our solitude we began to test new myths, to search for life on other solar planets, and finally to explore the planets of other stars. Of the ones that were like Earth, yours was the closest, so we began to study it with our unmanned capsules, which, as you know, soon established contact. Briefly, that is why we are here today, attracted by your intelligence, by the cleanliness of your atmosphere, and by the brilliant greens and blues of your planet. But now that we are beginning to realize how advanced you really are, we wonder why it was not you who first explored the Universe, and you who discovered us.

ALPHA CENTAURI Understood. It seems that your view of your world evolved as you gradually discovered it, so that your gods became insecure and your lonely curiosity became insatiable. We may also have gone through such a period; if so, we have forgotten it. As far as we can remember, we always knew what the Universe was like, and Who invented it and gave it its laws. Consequently our curiosity and our aim have been introspective; to perfect ourselves and our own planet . . . But you mentioned "adventure." This is a word we have not yet quite understood. What is it?

ARGO Adventure . . . adventure is to face the unknown, risking failure and oblivion, out of curiosity and because of the need to find new beauty. Haven't you ever felt that need?

ALPHA CENTAURI No, and to us it seems a foolishly dangerous need. We are concerned with peace, with equilibrium. That is why we have doubts about letting you land, though we do not wish to be unfriendly . . . You speak of beauty . . . do you only find it in risk? . . . what happened to a phrase we used to hear from your Earth . . . *la douceur de vivre?*

ARGO A lovely phrase, but old-fashioned . . . One moment . . . You had better speak directly to our captain . . . Perhaps *she* can explain . . . This is Argo's captain speaking. I see there is a great deal to be explained about our past before we land. If I may, I think I will read you the introduction of an old booklet with which we amused ourselves at the beginning of our trip, before we grew accustomed to doing nothing but think.

To discover is to rend the veil. It is to cross the frontier where science converges with religion. It is to know, step by step, sea by sea, what God hath wrought. . . .

BIBLIOGRAPHY

Even a modest bibliography for the subjects upon which we have touched would be huge. This is a minimal list that may be useful.

Part One: Homeric Island and Infinite Ocean

Homer, *The Odyssey*, translated by E. V. Rieu (Baltimore: Penguin Books, 1969).

Apollonius of Rhodes, *The Argonautica*, translated by R. C. Seaton, Loeb Classics (Cambridge: Harvard University Press, 1967).

Pierre Grimal, *Dictionnaire de la Mythologie Grecque et Romaine* (Paris: Presses Universitaires de France, 1958).

J.S. Morison and R.T. Williams, *Greek Oared Ships, 900–322 B.C.* (Cambridge University Press, 1968).

A. Nils Nordenskjold, *Periplus* (New York: Burt Franklin, 1897), originally published in Stockholm in 1897.

George F. Bass (ed.), *A History of Seafaring based on Underwater Archaeology* (New York: Walker, 1972).

Michael Calder, *The Weather Machine* (New York: Viking, 1975).

Kilmer, Crocker, and Brown, *Sounds from Silence: Recent Discoveries in Ancient Eastern Music,* a recording (Berkeley, Calif.: Bit Enki, 1976).

Part Two: The Complete World of the Renaissance

Christopher Columbus, *Diary*, edited by Bartolomé de las Casas.

Ferdinand Columbus, *Life of the Admiral.*

Ibn Khaldún, *Magaddima*, translated by F. Rosenthal (New York: Hakluyt Society, 1958).

Einar Haugen, *Voyages to Vinland* (New York: 1942), a translation of the Vinland sagas.

Antonio Pigafetta, *The Voyage of Magellan*, translated by Paula Spurlin Paige (Englewood Cliffs, N.J.: Prentice-Hall, 1969).

Pedro de Medina, *Regimiento de Navegación* 1563, facsimile (Madrid: Instituto de España, 1964).

Leo Bagrow and R. A. Skelton, *History of Cartography* (Cambridge: Harvard University Press, 1964).

Olaf Olsen and Ole Crumlin-Pedersen, *The Skuldelev Ships*, reprinted from *Acta Archaelogica* XXXVIII, Copenhagen, 1967.

José M. Martinez-Hidalgo, *Columbus' Ships* (Barre, Mass.: Barre Publishers, 1966).

Enrique Uribe White, *Edición Facsimilar de las Cartas de Vespucio* (Bogotá: Prensas de la Biblioteca Nacional, 1942).

Samuel Eliot Morison, *Admiral of the Ocean Sea* (Boston: Little, Brown, 1942).

Samuel Eliot Morison, *The European Discovery of America*, 2 vols. (Oxford University Press, 1971, 1974).

Music of Columbus' Day, a recording (Música Riservata, Director John Beckett) Philips 839714 LY.

Part Three: The Sea of Air and the Ocean of Space

René Chambe, *Histoire de l'Aviation* (Paris: Flammarion, 1958).

Charles Lindbergh, *The Spirit of St. Louis* (New York: Scribner, 1953).

Michael Collins, *Carrying the Fire* (Apollo 11) (New York: Farrar, Straus & Giroux, 1974).

Evgeny Riabchikow, *The Russians in Space* (Garden City, N.Y.: Doubleday, 1971).

A FEW REFERENCES

Ocean engendered Chaos	*Iliad* XIV, 246
Spirit of God moved over the waters	*Genesis* 1–2
Wisdom first possessed by God	*Proverbs* 8–22 and 29
Evolution in the *Argonautica*	*Argonautica* IV, 685
Steira	*Odyssey* II, 420
Description of boat Calypso helped Odysseus build	*Odyssey* V, 234–261
Mast crushes helmsman's skull	*Odyssey* XII, 410
Mast stepped	*Odyssey* II, 422–423
Mast lowered	*Odyssey* XII, 170
Number of oarsmen	*Iliad* XVI, 169; IX, 323
Stern-post height	*Iliad* XV, 716
Cyclopes had no ships	*Odyssey* IX, 125
Coast of Bronze	*Odyssey* X, 3
Voyage to the Russian steppes?	*Odyssey* XI, 128
Achilles: better alive than great	*Odyssey* XI, 488
Zeus' doves dare not fly over Stromboli	*Odyssey* XII, 61
Seventh century B.C. canal	*Herodotus* I, 13
No distinction between prophets	*Koran* I, 130
Abraham and Isaac	*Genesis* 22, I–18
Homer writing as sailor	*Iliad* XIV, 20

INDEX